Leroy Jones Halsey

Living Christianity; or Old Truths Restated

Leroy Jones Halsey

Living Christianity; or Old Truths Restated

ISBN/EAN: 9783337167486

Printed in Europe, USA, Canada, Australia, Japan

Cover: Foto ©Lupo / pixelio.de

More available books at **www.hansebooks.com**

LIVING CHRISTIANTY;

OR,

OLD TRUTHS RESTATED.

BY THE

Rev. LEROY J. HALSEY, D.D., LL.D.,

Emeritus Professor in Theological Seminary of the Northwest;
Author of "Literary Attractions of the Bible," "Beauty of
Immanuel," "Life-Pictures from the Bible," etc.

PHILADELPHIA:
PRESBYTERIAN BOARD OF PUBLICATION,
1334 CHESTNUT STREET.

PREFACE.

All religious truth is unto godliness, and the best test of religious truth is its tendency to produce a life of godliness. Some truths, however, are more prominent in the Scriptures than others, and they are deemed essential as being at the foundation of the Christian system and of all religious experience. The truths set forth in these chapters are of this class. They are all taken from the clear teaching of the word of God. The aim of the writer has been to discuss them from the standpoint of religious experience; not as speculative theological dogmas, but as the great realities of practical duty. The chief purpose of the volume is to give a scriptural and practical answer to two lines of inquiry—the first, What must I believe and do in order to be saved? the second, What must I do and what must I become in order to fulfill the law of Christ?

Another important object has been kept constantly in view through these pages. It has been to state the cardinal truths of the Bible in the light of our common salvation. The points on which all evangelical Christians agree are far greater than those on which they differ. Christianity is strongest when it plants itself on the common salvation—on its cardinal facts and doctrines. Even in the eyes of the unbelieving world the Church of God is to-day more glorious in its harmonies than in its differences.

It has long been a cherished hope of the author that he might be able to state the great essential doctrines of the common salvation—that is, the saving truths of the gospel—in such form as would commend them to the judgment and the cordial acceptation of God's children in all evangelical denominations. This volume is the contribution of a Presbyterian to that wider Christianity of the ancient past, and also of the future, in which it is hoped all evangelical Christians will ere long stand nearer together than they now stand, because they will learn to look less at their points of difference and more at the great principles of their common salvation. What the world needs is a living Christianity, and the Church can render it no better service than by proclaiming anew those old truths which are vital and saving.

CONTENTS.

CHAPTER I.
THE EXISTENCE AND CHARACTER OF GOD.................... 9

CHAPTER II.
THE FATHERHOOD OF GOD.............................. 16

CHAPTER III.
NATURE AND RESPONSIBILITY OF MAN.................. 23

CHAPTER IV.
THE FALLEN CONDITION OF OUR NATURE................ 29

CHAPTER V.
THE UNIVERSALITY OF SIN............................ 36

CHAPTER VI.
THE BROTHERHOOD OF MAN............................ 42

CHAPTER VII.
THE MEDIATORSHIP OF CHRIST........................ 53

CHAPTER VIII.
DIVINITY AND INCARNATION OF CHRIST................ 60

CHAPTER IX.
Christ the Light of the World...... 70

CHAPTER X.
The Supreme Miracle of Christianity...... 77

CHAPTER XI.
The Atoning Death of Christ...... 84

CHAPTER XII.
The Resurrection of Christ...... 93

CHAPTER XIII.
Divine Personality of the Holy Spirit...... 101

CHAPTER XIV.
The Law of God...... 109

CHAPTER XV.
The Forgiveness of Sins...... 121

CHAPTER XVI.
The Grace that Saves...... 130

CHAPTER XVII.
The Offices of Faith...... 139

CHAPTER XVIII.
Repentance unto Life...... 146

CHAPTER XIX.
The New Birth...... 151

CHAPTER XX.
The Conditions of Salvation.................................... 156

CHAPTER XXI.
The Christian Profession.. 165

CHAPTER XXII.
Consecration to Christ.. 171

CHAPTER XXIII.
The Spiritual Life.. 178

CHAPTER XXIV.
Religion as a Living Power....................................... 183

CHAPTER XXV.
Christian Life a Ministry of Love................................ 190

CHAPTER XXVI.
The Golden Rule... 195

CHAPTER XXVII.
The New Commandment... 200

CHAPTER XXVIII.
The Morality of the Gospel....................................... 205

CHAPTER XXIX.
Prayer a Duty and a Privilege.................................... 215

CHAPTER XXX.
The Inspired Word of God... 226

CONTENTS.

CHAPTER XXXI.
The Day of Rest and of Worship.................................. 234

CHAPTER XXXII.
The Two Sacraments... 240

CHAPTER XXXIII.
The Church of Christ... 248

CHAPTER XXXIV.
The Gospel Ministry.. 257

CHAPTER XXXV.
The Conversion of the World...................................... 264

CHAPTER XXXVI.
The Coming of the Lord... 273

CHAPTER XXXVII.
The Final Retribution.. 279

CHAPTER XXXVIII.
The Resurrection of the Body..................................... 286

CHAPTER XXXIX.
The Life Everlasting... 291

CHAPTER XL.
Three Experiences: Sin, Grace, Glory............................. 299

CHAPTER XLI.
The Supreme Good... 305

LIVING CHRISTIANITY.

CHAPTER I.

THE EXISTENCE AND CHARACTER OF GOD.

THE Bible does not discuss the question of the existence of God. To the sacred writers that is never an open question. They point, it is true, to his witnesses, to the manifestations of his power and Godhead in the works of creation and providence. "The heavens declare the glory of God," says David, "and the firmament showeth his handiwork." "The invisible things of him from the creation of the world," says Paul, "are clearly seen, being understood by the things that are made, even his eternal power and Godhead, so that they are without excuse." But the sacred writers attempt no formal argument for the being of God. They tell us, indeed, that the fool hath said in his heart, "There is no God," but they do not think it worth while to answer the fool. As for themselves, they either quietly assume, or else they simply declare, both the existence and the personality of the Divine Being. God is the ever-present burden of their thoughts, and the one perpetual theme of their instructions, but they no more think of stopping to prove there is a God than we would to prove there is a sun.

It is interesting to notice with what brevity of expression, and at the same time with what unquestioning certainty, the great idea of God is introduced by the sacred writers in the opening chapters of their several books. It is as if the thought of God were no new thing, but one that had always been familiarly and fully known both to them and to their readers. They are not startled by it themselves, nor do they expect to startle any one else by its distinct reiterated and most emphatic announcement. When they declare a message from heaven with the usual prelude of "Thus saith the Lord," there is never the semblance of a doubt whether mortal man might not call in question Jehovah's own existence as well as his right to speak. Such doubts and such discussions have been reserved for later and more skeptical ages. They were unknown to the writers of the Bible.

How impressive in its unquestioning belief in God, as well as in its sublime simplicity, is the style in which Moses opens the Pentateuch and begins with God, in the first verse of Genesis!—"In the beginning God created the heaven and the earth." In this brief narration of the six days' creation he repeats the term *God*, without definition or comment, no less than thirty-five times in the first thirty-four verses. In the book of Exodus, when the Lord appears to Moses in the burning bush at Mount Horeb, and sends him into Egypt with authority to deliver Israel, he gives no higher credentials than this brief yet sublime announcement of the Divine self-existence: "And

Moses said unto God, Behold, when I am come unto the children of Israel, and shall say unto them, The God of your fathers hath sent me unto you, and they shall say to me, What is his name? what shall I say unto them? And God said unto Moses, I AM THAT I AM; and he said, Thus shalt thou say unto the children of Israel, I AM hath sent me unto you. The Lord God of your fathers, the God of Abraham, the God of Isaac, and the God of Jacob, hath sent me unto you: this is my name for ever, and this is my memorial unto all generations."

In similar terms of brevity and of unchallengeable authority Isaiah opens his book of inspired prophecies: " Hear, O heavens: and give ear, O earth: for the Lord hath spoken," and closes it saying, " Thus saith the Lord, The heaven is my throne, and the earth is my footstool. Where is the house that ye build unto me, and where is the place of my rest? For all those things hath mine hand made, and all those things have been, saith the Lord, but to this man will I look, even to him that is poor and of a contrite spirit, and trembleth at my word." The patriarch Job is thought by many to be the earliest of all the sacred writers. But in all his deep affliction and throughout that elevated dialogue which he carries on, first with his three ancient friends and then with the younger Elihu, while greatly troubled with conflicting doubts and fears on other points, he raises no question, nor does Satan himself suggest one to any of the speakers, as to the Divine existence. They are all dumb with silence and awed into reverence before the overpowering majesty of the Almighty, and can only say, " Canst thou by searching find out God? canst thou find out the Almighty unto perfection? It is high as heaven, what canst thou do? deeper than hell, what canst thou know? Lo! these are parts of his ways, but how little a portion is heard of him! and the thunder of his power who can understand?"

If we turn to the New-Testament books, this tone of authority and brevity of expression, this reticence of discussion and certainty of conviction, are only increased. No one of the writers seems ever to have entertained a doubt on the being of God. God is a present reality to every mind. Thus the apostle John, like Moses, opens the Fourth Gospel with God in the foreground: "In the beginning was the Word, and the Word was with God, and the Word was God. The same was in the beginning with God. All things were made by him, and without him was not anything made that was made." So in like manner begins St. Paul's Epistle to the Hebrews: "God, who at sundry times and in divers manners spake in time past unto the fathers by the prophets, hath in these last days spoken unto us by his Son, whom he hath appointed heir of all things, by whom also he made the worlds."

Assuming, therefore, and declaring, the great primal fact of a personal and self-existent Deity as a truth sufficiently attested by the whole visible universe around us, as well as by man's own inner consciousness, the sacred writers content themselves with simply communicating to us those revelations which they had in various ways received from God, respecting his own person and character on the one hand, and his great works of creation, providence and redemption on the other. They tell us of his glory, his dominion, his everlasting kingdom. They tell us of all his natural and moral attributes—his almighty power, his incomprehensible knowledge, his infinite wisdom, his omnipresent and resistless rule over all worlds and all intelligences. They tell us of his creative skill, his providential care over all creatures, his moral government of angels and men. They tell us of his goodness, his justice, his truth, his holiness, his spirituality, his love, his acts of condescension, mercy and grace to the race of man. They tell us of his holy law, his condemnation of sin, his wrath against the wicked. They tell us of the tri-personality of his Godhead, and of the great mystery of godliness as revealed in the incarnation and redemptive work of Christ. And they tell us of that coming kingdom of glory and immortality which, through the work of Christ and the power of the Holy Ghost, he will establish on earth and in heaven to endure for ever.

The Scriptures abound in descriptions of surpassing sublimity setting forth the incommunicable attributes of the Divine nature, especially in the Psalms of David, the book of Job, Isaiah and all the prophets. Take, for illustration, the omnipresence and omniscience of Jehovah in the one hundred and thirty-ninth Psalm: "O Lord, thou hast searched me and known me; thou knowest my downsitting and mine uprising; thou understandest my thought afar off. Thou compassest my path and my lying down, and art acquainted with all my ways. There is not a word in my tongue, but lo, O Lord, thou knowest it altogether. Thou hast beset me behind and before, and laid thine hand upon me.

Such knowledge is too wonderful for me; it is high, I cannot attain unto it. Whither shall I go from thy Spirit? or whither shall I flee from thy presence? If I ascend up into heaven thou art there: if I make my bed in hell, behold thou art there. If I take the wings of the morning and dwell in the uttermost parts of the sea, even there shall thy hand lead me and thy right hand shall hold me. If I say, Surely the darkness shall cover me, even the night shall be light about me. Yea, the darkness hideth not from thee, but the night shineth as the day; the darkness and the light are both alike to thee."

It is, however, on the moral attributes of the Divine character that the revelations of Scripture shine forth in full-orbed beauty and perfection. This is the glory that excelleth all other glory in the communications from God, and raises the Bible immeasurably above every other book in the world. Isaiah had a vision of this infinite majesty of God when his train filled the temple and the winged seraphim cried one to another, "Holy, holy, holy, is the Lord of hosts, the whole earth is full of his glory." It was this moral excellence of the Divine character which was revealed to Moses when, in answer to his prayer "Show me thy glory," the Lord proclaimed himself merciful and gracious, long-suffering and abundant in goodness and truth, showing mercy to thousands, forgiving transgression while yet punishing the guilty—a God of inexorable justice to the wicked, but of mercy to the penitent.

But it is when we turn to the utterances of Christ himself that we find the fullest revelation of what God is, of what he has done for man, and of what he would have man to be. All Bible instruction on the character and attributes of God may be said to reach their culmination in the teaching of Jesus Christ. In a single brief declaration he has summed up all in one, and told us what God is and how he is to be worshiped: "The hour cometh, and now is, when the true worshipers shall worship the Father in spirit and in truth; for the Father seeketh such to worship him;" "God is a Spirit, and they that worship him must worship him in spirit and in truth."

This grand conception of the spirituality of God, so fully stated by our Saviour here, and so constantly implied in all his instructions, runs through all the Epistles of the New Testament, and it gave character from the beginning to all true Christian worship. The spirituality of God and of his worship had indeed been abundantly taught in the Old Testament, especially in the Psalms and the prophets. But the doctrine rose to a higher measure and a nobler expression under the teaching of Christ and his apostles. Thus we find it in the doxologies of St. Paul's Epistles: "Now unto the King eternal, immortal, invisible, the only wise God, our Saviour, to him be glory for ever and ever. Amen." The primal truth of all the Scriptures is the one supreme, spiritual, intelligent and eternal God of nature as proclaimed by Paul to the men of Athens: "God, that made the world and all things therein, seeing that he is Lord of heaven and earth, dwelleth not in temples made with hands, neither is worshiped with men's hands, as though he needed any thing, seeing he giveth to all life and breath and all things."

CHAPTER II.

THE FATHERHOOD OF GOD.

NO conception of the Divine character in the Scriptures is more assuring to our doubting hearts than that in which God reveals himself as a Father. This conception is all the more encouraging to our hesitating faith when it comes to us, as it so frequently does in the New Testament, through the revelations of Jesus Christ as the Son of God. As he stands in the relation of Son to the Divine Father, and at the same time of brother to our humanity, we are enabled to draw near to God with a confidence and a love which would be impossible without such a Mediator. No doubt one great purpose of the incarnation of Christ in human form was, that as the Son of God he might reveal to us most effectually the fatherhood of God. The evangelist John says, as if with this very thought in view, "No man hath seen God at any time; the only-begotten Son, who is in the bosom of the Father, he hath declared him." And we shall find through all his teachings that this one emphatic declaration of fatherhood predominates.

It is far from being the only manifestation or conception of the Divine character. The Scriptures reveal God as the self-existent Jehovah, as the Creator, the Almighty, the sovereign Ruler of men and nations, the Lawgiver and final Judge. These representations of his eternal power and Godhead everywhere abound throughout the Scriptures, especially in the Old Testament. But God appears in many passages even of the Old Testament in a more endearing character. It is that of a Father—a Father to his chosen people Israel, and a Father to all them that fear him. Thus David speaks in the one hundred and third Psalm: "Like as a father pitieth his children, so the Lord pitieth them that fear him: for he knoweth our frame, he remembereth that we are dust." And again in Psalm sixty-eight he says, " A Father of the fatherless, and a Judge of the widows, is God in his holy habitation."

It is, however, when we come to the teachings of Christ and his apostles in the New Testament that the conception of God as a Father is set forth in its most attractive light. There is probably no thought more conspicuous in the daily life and in the discourses and parables of our blessed Lord than this doctrine of God as a Father. As a name of God, Father is used not less than a hundred times in the New Testament. It seems to have been the favorite expression with John, and was evidently so with our Saviour himself. Both in his teachings and in his prayers he speaks of God far more frequently as a Father than under any other title. Thus in the Sermon on the Mount he taught his disciples to pray, " Our Father which art in heaven," and one of his last recorded prayers on the cross was, " Father, forgive them, for they know not what they do." He said, " Be ye perfect, even as your Father in heaven is perfect." "Love your enemies, and do good to them that hate you, that ye may be the children of your Father which is in heaven." He spoke the beautiful parable of the Prodigal Son, using the endearing relationship of the parent and the child to set forth the care and tenderness of our heavenly Father toward his erring children. Nor is there in human literature a single passage where the great doctrine of the fatherhood of God is more clearly taught as an illustration of the Divine character and as an incentive to human repentance. It would be difficult to see how the character of God could have been painted in more attractive colors, and how the sinful heart of man could have been more deeply touched or more surely won, than by this matchless parable. Yet our reconciled and forgiving heavenly Father, as he appears in this parable, gives us that ideal of the Divine character which was constantly in the mind of Christ and of his apostles.

It is in the character of Father more than by any other title or relation that God reveals himself to us in his attribute of mercy. This revelation of grace and love to the guilty and the perishing reaches its climax when his well-beloved Son Jesus Christ, "the brightness of the Father's glory and the express image of his person," comes into the world to suffer and die upon the cross, and thus to reconcile us to God by this unique and extraordinary display of the Divine clemency. Thus the fatherhood of God, as made known and exemplified in Jesus Christ, comes to us as the very seal of our redemption and the type of our adoption into the family of God.

The doctrine of the fatherhood of God is presented to us in the Scriptures under two different aspects. There is a wider, and there is also a narrower, view. There is a sense in which God is the Father of all, including all races and nations of men, and there is a peculiar sense in which he is the Father of his redeemed and reconciled children.

In the first of these senses the psalmist says, "God is good to all, and his tender mercies are over all his works;" "The eyes of all wait upon thee; and thou givest them their meat in due season. Thou openest thine hand, and satisfiest the desire of every living thing." In this sense our Saviour said, "He maketh his sun to shine on the evil and the good, and sendeth rain on the just and on the unjust." In this sense "God so loved the world that he gave his only-begotten Son, that whosoever believeth in him should not perish, but have everlasting life." In this sense the apostle Peter preached to Cornelius that "God is no respecter of persons; but in every nation he that feareth him and worketh righteousness is accepted with him." So also the apostle Paul, preaching to the Athenians on Mars' Hill concerning the eternal providence of God over all nations and races of men, declares this wide doctrine of God's universal fatherhood, and tells the Athenians that "in him we live and move and have our being," even as some of their own poets had said, "We are the offspring of God."

But it is in the narrower sense that the doctrine is more frequently presented in the Scriptures. Under the covenant of grace God is in a peculiar and endearing sense the Father of all those who acknowledge the relationship; that is, of those who obey the gospel, recognize him as their Father, and are reconciled to him by the death of his Son. It is their high privilege that they are adopted into the Divine family and receive that spirit of sonship by which they cry "Abba, Father." To all these the apostle Paul says, "Be ye followers of God as dear children." It is of this new and endearing relationship to God, as redeemed by his Son, that Paul says to the Galatians, "Ye are all the children of God by faith in Christ Jesus." Of this John says, with exultation, "Behold, what manner of love the Father hath bestowed upon us, that we should be called the sons of God."

As universal Father, God exercises toward all his creatures good-will and beneficence, but toward his own believing children he feels not only benevolence, but complacency and approval.

There was probably no method by which this great conception of the Divine fatherhood could be so impressively revealed to us as through the incarnation of Jesus Christ. When God comes to us in the character of a suffering fellow-man and a brother, he comes very near to our souls. It can be only as a Friend and a Helper that he thus appears. This he does when his own eternal Son, the brightness of his glory and the express image of his person, veils his Godhead for a season in the drapery of humanity, and approaches us in flesh and form with all the attributes of a brother-man. It would have been different had he come as a winged seraph from the burning throne or with the overpowering majesty of a God confessed. But, coming as he did in the lowliest guise of our nature, born of a human mother, educated as a child, and compassed about by every circumstance and condition of manhood, he speaks to our hearts as no other messenger from the skies ever did or could do. He comes from his Father, and assures us that his Father is our Father.

How could God come nearer to us than this? How could God do anything greater for us than this gift and mission of his Son? It is when we see him as a brother that we see God as a Father. "No man," said he to the disciples, "cometh unto the Father but by me. If ye had known me ye should have known my Father also; and from henceforth ye know him and have seen him. Have I been so long time with you, and yet hast thou not known me, Philip? He that hath seen me hath seen the Father, and how sayest thou then, Show us the Father? Believest thou not that I am in the Father and the Father in me? The words that I speak unto you I speak not of myself; but the Father that dwelleth in me he doeth the works. Believe me that I am in the Father and the Father in me, or else believe me for the very works' sake."

This union of the Father with the Son, this incarnation of God in man, is a deep, an unfathomable mystery. But it is one of the sublime doctrines of Christianity, shining out on all the pages of the New Testament. If we accept the doctrine as true, what a flood of light it pours over our fallen humanity, and what hope it inspires for immortality! Who can fail to see how it brings him, who otherwise had been the Unknown God, near to us, and reveals him to our hearts in all the tenderness of a wise, loving and almighty Father?

It is the pre-eminent distinction of Christianity that it proclaims God as the universal Father, caring for his whole rational creation, and yet taking special delight in those who revere his name and keep his commandments. The great record of Christianity, its fact of facts, is, that God has come into the sphere of our humanity, and that he has come for our help and deliverance. Other religions, it is true, have laid claim to such distinction, but it has been an empty boast. There is no historical basis for the claim. In Christ Jesus only has it been realized and demonstrated as a fact. The great announcement of the gospel was, at the beginning, and still is, that God has appeared in a human form, that God as Father has declared his love to men in the person of his only-begotten Son, and that "God was in Christ reconciling the world unto himself by the death of his Son, not imputing their trespasses unto them." The gospel as a scheme of Divine benevolence and mercy for man stands or falls on this announcement; and its verity is so anchored as a fact on the rock of the world's history that it is impossible to deny it without unsettling all human history.

CHAPTER III.

THE NATURE AND RESPONSIBILITY OF MAN.

THE Scriptures do not more distinctly set before us the existence and character of God as a Spirit, infinite, eternal and unchangeable in his being, wisdom, power, holiness, justice, goodness and truth, than they set before us a distinct and ineffaceable delineation of the nature and character of man as he has existed in all nations, in all ages and in all conditions.

This is the second great theme of revelation, and the information of the Bible on this point is as clear and full as it is on the first. But on this second subject we have an advantage which we did not possess on the other. We have some independent knowledge to begin with. We have all the light derived from our own experience and observation, and all the antecedent knowledge which has come down to us from past history, to teach us what man is, what is his character and what his capacity. Thus by what we know of him already from outside sources we are all the better able to test and to appreciate that picture of his nature, origin and destiny which the Bible gives.

It should be borne in mind that the Bible representation of human nature is no uncertain one. No picture was ever more distinctly drawn. It is consistent throughout from Genesis to Revelation. There are no false touches, no unmeaning strokes, and it is impossible to look upon it without feeling that it has come from the hand of a master. On this subject the Bible has come so completely within the range of our own knowledge, derived from experience and history, that it places us in a very favorable position to judge of the credibility of that information which it brings to us when it speaks on subjects beyond our range. For here we can compare its picture and its information with what we know already. And if in a thousand instances we know what it tells us to be true to life and nature, it would be hard to resist the conclusion that the book which never fails of truth here is worthy of credit when it speaks of the things which are unseen and eternal.

At the meeting of the General Presbyterian Alliance of 1880, in Philadelphia, one of its members, the Rev. Dr. E. P. Humphrey, in an able discussion of "Inspiration," made the deeply-significant statement that the Bible contained the proper names of not less than four thousand persons and places brought to view in its history; and that in no instance had recent investigations proved one of those names to be a myth or one of the localities to be misplaced. The argument is obvious. The book which has made no mistake in geography and history during a period of four thousand years and in four thousand examples can be safely trusted on other points. In like manner a book which has drawn a true picture of humanity for all times and places is to be trusted not only for time, but for eternity—not only when it speaks of men, but when it speaks of God and the supernatural world.

What, then, is the scriptural representation of our common humanity. It came directly from the creative hand of God, not by slow and gradual evolution of the forces of material nature, but by the immediate fiat of an omnipotent Creator. There can be no mistake that such is the plain teaching of the Bible, not only in the first chapters of Genesis, but through all its pages; nor is there any evidence that the scientific discoveries of recent times have invalidated the teaching. It stands out plainly on the very face of the ancient record that the human race began with two progenitors, Adam and Eve, and that these were called into being by God. He created them neither in an infantile state nor in a low savage state, but in a superior condition of intellectual and moral responsibility; that is to say, in his own image, in knowledge, righteousness and true holiness. For if they had at the start these three high attributes of personal responsibility, as we must believe they had from Moses' account of their actions in Genesis, it is clear that they were neither infants nor savages. We therefore stand by this ancient record as the best account that has ever been given of the origin and antiquity of man. After he had called into being all the lower orders of life, God said, "Let us make man in our image, after our likeness: and let them have dominion over the fish of the sea, and over the fowl of the air, and over the cattle, and over all the earth, and over every creeping thing that creepeth upon the earth. So God created man in his own image, in the image of God created he him, male and female created he them. . . . And the Lord God formed man of the dust of the ground, and breathed into his nostrils the breath of life, and man became a living soul." And God saw everything that he had made, and, behold, it was very good."

It is evident that our humanity came forth from the creative hand of God in a state of high perfection. It certainly lost its original righteousness and true holiness by the first transgression. But it did not lose its intellectual and moral faculties any more than it lost its bodily organs. When it came forth in perfection from the hand of God it possessed, as it continued to possess after the fall, a dual nature of body and soul. It had a material nature, like that of the lower creatures, kindred with the dust from which it was fashioned, and it had a spiritual nature, a living soul, the breath of God, claiming kindred with the skies. It was endowed with high and noble faculties, capable of knowing God, and allying it with spiritual intelligences. In each of its parts it was originally destined for immortality and for indefinite growth in knowledge. Although this boon of life was forfeited and lost at the fall, a way was provided by which it could be regained in Christ, the second Adam.

This earliest picture of human nature as composed of two distinct parts, a material body and a thinking soul, is presented throughout the Bible. Says Solomon, "Then shall the dust return to the earth as it was; and the spirit shall return unto God who gave it." And thus says Christ: "Fear not them which kill the body, but are not able to kill the soul; but rather fear Him who is able to destroy both soul and body in hell" (Matt. x. 28). Now, it is because of this twofold distinction in our nature, and in virtue of this higher spiritual part called the soul, endowed with reason and conscience and capable of knowing and worshiping God, that we find the Bible everywhere addressing men as rational, responsible beings. In the great matters of salvation God himself constantly appeals to men as free rational agents, calling upon them by all the highest motives of action to choose the good and turn from the evil. There is nothing in the Bible more striking than this perpetual appeal of the Almighty and his inspired prophets and apostles to men as free, intelligent, responsible beings who have power to choose life or death. His language is, "Come now and let us reason together, saith the Lord; though your sins be as scarlet, they shall be white as snow; though they be red like crimson, they shall be as wool;" "Choose ye this day whom ye will serve. If the Lord be God follow him, but if Baal, then follow him;" "Turn ye, turn ye, for why will ye die, O house of Israel?"

From this invariable tone of expostulation and warning, running through all the Scriptures, it is easy to see what is God's estimate of man. Assuredly that estimate is not a low one, whether we judge from God's appeals to our intelligence or from what he has done to save us. If we are to measure man by what is confessedly his truest measure, his immortal nature—that is, by the worth and dignity of his soul—and if we are to take the dimensions of the soul from what Jesus Christ has done and suffered to redeem it, it is obvious that we cannot raise too high our estimate of the value of this fallen humanity. Created at the first in a state of sinless perfection, and now sadly fallen from its pristine glory by the apostasy, it still holds a position of superiority and responsibility immeasurably above the brute creation. The men of all races and climes, however sunk in sin, are still endowed with reason, conscience, affection, and freewill. As such they are competent to receive or reject the knowledge of God, to accept or refuse the offers of his grace in the gospel.

Such is the picture presented us in the Scriptures: a complex being of body and soul, matter and spirit; created originally in the intellectual and moral image of God, but fallen from that high estate; still fearfully and wonderfully constituted even in his ruin; made at first for immortality and happiness, and still capable through Christ of being raised to that glory; greatly marred and weakened in all his intellectual, physical and moral powers, yet still capable, through grace, of rising again from his degradation, of being refashioned into the lost likeness of God, of holding communion with God in worship here and of being fitted at last for the companionship of God and angels in the life to come.

CHAPTER IV.

THE FALLEN CONDITION OF OUR NATURE.

THOUGH the first human pair came forth from the creative hand of God in perfection, fashioned after his own image, in knowledge, righteousness and holiness, and blest with communion with God, we do not have to read far in the sacred record to find them sadly fallen from that primeval condition. In fancied security, and in forgetfulness of God's command, they yielded to the seductive voice of temptation, put forth their hands in an evil hour to the forbidden fruit, and by sinful disobedience fell into an estate of apostasy and ruin. They lost God's approval, incurred the just penalty of his violated law, and so brought condemnation and death upon themselves and their posterity. The forfeited bliss of Eden was lost, its gates were closed against them, and they were left to that fearful heritage of sin and misery which has been the doom of all the race descending from them.

Simply and briefly is this momentous story of transgression told in the opening chapters of the book of Genesis. It is the one short tale of death and woe on which the sublime genius of Milton essayed its utmost strength when it wrought out for us the great epic drama of *Paradise Lost*. It was the first human misdeed, the beginning of all man's transgressions, and it has sent its disastrous influence down to the latest hour. Its fearful results were soon developed in many diverging lines of violence and Heaven-defying wickedness, from the murder of Abel by a brother's hand to that almost universal criminality which soon overspread the earth, filled it with violence and brought down the wrath of God in the destruction of the deluge. Sin had entered the world, and death by sin.

No man can read the Scriptures in any part of them without being struck with the prominence given to the topic of sin, and with the frequent denunciation of God's displeasure against it. While the inspiring keynote of the Bible from beginning to end is salvation, there is a deep and solemn undertone of sin and guilt which swells up unceasingly and gives character to all its music. In truth, the one is but the counterpart to the other; the one necessitates the other. It is because we are sinners that we need salvation. It is because we are all sinners, and because sin is so fearful a malady, that God has given us a book revealing a remedy for sin in the salvation of the cross. Had there been no sin, there had been no Bible and there had been no cross.

Probably on no one point is the demonstration of the truth of the Bible more complete than on the subject of human sinfulness. Under the varying terms of sin, guilt, iniquity, transgression, apostasy, depravity, wickedness, ungodliness, the idea is reiterated over and over in the Bible more than a thousand times. Through a history of forty centuries, and through an authorship of fifteen, it is the one charge against our fallen nature which is never withdrawn and never concealed, and it is everywhere presented as the indictment and the testimony of God himself. Some of the deep thinkers of our day have been striving hard to bring the Bible into conflict with the alleged facts of science and with some of the ascertained facts of history. We venture to say that there is no conflict between the Bible and facts on the subject of sin—no conflict either in the history of the past or in the realm of present experience.

What is the written history of the past but a record of human sinfulness, of "man's inhumanity to man," of tyranny and oppression and deceit, and all manner of wrong-doing? A thousand wasting wars and the innumerable bloody battles that have dotted over the earth's surface, all proclaim with trumpet tongue that the book of God is right, and in no conflict with the facts of history and experience, in arraigning man as a sinner. The inward consciousness of every candid man bears witness that the charge is true. There are historians whose facile pens have narrated all these things without any mention of the word "sin." There are great historians, like Gibbon, who have eloquently related deeds of darkness, with no mention of sin except for derision or for contempt. Still, the fact itself of sin remains a dread reality on every page, despite omission or derision and contempt. No gilded eloquence of narration, no concealment of the truth under the colors of sophistical philosophy, can set aside what is the most patent fact of all history and experience—that man is in a state of apostasy, a sinner against his God and a wrong-doer to his fellow-man.

This is the Bible testimony everywhere, and we know that the witness is true. In this the Bible carries along with it its own complete vindication, for it utters a language on this point which is only that of universal history and experience. No other book claiming to be a revelation from God has ever uttered a voice so distinct and borne a testimony so consistent with all the facts of human nature. If we had no other evidence, this would go far to convince us that the Bible is from God, for no one fact is more momentous in itself or better established by experience than the fact of sin. We see it everywhere in the world, and we feel its bitter presence in our own hearts.

Upon this stern and awful reality, the fact of sin, which we can no more dispute than we can our own existence, the Bible throws a light of information that can be derived from no other quarter. It tells us of its origin, its primal author, its extent, its enormity, its sad consequences. It tells us how it came into the world, and how it has prevailed among men. It tells us of the ruin it has wrought, how it has dug the graves of the race of men, and how it has dishonored God. It tells us of its wages, death and hell, and also of the remedy which God has provided for the removal of its curse. In brief, sin is the deep and deadly malady which has fallen upon human nature, and for which there is but one cure, the salvation of Jesus Christ. The book which so frequently warns us of the disease tells in the same breath of the antidote and points to the Great Physician.

Of the origin of sin the Bible writers speak with no uncertain voice. They inform us that it began with the first parents of our race, who, tempted by the devil, transgressed the command of God: "By one man sin entered into the world, and death by sin; and so death passed upon all men, for that all have sinned;" "By one man's disobedience many were made sinners." Whether or not we can explain all the difficult problems connected with the doctrine which traces all human sinfulness back to Adam as its primal originating cause, evidently no other theory has been propounded which is more rational in itself or attended with less difficulties. Men may speculate and philosophize on this plain statement of the Bible as to the origin of sin, but thus far no man has told us anything on the subject more worthy to be believed than the simple fact that the first man sinned, and by that transgression brought sin and death upon all his descendants.

As to the extent and prevalence of sin the sacred writers are equally explicit. All men are sinners. Says the apostle Paul: "All have sinned, and come short of the glory of God;" "There is none righteous, no, not one;" "That every mouth may be stopped, and all the world may become guilty before God." Says John: "The whole world lieth in wickedness." And said the prophet Jeremiah: "The heart of man is deceitful above all things, and desperately wicked. Who can know it?" King David said: "I was shapen in iniquity, and in sin did my mother conceive me." So, again, Paul records one of his deepest experiences when he says, "For I know that in me, that is, in my flesh, dwelleth no good thing." From passages like these we can come to no other conclusion than that of the universal sinfulness and corruption of man in his natural state. Our human nature, as it came from the hand of God, was good, being created after the image of God in knowledge, righteousness and holiness. But by the apostasy in Eden it was brought into an estate of sin and misery, losing its original righteousness and the divine favor, being thenceforth inclined to that which is evil, and exposed to the wrath and curse of God, or as Paul expresses it, "dead in trespasses and sins."

It may well be called a sad heritage. The true children of God in every generation have found it so. "Fools," says Solomon, "make a mock of sin." No man in his senses, who has ever been led to see the reality and enormity of sin, can make a mock of it. No sane man can treat with levity that which has filled the world with woe and all human hearts with sorrow and with fear. It was only after Paul had come to understand the subject fully, having felt what sin was in his own heart and seen what it was in the light of God's law, that he cried in deep bitterness of spirit, "Oh, wretched man that I am! who shall deliver me from the body of this death?" The man who has no sense of sin, no conviction of guilt, is the man who has no thorough knowledge of his own heart, and no appreciation of the character of God or of his holy law. "Know thyself" was a wise maxim even in a pagan philosopher: how much more essential is such knowledge in a man of God! The holiest men of old were those who had made the deepest discoveries of their own sinfulness through the illuminating power of God's law and the Holy Ghost.

It was through these deep heart-searchings and many painful conflicts in the days of trial and adversity that the patriarch Job was led at last to say, "I have heard of thee by the hearing of the ear, but now mine eye seeth thee; wherefore I abhor myself and repent in dust and ashes." It was when the inspired Isaiah had seen a vision of the divine glory in the temple that he cried, "Woe is me, for I am undone, because I am a man of unclean lips, and I dwell in the midst of a people of unclean lips; for mine eyes have seen the King, the Lord of hosts." It was this discovery of God's character, and of the deep-seated depravity of his own heart in the light of God's law, that led David to indite that penitential psalm whose every utterance is a confession of guilt or a prayer for forgiveness: "Have mercy upon me, O God, according to thy lovingkindness; according unto the multitude of thy tender mercies blot out my transgressions. Wash me throughly from mine iniquity, and cleanse me from my sin. For I acknowledge my transgressions, and my sin is ever before me."

The way of transgressors is hard. It is an evil and a bitter thing to commit sin. It biteth like a serpent and stingeth like an adder. It pierceth the soul through with many sorrows. Unless it is repented of and forgiven, it will be the soul's eternal undoing. To live in sin and to die a rebel and wrong-doer in the sight of God is a fearful doom. The world is full of the evils of sin, and hell is made up of its victims. Yet by nature it is within us all. How shall we escape it? There is but one way.

CHAPTER V.

THE UNIVERSALITY OF SIN.

THE sinfulness of human nature manifests itself in many different forms and in varying degrees of intensity as men are exposed to temptation. It would be a great mistake to suppose that no sin exists in those amiable characters who have never encountered temptation and exhibited any outward acts of depravity. The heart is a deep fountain whose bitter waters may not always overflow, simply because they have been walled around by God's providence or restrained by his grace. Some superficial theorists have maintained that there is no sin except in the overt act of willful transgression. But this opinion is contradicted both by Scripture and by experience. It falls utterly short of that deep malady, that foul leprosy of a sinful nature, which the Bible depicts in such fearful terms, and which the best men in the world have mourned over all their lives. In all ages the children of God, though partially sanctified by grace, have still been sadly conscious of an abiding depravity, against which they have struggled, though it found no expression on the lips or in overt acts of transgression.

In fact, there are three distinct forms or stages of this natural depravity; and no man can be said to have fully known his own heart until, in the light of God's law, he has found them out. It is the true function of the Divine law to reveal this self-knowledge to us. "By the law," says Paul, "is the knowledge of sin. I was alive without the law once (that is, had a good opinion of myself), but when the commandment came sin revived and I died."

There is, first, the class of outward and flagrant acts of transgression as expressed in wicked words and deeds. No one can deny that these are sinful violations of the law of God, making the offender amenable even at the bar of human justice. And how large a portion of men's lives and of the world's history is but the dark record of such outward acts of violence and wrong-doing!

There is, secondly, that phase of depravity which lies back of all overt acts of sin, which often leads to such overt acts, but which may exist where no outward action gives expression to the sin, and where no eye but that of God can discern it. It is the secret sin of bad intention, of a deliberate purpose to do wrong; and it is the antecedent stage of most of the actual wrong-doing in the world. This secret purpose in the heart, this deliberate choice of the will to do wrong, is the very essence of transgression, even when no outward act gives expression to it. The thwarted or unexecuted intention of crime is as certainly sinful in the sight of a holy God as is the criminal act. When God says, "Thou shall not covet," it is as real a prohibition of sin in the heart as when he says, "Thou shalt not kill, or steal or commit adultery." However it may be with human laws, the Divine law is as truly violated by the sinful purpose of the heart as by the sinful word or the sinful deed. The word of the Lord, we are told, is "quick and powerful," and it is "a discerner of the thoughts and intents of the heart." His commandments are exceeding broad. When Ananias and Sapphira fell dead at the feet of the apostles under the just judgment of God for having lied unto the Holy Ghost, the very essence of their guilt, as charged by Peter, was that they "had conceived this thing in their hearts." When Simon Magus proposed to purchase the gift of the Holy Ghost with money, it was this evil intention that brought forth the stern rebuke of the apostle, who exhorted him to repent, "if perchance the thought of thine heart may be forgiven thee."

But this does not measure the whole extent of man's sinfulness. Back of his actions, and back of his voluntary purposes of action, there is a still deeper malady in his fallen nature. There is a fountain of evil within him, from which the stream of his evil acts and his evil intentions is constantly flowing. The saddest part of this heritage of sin is that innate evil heart, that bias of his moral nature, which makes him averse to good and inclined to evil from the earliest dawn of his free agency and responsibility. All history and all experience prove what the Scriptures so abundantly teach us, that when the child of Adam comes into the world it is not a sinless angel that the mother's arms enfold, but a creature whose opening moral agency will show it to be a transgressor of God's law—a creature which if not corrected and restrained by grace may soon grow into an enemy of man and a rebel against God.

This is the doctrine of Scripture, and this is the fact

of all experience and history. The penitential conviction of David recognized this when he cried, "Behold, I was shapen in iniquity, and in sin did my mother conceive me. Create in me a clean heart, O God, and renew a right spirit within me." "The wicked are estranged from the womb," said he; "they go astray as soon as they be born, speaking lies." The perfect man of Uz, the upright Job, confessed this when he cried, "Behold, I am vile: what shall I answer? I will lay mine hand upon my mouth. I have heard of thee by the hearing of the ear, but now mine eye seeth thee. Wherefore, I abhor myself and repent in dust and ashes." The beloved and venerable apostle John, with all his saintliness, confessed this when he wrote, "If we say that we have no sin we deceive ourselves, and the truth is not in us." The great apostle of the Gentiles from the inmost experience of his soul saw and confessed this deep and dreadful malady of a corrupt nature when he described the struggle between the natural and the spiritual in the seventh chapter of the Epistle to the Romans: "For I know that in me (that is, in my flesh) dwelleth no good thing: for to will is present with me, but how to perform that which is good I find not." "I find then a law, that, when I would do good, evil is present with me. For I delight in the law of God after the inward man: but I see another law in my members, warring against the law of my mind, and bringing me into captivity to the law of sin which is in my members. Oh, wretched man that I am! who shall deliver me from the body of this death?"

In no part of the Bible is this doctrine of the inborn

sinfulness of human nature more vividly set forth than in the words of our blessed Lord. In repeated passages he traces all outward forms of depravity to that unbending will which will not come to God, or to that evil heart which loves darkness rather than light, because its deeds are evil. "This is the condemnation," said he, "that light is come into the world, and men love darkness rather than light, because their deeds are evil;" "And ye will not come unto me because your deeds are evil." What great ethical philosopher ever struck the key of human nature so truly as when he said, "A good man, out of the good treasure of his heart, bringeth forth good things; and an evil man, out of the evil treasure, bringeth forth evil things;" "Either make the tree good and his fruit good; or else make the tree corrupt and his fruit corrupt; for the tree is known by his fruit;" "Do men gather grapes of thorns or figs of thistles? Even so every good tree bringeth forth good fruit; but a corrupt tree bringeth forth evil fruit. A good tree cannot bring forth evil fruit, neither can a corrupt tree bring good fruit. Every tree that bringeth not forth good fruit is hewn down and cast into the fire. Wherefore, by their fruits ye shall know them." Can any teaching be more explicit than this—that man's nature is as are his acts; and, inasmuch as all history proves his actions to be sinful, it must be a sinful nature at the root which bears such fruits?

We are not, however, left merely to the analogy and the logic of the case. Christ has laid down the doctrine in the most explicit and didactic statements elsewhere. He says, "Those things which proceed out of the mouth come forth from the heart, and they defile the man;" "For from within, out of the heart of men, proceed evil thoughts, adulteries, fornications, murders, thefts, covetousness, wickedness, deceit, lasciviousness, an evil eye, blasphemy, pride, foolishness: all these evil things come from within, and defile the man."

It is very clear, then, from the Scriptures, that human nature is sadly marred and fallen from its high estate. The malady is deep, and it is universal. It has reached every man, and every man is by nature under condemnation on account of sin. There is no exemption and no relief from the curse except by grace. After all that God's restraining grace has done under the gospel, violence and crime prevail and the wickedness of man is great in the earth. Now, as at the flood of Noah, it may be said of man that "every imagination of the thoughts of his heart is only evil continually."

When we look on this sad estate of our fallen humanity, in which the whole head is sick and the whole heart faint, what are we to do? Is there no balm in Gilead, no physician there? In the infinite goodness of God there is a remedy, there is One who can heal. The remedy is found at the cross; it is found in Christ. From the deepest discoveries and convictions of our own utter sinfulness and impotence, and from the condemning sentence of the law, we are able to turn with confidence to the pardoning and restoring grace of the gospel, and to cry out with Paul, "Thanks be unto God, who giveth us the victory through our Lord Jesus Christ!"

CHAPTER VI.

THE BROTHERHOOD OF MAN.

FROM the established truth of the fatherhood of God follows, by logical sequence, the related doctrine of the brotherhood of man. If by creation and providence we are all children of one Father, then we are all brothers of the same family and bound to recognize the kinship of a common humanity. And what is thus true in the realm of nature is equally true in the kingdom of grace, so far as grace has extended. If in Christ Jesus we have one reconciled God and Father, and have been made partakers of his redemptive work by grace, then are we all to whom this new tie is given brethren of one family, and equally bound to recognize the nearer relationship. In this redeemed family of Christ, who have all put on the new man and been renewed in knowledge after the image of Him who created them, we are told, "There is neither Greek nor Jew, circumcision nor uncircumcision, barbarian, Scythian, bond nor free; but Christ is all and in all." This is the broad brotherhood of the saints, as exemplified in the one universal or catholic Church of all ages, and completed when all that Church shall be gathered together in Christ its Head at the end of the world.

But besides this common brotherhood of the saints, so clearly taught in the Scriptures, there is a still broader brotherhood of the human race taught with equal clearness both by Scripture and by the light of reason. "God," declares the inspired apostle, to the Athenian sages on Mars' Hill, "hath made of one blood all nations of men, to dwell on all the face of the earth; and hath determined the times before appointed, and the bounds of their habitation." The gospel which thus proclaims all men "the offspring of God," and the men of all nations as originally "made of one blood, and created in the image of God," is equally explicit in telling us that all who are redeemed in Christ are redeemed out of "every nation and kindred and tongue and people" by the one blood of the Son of God. The one blood of redemption shed upon the cross, by which all who are in Christ are united as brothers for evermore, is but the counterpart of that one blood of a divine creation by which the men of all races and nations to the end of the world belong to one great family and constitute the common brotherhood of humanity.

The subject is a fruitful one, but three points suggested by it claim special consideration.

The first is, that the doctrine of a universal human kinship is the clear and unmistakable teaching of Scripture. The last proclamation of the great Founder of Christianity, delivered with solemn emphasis when he ascended to heaven, involves it in every utterance. He said, "Go ye into all the world, and preach the gospel to every creature. Go ye and teach all nations. He that believeth and is baptized shall be saved. He that believeth not shall be damned." The mighty angel of the Apocalypse also virtually proclaims it when he is seen flying through the midst of heaven, having the everlasting gospel to preach unto them that dwell on the earth, to every nation and kindred and tongue and people. As in the New Testament there is but one gospel, one redemption, one "common salvation" for men, so there is but one humanity, one organic race of men, as distinguished from all other beings, and one common nature fashioned originally in the likeness of God. To our own conception it is as clear that the Scriptures everywhere teach or imply this doctrine as it is that they teach anything. When the Scriptures announce those great fundamental truths—there is one God, and one Mediator between God and men, the man Christ Jesus, who gave himself a ransom for all, to be testified in due time—how more impressively could they have taught the oneness of the human race and the common brotherhood of all the nations?

The second thought worthy of special notice is the slowness of mankind in accepting the doctrine of a common origin and a common brotherhood, and the reluctance of human philosophy and statesmanship to learn the great practical lessons which result from it. Had the doctrine been accepted and its lessons practiced, how would wars have ceased to the end of the earth! What untold horrors and desolations have been entailed upon mankind from age to age by the old idea, still prevalent among nations, that each great power may lawfully stand in an attitude of armed resistance against all the rest, and that the weaker nations and the uncivilized races have no ties of brotherhood which the stronger are bound to respect! How would the whole bloody history of the world from the beginning till now have been reversed if the plain New-Testament doctrine of peace on earth and good-will to men, on the basis of a common brotherhood, had been accepted and obeyed! Alas for the civilized statesmanship of the nineteenth century and for the Christianity which it represents! Alas, too, for the boasted science and philosophy on which our civilization and our Christian statesmanship rest, when our great states and nations, now holding the dominion of the globe, have yet to learn the first principle of a true Christian ethics—namely, that before God all men, whether civilized or savage, are brothers and should be treated as brothers!

A third point suggested by the subject is the grand argument it furnishes in vindication of Christianity as the true religion of heaven and the one divine religion for man. As things are, we do not know any better proof that the gospel of Christ is from God, and not of man's devising, than that it comes to us with this great doctrine of the common brotherhood of man. We should be willing to take our stand in defence of it, before all reasonable men, on that ground alone, even if there were no other. For we feel in our inmost soul that the doctrine is true and the doctrine is right, whatever human science and philosophy may choose to decide about it. We rejoice that Christianity from the first has so boldly committed itself to the doctrine. We rejoice that on this one great truth of human brotherhood Christianity has always been in advance, not only of all other religions, but of all human civilization. It stands in that advanced position to-day. In that position it is now, as it always has been, in the lead of the world's advancing civilization. For a hundred years, in all parts of the globe, the progress of modern missions to the heathen has vindicated the truth of that position. Every new triumph which the gospel wins amongst barbarous or semi-civilized tribes or nations is but an added demonstration of the great doctrine proclaimed by Christianity from the beginning, that all men are brothers by nature and in Jesus Christ may be made both brothers and equals. This is one of the instances in which we do not reason that a doctrine is true because it is taught by Christianity—as, for example, the resurrection of the dead—but in which we rather reverse the reasoning, and feel that Christianity is true and must be divine because it has taught the doctrine, and is to-day illustrating it around the globe by preaching a gospel alike adapted to all men.

It is the fashion in our times to hold the Church up to disparagement and ridicule because it has not lived up to the ideal of its great Founder, and has never fulfilled his last commission to give the gospel to all mankind. It is alleged that the Church is mercenary, selfish, ambitious, seeking only the welfare of its own members, and caring naught for the poor and the perishing of a world lying in wickedness. Now, we have only to point to the history of Christian missions all around the globe during the last hundred years to prove the charge an unwarranted slander. We have only to point to hundreds of missionary stations and to thousands of missionaries and teachers, male and female, and to hundreds of thousands of converts won from paganism by their labors, to demonstrate that the doctrine of the brotherhood of man and of care for the poor is held by the churches of evangelical Christendom, not as a dead letter of the creeds, but as a grand practical reality, in which hundreds of the noblest men and women of the Church—the Livingstones, Duffs, Wilsons, Hebers, Morrisons, Judsons, Newells, Martyns, Williamses, Vanderkemps, Moffats—have been willing to spend or sacrifice their lives. We are justified, in the light of such labors and after the testimony of such lives, to hurl back the slander in the teeth of those who make it.

Who raised up and educated and sent out those missionaries, and who sustained the cost of their going, to the extent of millions of dollars and at the risk of the lives of their own loved sons and daughters? It is the evangelical Christian Church of all denominations and in all lands that has done it, and done it with no earthly selfish motive, but out of simple obedience to Christ's command and a yearning sympathy for the souls of the perishing. The Church has done it because the Church believes that one gospel was intended for all mankind, and that all men of all races and nations are brothers and equals, alike precious in his sight.

While skeptical unbelievers at home are finding fault with the Church as being out of sympathy with humanity, and as being out of sympathy with the progressive spirit of the age, the Church by her missionaries abroad is daily refuting the imputation, and proving beyond question that her sons and daughters are doing more to help the perishing and to spread true civilization around the globe than all other agencies put together. This demonstration of a divine origin, and of a practical philanthropy in the face of toil and danger and death, Christianity is now giving in every heathen land to which the Christian missionary and the Christian teacher have gone. Nor do we see that the demonstration is any less remarkable and conclusive in the eyes of the men of this generation than was that earlier demonstration which God gave to the men of the first century when his inspired apostles first carried the glad tidings of salvation to the Gentiles.

Christianity has always been better than the governments, or even the churches, professing to be guided by its precepts. It is not responsible for man's inhumanity to man, nor for the crimes committed in its name by great civilized nations calling themselves the exponents, *par excellence*, of Christian civilization. No government in the world has ever yet practically lived up to the principles of peace and philanthropy inculcated by Christ. Instead of treating the inferior races as their fellow-men, all children of the same Father, the great nations of Christendom have too often pursued them unto death as enemies. It has been reserved for the evangelical churches to demonstrate on a hundred mission-fields the true doctrine of the universal brotherhood of man, and to proclaim among the nations that divine law of peace and good-will to all men which was first proclaimed from heaven at the birth of Christ. If ever the golden age of bards and prophets, when the nations shall "beat their swords into ploughshares and their spears into pruning-hooks," shall be realized in this world of selfish ambition and tyranny, it will be only as the beneficent principles of the gospel of Christ shall prevail over the world's maxims of cupidity and selfishness.

All men admire, or profess to admire, the virtues of benevolence, charity, philanthropy. We are sometimes told that the Church is deficient in not giving a higher illustration of these qualities, and that if it would conquer the world it must preach a gospel broad enough to include all humanity. If there be any one sentiment that, as an abstract theory, may be said to be fully incorporated among the virtues in the judgment of civilized nations, it is this sentiment of common brotherhood. "I am a man, and nothing human is foreign to me." This creed of the old Roman poet is now the lauded creed of the world. This is the "one touch of nature which makes the whole world kin."

Such, at least in profession, is the beautiful theory of the world's religion. The practice of it is a different thing. Without stopping to inquire whence this much-applauded sentiment originated, and how it has grown so popular, it is more to our present purpose to notice the immense discrepancy often exhibited between the profession and the practice of this religion of universal humanity. Possibly it may be found, after all, that it is only within the bosom of the Christian Church that there is anything like an approximation of the practice to the theory. When the world desires to learn what its own favorite ideal of the religion of humanity can do as an actual experience amongst men, it may be found that it will have to go into the Church to see the examples and learn the lesson. Poets can sing of it very sweetly, and philosophers extol, but only Christian heroes do the work. From the days of Terence until now, history does not contain the record of many splendid poets or great philosophers, or even founders of religions, who have actually gone into the world's great field of action to teach men by living example how to practice this blessed evangel of common humanity, this universal brotherhood of man to man and nation to nation.

On the contrary, notwithstanding all the light and all the high sanctions of divine example by which Christianity has illustrated and enforced the sentiment of human brotherhood, cases are constantly occurring in which great Christian nations practically set it aside and act on the opposite principle of a narrow, selfish exclusivism. The leaders of public opinion, in the teeth of all their professions of liberality and broad philanthropy, not only "give up to party what was meant for mankind," but sacrifice every principle of right and justice on the altar of a mere temporal aggrandizement, or, as it is called in the convenient phraseology of modern diplomacy, "in protection of the national interests"—a principle on which every war of conquest or of ambition under heaven has been waged and vindicated. Where is the beautiful sentiment of humanity and brotherhood, the world's blessed religion, when weighed in the balances against self-interest, individual, local or national? What does all the fine poetry or the philosophy or the religion avail in worldly minds when it comes to a struggle against the lust of power, the greed of gain, the demon of ambition?

Men who discard Christianity discourse eloquently to the Church about a broad and liberal religion large enough to clasp in its loving bosom all men as brothers. They denounce all narrow sectarian shibboleths of the creed as a breach of the great law of humanity. In the mean time, what are they doing, and what have they ever done, to illustrate the common brotherhood of man? What hospitals of mercy at home have they founded, what orphan asylums have they erected, what missions of civilization established among the heathen? We much fear that a gospel left to such defenders would soon perish in the hands of its own apostles.

But not so: the true gospel of humanity is safe; it is in other and better hands. It is where it was placed eighteen centuries ago, in the keeping of the Church of God. That world-wide gospel of love and brotherhood, peace on earth and good-will to men, first proclaimed by its divine Founder, and illustrated in the career of its chosen apostle to the Gentiles, has won its way hitherto over all obstacles of race and prejudice, and to-day is winning its sure and predestined way to a universal dominion. This is the grandest fact in all modern history. Thousands of educated men and women in every nation around the globe, civilized or pagan, are to-day exemplifying the true religion of humanity precisely as it was taught by Jesus Christ and illustrated in the life of Paul. With them the religion of humanity is no mere dream of a poet's fancy, no philosophic theorem of the cloister: it is a living reality. With them human brotherhood is both a theory and a sentiment, both a doctrine and a fact. They are the living epistles of its truth, known and read of all men amongst whom they have gone preaching this gospel of the kingdom. The poor heathen, blind as they are, see it and admit it. Thousands of them have already thrown away their idols in attestation of its superior power. Our great men and philosophers at home must be fools indeed if they cannot see it. Does the scientific, cultured world of our day demand a sign from heaven, a true miracle of unselfish humanity laboring for the good of others? Here it is in the advanced guard of Christianity on every heathen shore, preaching and practicing the doctrine of human brotherhood. The great poet of sentiment, Robert Burns, was not truer to human nature than he was to Christianity when he wrote the lines—

> "Then let us pray that come it may,
> As come it will for a' that,
> That man to man, the wide world o'er,
> Shall brothers be for a' that."

CHAPTER VII.

THE MEDIATORSHIP OF CHRIST.

THE whole contents of the Bible may be expressed in three words—God, the Mediator and man. The extreme terms, God and man, give us a vast chasm, which can be bridged over only by the third, the Mediator. Between the extremes lies all religion, and in this middle term alone the idea of salvation becomes possible. In his return to God man needs a voice of truth and a guide of conduct. Nothing in this world can ever supply that want but a Mediator who has come from God and gone back to God. He alone has authority to say, "I am the way and the truth and the life. No man cometh unto the Father but by me." Clearly, there can be no salvation for any human soul without mediation, and no mediation is available between God and man except by one who is authorized and competent to fill the great office.

Accordingly, we find the apostle Paul in the First Epistle to Timothy rising to one of his grandest generalizations of essential doctrine when stating this central truth of the Christian system in terms which admit of no uncertainty and no mistake: "For there is one God, and one Mediator between God and men, the man Christ Jesus, who gave himself a ransom for all, to be testified in due time." Here we have the fundamental facts of the scheme of salvation: the one God and Father of all, the one sinful, ruined race of man to be redeemed and restored to God, the one Mediator competent and authorized to intercede and save, the Divine man Jesus Christ, and the one ransom of his sacrificial vicarious death adequate for all and offered to all. This is without controversy the sum and substance of the gospel. This plan of salvation through a Mediator, Immanuel, who is himself God manifest in the flesh, and therefore mighty to save even to the uttermost, is the great mystery of godliness which gives the gospel its vast significance and its infinite value.

Inasmuch as the Mediator is one who comes between offended and alienated parties in order to reconcile them, it was needful that Christ Jesus, in order to be an adequate Mediator between God and man, should represent both and possess the nature of both. A mediator, says Paul, is not of one party, but of both. So our great Mediator, being the eternal Son of God, and becoming by his incarnation the Son of man, "born of a woman and made under the law," with a true body and a rational soul, had in himself this essential condition of true mediation. "He took not on him the nature of angels; but he took on him the seed of Abraham"—that is, our human nature. Both he that sanctifieth and they who are sanctified are all of one. "Wherefore," says the apostle, "it behooved him to be made like unto his brethren, that he might be a merciful and faithful high priest in things pertaining to God, to make reconciliation for the sins of the people."

The mediatorial work of Christ includes all that he

accomplished for our redemption in his two estates of humiliation and exaltation, and in his three offices of Prophet, Priest and King. Much of the New Testament—indeed, we may say, all of the New Testament—with a large portion of the Old, gathers around this mediatorial work of the incarnate Redeemer. Volumes have been written in elucidation of it. Only a few of its essential features can be noticed here. But even these will be sufficient to indicate how fundamental to our salvation was that work, and how pre-eminent were the qualifications of our adorable Lord to assume it.

First, it was in virtue of his mediatorship that Christ came to reveal the true knowledge of God. In this respect he was, as he often declared, the "Light of the world." "He was the true light," says John, "that lighteth every man that cometh into the world;" "No man hath seen God at any time; the only-begotten Son who is in the bosom of the Father, he hath declared him." Until Christ came the world by wisdom knew not God. In fact, the world at its highest estate, including a large portion of the Jewish race, had lost all true saving knowledge of God.

In this character of Revealer and Teacher, Jesus Christ came into our sin-darkened world to bear witness unto the truth. In this character he fulfills the first great mediatorial office of Prophet from God—the one Prophet of whom all other inspired prophets had spoken, to whom all the apostles bore witness. Thus the apostle Paul, in opening his sublime discussion in the Epistle to the Hebrews, on the person, character, and work of Christ, says: "God, who at sundry times and in divers manners, spake in time past unto the fathers by the prophets, hath in these last days spoken unto us by his Son." It is in this voice of the Son of God that we have an infallible guide to heaven, the way of life revealed and the knowledge of God and immortality brought to light by the gospel.

In the next place, Christ as Mediator came to assert the law of God and to exemplify it in his own perfect life. Men had denied its claims, perverted its meaning, trampled its authority in the dust. It needed a Divine Vindicator, a perfect human example, that should fulfill all righteousness and teach men how to live and how to die. Christ's immaculate life, a man approved of God and all the people, holy, harmless and separate from sinners, was the lesson for all time. The language of his life was, "I delight to do thy will, O my God;" and of his death, "Not my will, but thine be done." Thus he magnified the law and made it honorable. Thus he glorified God on the earth by an absolutely sinless obedience, and finished the work God had given him to do.

Another essential part of our great Mediator's work consisted in his satisfying divine justice and paying the penalty of transgression due to man's sins. This Christ did once for all by his sacrificial death upon the cross. By that one great immolation he hath reconciled us to God and God to us, so that God can be just and yet justify the ungodly. By that great atonement through his blood, which no other being in the universe was competent to make, " he tasted death for every man " and " perfected for ever them that are sanctified." Thus said the prophet Isaiah: "He was wounded for our transgressions, he was bruised for our iniquities; the chastisement of our peace was upon him; and with his stripes we are healed. All we like sheep have gone astray; we have turned every one to his own way; and the Lord hath laid on him the iniquity of us all." Thus said the prophet Daniel: "He finished transgression, made an end of sins, made reconciliation for iniquity, and brought in everlasting righteousness." So when the great Redeemer had paid this ransom on the cross he cried with his dying breath, "It is finished." All this he accomplished in virtue of his mediatorial office as our great High Priest, and then ascended to the heavens. Being delivered for our offences, he was raised again for our justification.

His atoning work on earth being now finished, it remained for him to fulfill another part of his great mediation. It is that of intercession for his redeemed people before the throne of God in heaven. Isaiah had described him as "bearing the sins of many and making intercession for the transgressors;" "He saw that there was no man, and wondered that there was no intercessor; therefore his arm brought salvation unto him, and his righteousness, it sustained him." And thus the apostle Paul, in the Epistle to the Hebrews, after describing the completed work of Christ's priesthood in this world, tells us of that exalted intercession in heaven which is still going on before God's throne: "But this man, because he continueth for ever, hath an unchangeable priesthood. Wherefore he is able to save them to the uttermost, that come unto God by him, seeing he ever liveth to make intercession for them." In his character of Intercessor he has gone to appear before God and to make continual intercession for his people. In his life of humiliation here and his death of sacrifice he had revealed God and wrought out redemption for man. In his intercessory glory above at God's right hand it is his office to introduce redeemed and sanctified man to his God. The theme is a fruitful one, but we cannot dwell upon it now.

Yet one more point must be mentioned. It is that essential part of the Mediator's work which belongs to his kingly office. The Scriptures, which declare him to be a priest for ever after the order of Melchisedec, also proclaim him "King of kings and Lord of lords;" "Thy throne, O God, is for ever and ever." "Christ," says the Westminster Catechism, "executeth the office of a King, in subduing us to himself, in ruling and defending us, and in restraining and conquering all his and our enemies." This kingly office began in his estate of exaltation, when he rose from the dead and ascended into heaven, and it will be carried forward to the end of the world, when all his enemies shall be put under his feet.

In this exalted state our divine Redeemer is now seated on his mediatorial throne, crowned with glory, reigning and ruling over all nations, and administering all things for the welfare of his redeemed Church. This great work still goes on, as for more than eighteen centuries it has gone on, with irresistible power. And it will go on with increasing glory to the end; for every knee must bow to him, and every tongue confess that Jesus Christ is Lord, to the glory of God the Father. When the works of the devil are destroyed, all things subdued by the power of Christ, and even death, the last enemy, destroyed, then only shall come to pass that sublime consummation mentioned by Paul in the First Epistle to the Corinthians, when he shall deliver up the mediatorial kingdom to God.

CHAPTER VIII.

THE DIVINITY AND INCARNATION OF CHRIST.

IT is worthy of notice that three of the New-Testament writers, Mark, John and Paul, introduce three of the most important treatises in the volume with a distinct and formal recognition of the supreme divinity of Jesus Christ. The other writers refer to it also, and recognize it in many passages with more or less fullness, but it is not without significance that these three have set it forth boldly in the foreground, as forming the very text and subject of what they had to write. Mark gives it to us in the very title of his book: "The beginning of the gospel of Jesus Christ, the Son of God." John does the same in the opening verses of his Gospel: "In the beginning was the Word [the Logos], and the Word was with God, and the Word was God. The same was in the beginning with God. All things were made by him, and without him was not anything made that was made. In him was life, and the life was the light of men." He does the same again in the first of his Epistles: "That which was from the beginning, which we have heard, which we have seen with our eyes, which our hands have handled of the Word of life, that declare we unto you, that ye may have fellowship with us, and truly our fellowship is with the Father, and with his Son Jesus Christ."

In like manner the apostle Paul devotes the first chapter of his Epistle to the Hebrews to a formal presentation of the proof that Jesus is the Son of God, and opens the discussion in these weighty words: "God, who at sundry times and in divers manners, spake in time past unto the fathers by the prophets, hath in these last days spoken unto us by his Son, whom he hath appointed heir of all things, by whom also he made the worlds; who being the brightness of his glory and the express image of his person, and upholding all things by the word of his power, when he had by himself purged our sins, sat down on the right hand of the Majesty on high; being made so much better than the angels, as he hath by inheritance obtained a more excellent name than they." It is impossible that any fair and candid criticism can ever explain away or break the force of the argument for the supreme divinity of Christ which the apostle sets before us in this chapter. It is only one of many similar passages in the Bible, but even if it stood alone it would establish the doctrine. For the inspired writer here, without limitation, has ascribed to Jesus Christ the very names, titles, attributes, works and worship of supreme Godhead. He is the "Son of God," "the brightness of the Father's glory and the express image of his person." He is the almighty Creator, by whom "the worlds were made," the God of providence, "upholding all things by the word of his power." He is the Redeemer of the soul, having "expiated our sins by his death," and then "sat down on the right hand of the Majesty on high." Of him the Father says, what was never said to any one of the angels, "Thou art my Son; this day have I begotten thee;" "And to the Son he saith, Thy throne, O God, is for ever and ever;" "Thou hast laid the foundations of the earth, and the heavens are the work of thy hands." Men are never required to worship men, nor angels to worship angels. But the command of the Father is, "Let all the angels of God worship him;" and he himself taught that "all men should honor him even as they honor the Father."

The supreme divinity of Jesus Christ, as being the only-begotten and eternal Son of God, is as clearly taught throughout this passage as any truth can be taught. The demonstration is satisfactory and complete when the highest worship of earth and heaven is ascribed to him as his right, and when he is expressly declared to have created all worlds by his power and wisdom, to have upheld all creatures by his providential sway, and to have redeemed all souls by his blood.

If Jesus Christ did these things, it is impossible to believe that he could be less than God, for none but God could do them. But Paul, both here and elsewhere, asserts without qualification or ambiguity that he did them. And with him all other New-Testament writers, as well as Moses and the prophets, agree. The Old-Testament prophets announced the great doctrine of his Godhead and the fact of his incarnation when they said, "Behold, a virgin shall conceive, and bear a son, and shall call his name Immanuel, God with us. The government shall be upon his shoulder. Of the increase of his government and peace there shall be no end.

And his name shall be called Wonderful, Counselor, The mighty God, The everlasting Father, The Prince of peace." The angels heralded that advent at Bethlehem, and the inspired evangelists confirmed the same wondrous tidings to all nations when they gave their united testimony and sealed it with their blood, saying, "The Word was made flesh and dwelt among us, and we beheld his glory, the glory as of the only-begotten of the Father, full of grace and truth."

In the first chapter of the Epistle to the Colossians the pre-existence and the supreme divinity of Christ are set forth with unmistakable distinctness. "He," says Paul, "is the image of the invisible God, the first-born of every creature," or, as it would be better rendered, "the first-begotten before all creatures;" "For by him were all things created that are in heaven, and that are in earth, visible and invisible: whether they be thrones, or dominions, or principalities, or powers: all things were created by him and for him, and he is before all things, and by him all things consist. And he is head of the body, the Church; who is the beginning, the first-born from the dead: that in all things he might have the pre-eminence. For it pleased the Father that in him should all fullness dwell; and having made peace through the blood of his cross, by him to reconcile all things unto himself—by him, I say, whether they be things in earth, or things in heaven." Farther on the same apostle says: "In him dwelleth all the fullness of the Godhead bodily."

No doctrine of Christianity is established on more abundant evidence than the divinity of Christ, and no doctrine is more essential to the gospel plan of salvation; for it is impossible to see how he could forgive sin as he claimed to do, and how he could take away the sins of the world, unless he was divine. A merely human Saviour would be no Saviour. It is on the divine ability of Christ to save, and to save to the uttermost, all that come to God through him that our hopes of heaven depend. The incarnate divine Saviour, Immanuel, God with us and God for us, is the very keystone in the arch of our salvation, as he is the cornerstone in its foundation. But if Christ is God, and the Holy Ghost is also God, as the Scriptures affirm, then we have the great doctrine of the Holy Trinity as held by the fathers and by all the great churches of Christendom, Greek, Roman and Protestant.

The Scriptures teach the unity of God: "Hear, O Israel, the Lord our God is one Lord;" "There is one God and one Mediator between God and men, the man Christ Jesus." But they teach also the tri-personality of the Godhead. There are three Persons in the Godhead. The doctrine of the Trinity is revealed to us chiefly in the history of redemption. Our salvation is the joint work of God the Father and the Son and the Holy Ghost. These three perform an essential part in it from beginning to end. Thus the three divine Persons are associated in the formula of Christian baptism. It is administered in the name of the Father and the Son and the Holy Ghost. To each of these divine Persons the Scriptures ascribe the attributes, works and worship of the one essential Godhead.

We do not attempt to explain this great mystery of the Trinity of the Godhead, any more than we do that of the divine nature or being. But when we prove from Scripture the incarnate deity of Christ and the deity of the Holy Ghost, we cannot do otherwise than accept the doctrine of the Holy Trinity as true. When we believe in the Father and in the Son and in the Holy Ghost, as formulated in the Apostles' Creed and in all the earlier creeds of the Church, we only accept the doctrine of a tri-unity of Persons in the Godhead as it is taught in the Scriptures.

Now, the Scriptures, so far from denying, are bold to confess, that this is a great mystery. Nor do the sacred writers feel called upon to reject or doubt it because it is a mystery. It is precisely when speaking of the incarnate divinity of Jesus Christ that Paul says, "Without controversy, great is the mystery of godliness." Writing to the Philippians, he gives us the nearest approach to an explanation of the facts which the case admitted of, in that remarkable passage which describes the three states of the Incarnate One—his pre-existent state of glory with the Father, his assumed mediatorial humiliation in the flesh, and his subsequent exaltation at God's right hand: "Who, being in the form of God, thought it not robbery to be equal with God, but made himself of no reputation, and took upon him the form of a servant, and was made in the likeness of men; and being found in fashion as a man he humbled himself and became obedient unto death, even the death of the cross. Wherefore, God also hath highly exalted him and given him a name which is above every name, that at the name of Jesus every knee should bow, of things in heaven, and things in earth, and things under the earth, and that every tongue should confess that Jesus Christ is Lord, to the glory of God the Father."

The nativity and the ascension are two great facts that stand out prominently on the pages of the life of Jesus Christ. Two others of equal significance, the crucifixion and the resurrection, intervene to fill up the mystery and complete the grand work of man's redemption. Incarnation, crucifixion, resurrection, ascension, are four events in the most wonderful life, four stages in the most eventful history, four acts in the most stupendous drama, the world has ever seen. It is an old story, but it loses nothing of its deathless interest. The centuries and the generations as they pass only concentrate the thoughts of men upon it, and develop more and more its far-reaching results. "His name," said the ancient prophet, "shall be called Wonderful." Nothing could be more wonderful than that the career of Christ on earth should open and close as it did. The sublime ascension was but the fitting finale and counterpart to the unique and marvelous advent.

In the one we have the advent of a new era in the world's history, the fulfillment and realization of all the ancient oracles that pointed to Immanuel, God manifest in the flesh; in the other, the sublime attestation that his mission on earth was completed and approved in heaven. At the nativity we have the stupendous fact that the Son of God had taken a human form and become the Son of man; at the ascension we behold the correlated fact, of equal significance and wonder, that the Son of man had gone up with our redeemed and glorified humanity to take his mediatorial throne at God's right hand. In the one, God comes down to dwell with men; in the other, ascends to reign with God.

There is a striking parallel and agreement between the occasions. Both alike are attended and announced by angelic messengers. At the nativity an angel of the Lord came down and proclaimed to the shepherds of Bethlehem, "Behold, I bring you good tidings of great joy, which shall be to all people. For unto you is born this day, in the city of David, a Saviour, who is Christ the Lord. And suddenly there was with the angel a multitude of the heavenly host, praising God and saying, Glory to God in the highest, and on earth peace, good-will toward men." At the ascension "he led them out as far as to Bethany, and while he blessed them he was parted from them;" "and a cloud received him out of their sight. And while they looked steadfastly toward heaven as he went up, behold, two men stood by them in white apparel, who also said, Ye men of Galilee, why stand ye gazing up into heaven? This same Jesus who is taken up from you into heaven shall so come in like manner as ye have seen him go into heaven." And as at the nativity the multitude of angels praised and worshiped God with songs of gladness for a Saviour descended, so at the ascension it is recorded that the disciples who witnessed that transcendent scene, a Saviour ascended to God, "worshiped him and returned to Jerusalem with great joy" (Luke xxiv. 52; Acts i. 9–11).

Both events alike are supernatural and mysterious, or rather they are parts of the one grand mystery of redemption. It is worthy of notice that the apostle Paul, in epitomizing the prominent facts of the gospel history in his First Epistle to Timothy, singles out these two as the first and the last of the remarkable summary. He begins with the incarnation and ends with the ascension, in that sublime confession of faith which rises into a doxology of wonder, saying, "And without controversy, great is the mystery of godliness; God was manifested in the flesh, justified in the Spirit, seen of angels, preached unto the Gentiles, believed on in the world, received up into glory" (1 Tim. iii. 16). It must not be forgotten that when Christ was born, his nativity ushered in his estate of humiliation and suffering. On the contrary, when he ascended it was in his estate of exaltation and glory, which began with his resurrection and was consummated when he sat down on his kingly throne in the heavens, exalted at God's right hand to give repentance and remission of sins.

It is in striking harmony with the glory of Immanuel in his ascended state that on the only two occasions recorded in the New Testament on which he ever again appeared to men he appears with such overpowering majesty of supreme Godhead that the human senses cannot endure the vision, and this frail mortality, dazzled with excessive light, falls in adoring homage at his feet. The one appearance is to Paul at his conversion on the way to Damascus, when he fell to the earth, trembling and astonished at the voice of him whom he was persecuting, and was led blind to Damascus, and remained three days without sight. The other appearance is to John in the isle of Patmos in the sublime epiphany of the opening chapter of the Apocalypse, when he is seen indeed as "One like unto the Son of man," but in such transcendent and ineffable glory of Godhead—"His countenance was as the sun shineth in his strength"—that the venerable apostle tells us, "When I saw him, I fell at his feet as dead. And he laid his right hand upon me, saying unto me, Fear not, I am the first and the last; I am he that liveth and was dead; and behold I am alive for evermore, Amen; and have the keys of hell and of death" (Acts ix. 4–9; Rev. i. 17, 18).

Now, it is plain that these two great affiliated doctrines of the incarnation and the ascension of Christ are fundamental to Christianity. That God has come into the world in the form of man, and that he has then taken that human form back to heaven, are stupendous and mysterious facts which involve all the rest and explain all the rest. If a man can accept and believe them, there is nothing more difficult in all the Bible at which he need stumble. If he cannot believe them, he has no right to say he accepts Christianity, for he clearly rejects that which is fundamental to the system.

But how, on the other hand, can any intelligent man reject them? They come to us on well-established human and divine testimony, interlinked with all the other facts in the life of Jesus, and so interlinked with a large part of the world's history that to reject them would be to reject everything, and, in fact, to shake our faith in all human knowledge. We must believe them; we cannot help believing them if we believe anything.

CHAPTER IX.

CHRIST THE LIGHT OF THE WORLD.

THE apostle John delights in a few brief, expressive terms, which he frequently uses in his Gospel history, in his Epistles, and occasionally in the Apocalypse. He no doubt heard them first from the lips of his divine Master; indeed, he often recites them as being spoken by Christ. Such words must have made an impression on the minds of the other disciples, and they may be traced in all the New-Testament writers, including Paul himself. But they seem to have made the deepest impression on John, and so have become the striking characteristic of his writings. The life, the truth, the light, the love of God, the resurrection, the true God, the eternal life, the Word of God, the way, the light of life, the Lamb of God, the bread of life, the book of life, the water of life, are some of the favorite simple or combined terms with which the beloved disciple has so tenderly recounted the wonderful and never-wearying story of the Cross.

If we could suppose a candid and well-informed man to have read and studied the first three Gospels without knowing that there was a fourth, we might well imagine that in reading for the first time this wonderful record of John he would feel that he had indeed the same old story, but in a form of phraseology so new and peculiar as to throw over it the charm of a profound and sublime originality. He would scarcely know whether to admire most the deep import of the thoughts conveyed in these brief words and sentences, or the surpassing simplicity of the style in which the thoughts are expressed. Where there is so little to meet the eye, what endless wonder is it that there should be so much to fill the mind? Nor will the wonder diminish by studied, oft-repeated and protracted reading. The veteran minister of God in the closing years of life ponders those brief words with far deeper meditation than when he first read them as a boy. The men of this nineteenth century, with all their advanced knowledge of the universe, read the same words to-day with as profound a reverence and wonder as did the Jews, Greeks and Romans, toward the close of the first century, when this last remaining apostle gave them to the world.

He who tells us that God is love declares also that God is light and in him is no darkness at all (1 John i. 5 and iv. 8). But he who tells us so emphatically that God is light claims for Christ all that is involved in this sublime and beautiful emblem of essential Godhead. For he asserts it at the very opening of his Gospel. "In him was life, and the life was the light of men. That was the true Light, which lighteth every man that cometh into the world" (John i. 4, 9). How strikingly, too, does the sublime ascription of all true light to Jesus Christ accord with what the other sacred writers declare of him as being the brightness of the divine glory, and the express image of his person, the light that should enlighten the Gentiles, and the glory of his people Israel (Heb. i. 3 and Luke ii. 32). But nothing can be more emphatic and decisive than the terms in which this chosen emblem of supreme divinity is assumed by Jesus Christ himself as the most fitting description of his own character and the very designation of his position in the world. In two distinct passages of John's Gospel, uttered on two different occasions, we have substantially the same grand outline of the office and mission of Christ as the author of light, the revealer of light and the giver of light to this darkened world.

In chapter viii. 12 he says, "I am the light of the world; he that followeth me shall not walk in darkness, but shall have the light of life." In chapter xii. 46 he says, "I am come a light into the world, that whosoever believeth on me should not abide in darkness." The two texts together declare his relation to the world—the fact of his coming into the world, the effect and result of that coming on the world, and the one method by which both the world and the individual soul may receive these benefits. The best exposition of the passages would be just to combine them into one double or parallel statement, thus: "I am come a light into the world, and I am the light of the world, that whosoever believeth on me and followeth me should not walk in darkness, and should not abide in darkness, but should have the light of life."

Now, in whatever sense Christ is the light of the world, he is also the light of the human soul. He comes to a world in darkness, and he comes to each soul in its darkness. He finds both alike in utter darkness as it regards all the great things of God and holiness and immortality; he is the light of the world by being the light of the human soul in all its relations toward God and eternity. And he becomes the light of the world in the wider sense just in proportion as he becomes the light of individual souls within their narrower personal sphere. He is the one Mediator between God and man, and whatever light he brings to a darkened world must be that true light from God which by him and through him shines in upon the soul in its darkness. We shall understand, then, how Christ is the light of the world by understanding in what sense he is the true light of the soul.

There are three distinct and important aspects under which the Scriptures set forth Christ as the true light of individual men and the true light of the whole world.

He is, first, the light of truth. He brings to us by his word, by his Spirit and by his personal character, as well as by his express declarations, the knowledge of the unknown God and of the spiritual world. By nature the whole world is in the darkness of ignorance on these great themes. The world by wisdom knew not God. "No man," says John, "hath seen God at any time; the only-begotten Son, which is in the bosom of the Father, he hath declared him" (John i. 18). And says Paul, "For God, who commanded the light to shine out of darkness, hath shined in our hearts, to give the light of the knowledge of the glory of God in the face of Jesus Christ" (2 Cor. iv. 6). With what depth of meaning, then, did He, the revealer of the unknown God to the world, the great teacher of all spiritual light and truth to the soul, say to his disciples when about to leave the world, " Believe in God, believe also in me; I am the way, the truth and the life; no man cometh unto the Father but by me. If ye had known me, ye should have known my Father also; and from henceforth ye know him, and have seen him" (John xiv. 1, 6, 7). It is in this light of revealed truth that the beloved disciple declares with such certainty, "We know that the Son of God is come, and hath given us an understanding, that we may know him that is true, and we are in him that is true, even in his Son Jesus Christ. This is the true God and eternal life" (1 John v. 20).

But as truth is in order to godliness, so Christ brings to the world and to the soul of man the light of holiness, or moral purity. The world is not only in the deep darkness of error, but in the deeper darkness of sin and corruption. Christ is the light of the soul and of the world to enkindle again this pure light of holiness which had been extinguished by the universal depravity. He comes into our fallen humanity with a divine and absolutely perfect character. He wears our human nature, but he is sinless, he is immaculate; one of us, but yet holy, harmless, undefiled and separate from sinners; since the fall of Adam his is the only perfect manhood ever seen on earth. The world needed the great Example; the soul, sunk in sin, needed such a life to uphold and embody the perfect law of God. "The Word was made flesh," cries John, "and dwelt among us, and we beheld his glory, the glory as of the only-begotten of the Father, full of grace and truth" (John i. 14). To all who follow his example, and by faith come into living contact with him, he communicates in some good degree this pure light of moral purity, and they in turn exhibit in their lives and characters that heavenly light. Hence they are appropriately called the "children of the light." So Christ said to his disciples, "Ye are the light of the world, ye are the salt of the earth." The beloved John evidently has in view this light of moral purity and holy living when he writes, "If we say that we have fellowship with him, and walk in darkness, we lie and do not the truth; but if we walk in the light, as he is in the light, we have fellowship one with another, and the blood of Jesus Christ, his Son, cleanseth us from all sin. We know that when he shall appear we shall be like him; for we shall see him as he is. And every man that hath this hope in him purifieth himself, even as he is pure" (1 John i. 6, 7 and iii. 2, 3).

Again, as truth and godliness are both unto salvation and eternal life, so Christ is the true light of immortality. He declares himself "the light of life." " I am the resurrection and the life. He that believeth in me, though he were dead, yet shall he live; and whosoever liveth and believeth in me shall never die" (John xi. 25, 26). Thus he has brought life and immortality to light by the gospel.

Since the apostasy in Adam a threefold darkness has fallen on every human soul and enveloped the world in hopeless despair—the darkness of ignorance and error, the darkness of sin and the darkness of death. Christ came as the great Deliverer of our ruined humanity. He came as the true light of the soul—the light of truth to redeem from error, the light of holiness to save from sin, the light of immortality in the darkness of the grave. Human speech never announced a grander truth: the light of the world is Jesus.

CHAPTER X.

THE SUPREME MIRACLE OF CHRISTIANITY.

MANY writers of our time have been led to regard the character of Jesus Christ as the supreme miracle of Christianity. Able discussions calling attention to this point have from time to time appeared, as those of Dr. Young in the *Christ of History*, Dr. Channing, Dr. Bushnell, Dr. Alexander and Dr. Arthur Mitchell.

There are many reasons for this pre-eminence. Character is that in which religion culminates—that, indeed, without which all pretensions to religion are vain. The human race has been experimenting on character long enough to show that a perfect model of it does not come by chance and is not likely to be a merely human production. When, therefore, such a character as that of Jesus stands out in its bold originality on the dark background of the most corrupt era known to history, it cannot be otherwise than that the hand of God is in it. There is no rational solution of the character except on the ground of supernatural power. It must be a miracle; and, if a miracle, it is impossible to overestimate its importance and its results.

If the death of Christ be the pre-eminent fact of Christianity regarded as a scheme of salvation, and his resurrection from the dead its pre-eminent fact in the chain of evidence on which the system rests, still we must regard the personal character of the great Founder as the supreme attraction and the supreme miracle, giving reality and power to all the rest. He certainly implied so much when he said, anticipating his death on the cross, "And I, if I be lifted up from the earth, will draw all men unto me." There are many ways and many cords of influence by which he draws—his providence, his Spirit, his word, his cross. But who can measure the attractive power of his immaculate character? When we consider its origin, its environments, its development in a brief life of thirty-three years, and its subsequent influence on mankind, who can deny that this is the supreme miracle of all history?

Among all the New-Testament miracles the character of Christ is an ever-present and ever-living reality to the hearts of men. It stands out on every page of the gospel history with such distinctness of outline and such power of reality that it is impossible to read the book without beholding the man.

And yet we cannot behold the man without feeling that God is here. No man can utter these words and do these mighty works unless God be with him. It is a true man who lives and speaks and acts. But if he is true he is more than man, for he claims equality with God. Is it too much to say that the unique character of Jesus Christ is God's perpetual demonstration, wrought out before the eyes of all generations, of the truth of Christianity? Yes, here is one miracle which we can all examine at our leisure—which we can in a sense see and hear and handle, of the Word of life.

We have not seen him die on the cross; we did not see him and converse with him after he rose from the dead. These and other facts we receive on the testimony of eye-witnesses who recorded them. But can we read the New Testament without seeing and feeling the living reality of the character of Jesus in its matchless perfection, in its human tenderness, in its divine glory? Is not the character there before our very eyes as truly and as vividly as if its possessor still lived and walked amongst us? Can we mistake it? can we fail to see what it is, and what it means?

Some one may say in reply, "We have the character, after all, only on the recorded testimony of those who reported the facts." True; but how could they delineate such a character if it had no existence in a living man? If they had no living example to draw from, if the real Jesus of the Gospels was not before their eyes, then they *created the character*. How could such men, in such an age, create out of nothing such a character of absolute originality and perfection? The greatest geniuses who have appeared in history, under the most favorable inspiration of clime and country, have often essayed their utmost endeavor and accomplished no such result. How could the isolated and comparatively rude fishermen of Galilee do it without a living original? To say they did would be to account for one miracle for which there is evidence by taking refuge in another for which there is none. It is far more rational to believe that Christ lived and acted out before the eyes of his disciples the character which they have reported in the New Testament than to believe that they could draw such a picture of godlike excellence without the living Christ before them.

If, therefore, we have before our eyes to-day, in these sacred pages, the very character which the apostles saw and admired and adored, then has God given to us, even as he did to them, the most sublime of all miracles, the most complete and satisfactory of all demonstrations that Christianity is true. The miracle of miracles, the proof of proofs, is the life and character of his Son. It is the one miracle which both wins the heart and satisfies the intellect. When we see it as we do in the New Testament, we are compelled to feel that "God has spoken by his Son."

If a man cannot or will not receive this evidence of character, if he has no heart to appreciate and admire it, if there be nothing within him responding in homage to the character of this Christ of the New Testament and of history,—then we fail to see what further God could do or ought to do to convince and save such a man. Not to appreciate the character of Christ is to disown the highest exhibition of moral excellence the world has ever seen. What grander miracle could God work before the eyes of men than to give the world this perfect image of his own moral perfections in human form, in the life and character of his own Son?

When a man tells us he cannot see in all this any evidence of truth, what is it but to admit that the highest virtue, the sublimest excellence, the purest moral character of which the mind can conceive, has lost its charm in his eyes, its hold upon his heart? When godlike virtue loses its attractions to a human mind, that mind is lost to virtue, lost to hope, lost to heaven, lost to God. "If our gospel be hid," says Paul, "it is hid to them that are lost: in whom the god of this world hath blinded the minds of them which believe not, lest the light of the glorious gospel of Christ, who is the image of God, should shine unto them" (2 Cor. iv. 3). If this pure light of divine character be so hidden from a man that he can neither see nor admire it, can we think of a more hopeless case? What can illume and save a soul when this pure light of heaven, this sublime miracle of character, makes no impression on it?

If Jesus was a mortal man and nothing more, it was a tremendous thing for him to say, "He that believeth not on me shall be damned." But if he was, as he always asserted and died affirming, the Son of God, then it was the true thing and the right thing to say. His Godhead is sufficient reason for the sublime arrogation of his claim. And it is a sufficient reason, too, why, under the gospel, the eternal destiny of every man who hears it is made to turn on his acceptance or rejection of this light from heaven—this revelation of God's own character, and of the highest human perfection, in the person of his Son. If a man turns away from this light after having seen it, and prefers the dark depravity of sin to the holiness of heaven as embodied in Jesus Christ, what is it but to exclude himself from God's presence, and thereby seal his own damnation?

In a discourse entitled "The Portrait of Christ the Proof of Christianity," Dr. Arthur Mitchell sums up his argument in the following weighty and suggestive sentences: "The picture of Jesus Christ could never have been drawn had there not been a living Christ from which to draw it. The life, the character, the teachings of Christ could never have been written by mortal man if that life had not first been witnessed, if that character had not been seen, if those teachings had not been heard. If this is so, then the simple existence of these books is sufficient proof of their historic truth, for the reason that what they describe is beyond human invention. Here is the marvelous picture. Here are the books. They must in some way be accounted for. No respectable scholar denies that they have been in the world from the earliest Christian age. Either Jesus Christ lived and this is a natural record of a real life, or somebody of that age invented it. For four unknown and unlettered men to conceive of such a character as that, actually to set him in motion with all the graces and virtues of an inimitable and noble manhood, to supply wisdom for him, to furnish him with the strength and loveliness of Jesus Christ, to carry through consistently a being making such stupendous claims, to make that airy fiction the source from which stream all our best thoughts of God, and to make him, at the same time, a real brother-man, so real that we may clasp him as our own flesh and blood,—for four unknown men, I say, to have risen in the darkness of the old Roman world and to have done that is a miracle of *authorship* which surpasses any miracle of the New Testament. The character of Jesus is the supreme miracle. It is far easier for me to believe that Jesus Christ came down from heaven, as these men say he did, than to believe that they manufactured him."

CHAPTER XI.

THE ATONING DEATH OF CHRIST.

THE three mediatorial offices of Christ are so related that his priesthood laid the foundation of his throne. In his priestly office he interceded with God, paid the penalty of the violated law, satisfied divine justice, removed the curse of sin and brought out an everlasting righteousness for his redeemed people. Without this there could be no kingdom to reign over. Without this there could have been no glad tidings of salvation to announce in virtue of his prophetical office. Thus, in humiliation, suffering and death, his priestly work constituted the basis of that mediatorial kingdom which he proclaimed as our Prophet and over which he reigns as our King. The Scriptures which declare, "Thy throne, O God, is for ever and ever," had also declared, "Thou art a Priest for ever, after the order of Melchisedec." The mediatorial crown was the outgrowth and reward of the mediatorial cross.

It is not without reason that the Scriptures attach so much importance to the death of Christ, and that one epistle, the Epistle to the Hebrews, is so largely devoted to a discussion of his priestly character. He had himself indicated the pre-eminence of this work on the cross when he said, "I, if I be lifted up, will draw all men unto me," and also when he instituted that memorial, the "new testament in his blood," which should "show the Lord's death till he come." It was in immediate anticipation of this great sacrificial immolation that he said, "I have finished the work which thou gavest me to do;" and it was while on the cross, in the very act of performing that oblation, that he cried with his dying breath, "It is finished."

The *word* "atonement" is used but once in the English version of the New Testament. In Rom. v. 10, 11 Paul says, "If, when we were enemies, we were reconciled to God by the death of his Son, much more, being reconciled, we shall be saved by his life. And not only so, but we also joy in God, through our Lord Jesus Christ, by whom we have now received the *atonement*." The doctrine expressed by this word, and by several others of the same import both in the English and the Greek of the New Testament, is one of the cardinal truths of the Bible. No one thing is more fundamental to the gospel than that sacrificial work of Christ which, in virtue of his priesthood, he wrought out for us on the cross. Thus, Paul said to the Corinthians in his First Epistle, "I delivered unto you first of all, that which also I received, how that Christ died for our sins according to the Scriptures." This great expiation, or sacrifice of himself on the cross, is variously set forth in Scripture by the terms "atonement," "reconciliation," "ransom," "propitiation," "redemption through his blood," and "the once offering of himself to God." These and other expressions, some of them of frequent occurrence, all refer substantially to the same thing—namely, deliverance from sin and condemnation through the vicarious atoning death of the incarnate Redeemer. No one word better describes what was done by Christ in his death than the term "atonement," or the making of God and man *at-one*.

In the Old Testament the idea of atonement is a familiar one. The word itself occurs more than forty times. The whole ceremonial law, as revealed to Moses and set forth in the book of Leviticus, was pervaded by the idea of atonement. The numerous burnt-offerings under that law were for the purpose, as it is variously expressed, of "making an atonement for sin," "an atonement for the people," "an atonement for the soul." There was no one ordinance among the Jews which was more solemnly enforced and attended with more imposing ceremonials than the great day of atonement celebrated every year as a holy sabbath. On this day the high priest went alone into the inner sanctuary with the blood of sacrifice, which he there offered for himself and for the sins of the people. "This," said the Lord, "shall be an everlasting statute unto you, to make an atonement for the children of Israel for their sins once a year."

Now, this whole ceremonial law, with its significant types and symbols, its burnt sacrifices and its annual feast of atonement, was but a perpetual prophecy of Christ, the Mediator of the New Testament. He, the great High Priest for whom all other priests had prepared the way, and to whom the shed blood of all the sacrifices had pointed, as Paul tells us, "by his own blood has entered in once into the holy place, having obtained eternal redemption for us." "For," argues he, "if the blood of bulls and of goats, and the ashes of an heifer, sprinkling the unclean, sanctifieth to the purifying of the flesh; how much more shall the blood of Christ, who through the eternal Spirit offered himself without spot to God, purge your conscience from dead works to serve the living God?"

He also is the true Passover prefigured in that annual festival which from the time of the exodus for fifteen centuries had commemorated Israel's redemption from bondage and from sin. And thus the forerunner of Christ on the banks of the Jordan pointed to Him in whom all these things culminate, the Lamb of God that taketh away the sin of the world.

The word "atonement" is used to express two different but closely-related ideas. It may express a result accomplished—that is, an actual agreement when two alienated parties have been brought together and harmonized. We speak of this result as a reconciliation, an atonement. Or it may denote the antecedent cause or means by which that end has been accomplished. Looking at the ground or means of reconciliation which some third party has provided, we call that intervention, whatever it be, an atonement or basis of agreement, though no actual reconciliation between the parties has yet taken place or may ever take place. In the first use of the term the atonement is a personal experience—something produced within the bosoms of the parties themselves. In the second it is an act external to the parties, and denotes something done by another in order to bring together those who had been alienated. Now, the atonement wrought by Christ in his redemptive work is this act of mediation between God and men. It is the ransom which he paid for us, the propitiation which he offered to God in his blood to satisfy divine law and justice in the sinner's place, so that God might be just and yet justify the ungodly. At the same time, reconciliation or atonement, in the first sense—that is, a result accomplished in the heart of every one who believes in Jesus—is effected and secured by the operation of the Holy Ghost applying Christ's redemption to the soul of the believer and reconciling him to God through Christ.

This great salvation of the gospel is therefore no half work. It belongs to both the second and the third Persons of the Godhead. As an actual historical fact, it was once for all wrought out and completed by Christ; and as such it was ample, adequate and sufficient for the whole race of man, whether saved or lost. It was the greatest atonement possible; all was done that could be done to make it wide enough to save the whole world. If the whole world had, in fact, been reconciled to God by it and brought home to glory, nothing more could have been added to its value. Its atoning merit was infinite because of the infinite merit of Him—the eternal Son of God—who made it.

But as a living experience in the hearts of men it is not, in fact, thus universal and unlimited. It is sufficient for all men and is freely offered to all, but it does not secure the actual restoration of all men to God at the cross, inasmuch as it becomes effectual as a living experience only to those who are wrought upon by the regenerating and sanctifying power of the Holy Ghost. And we know that this work of the Spirit, regenerating, sanctifying and saving men, is far from being as wide as the human family. Redemption, reconciliation, atonement as a personal experience, instead of being as broad as the redemptive work of Christ, has in fact in every age, so far as we can judge, been limited to those who believe on Jesus. Hence the often-mooted question whether the atonement is unlimited or limited will turn upon the point whether we speak of atonement made by the redemptive work of Christ or the actual reconciliation effected by the Holy Ghost.

As a ground of pardon and justification before God, an act of satisfaction to the law and justice of God, and a means of securing the soul's restoration to God, the ransom paid by Christ on the cross was complete and perfect. Nothing was lacking to give it worth and dignity sufficient to cover the sins of the whole world. If the entire human race, instead of a part of it, had been saved, no different atonement needed to be provided. In this sense of sufficiency it was absolutely unlimited. But then the sinner himself needed to be reconciled; and this second part of salvation is the work of the Holy Ghost applying to the hearts of men what Christ has done for them by persuading and enabling them to come to God through Christ. But all do not come. The Scriptures teach that men may, and often do, resist and even blaspheme the Holy Ghost, to their own eternal undoing.

This obvious distinction between the sufficiency of

the atonement as a work of unlimited merit and intrinsic value adequate to save all men, and the actual efficiency of the atonement as applied by the power of the Holy Ghost to the hearts of men, will serve to explain all those passages of Scripture which speak of Christ's redemption as being made for all men, while we know from other passages, as well as from observation, that it does not in fact avail to save all men. It is obvious that none can be saved by it, however wide its provisions or great its merit, except those to whom it is applied. In the economy of grace there is but one power that can effectually apply it: that power is the Holy Ghost. And this renovating power of the Spirit is as essential to salvation as is the redeeming work of Christ. We can accept, therefore, in their wide extent, as referring to the redemption purchased by Christ on the cross, such passages as the following: "And he," says John, "is the propitiation for our sins, and not for ours only, but also for the sins of the whole world." Says the Epistle to the Hebrews, "We see Jesus, who was made a little lower than the angels for the suffering of death, crowned with glory and honor: that he, by the grace of God, should taste death for every man." To Timothy, Paul writes: "This is good and acceptable in the sight of God our Saviour; who will have all men to be saved, and to come unto the knowledge of the truth. For there is one God, and one Mediator between God and men, the man Christ Jesus; who gave himself a ransom for all, to be testified in due time." Thus said the Saviour himself: "God so loved the world that he gave his only-begotten Son, that whosoever believeth in him should not perish, but have everlasting life." And thus runs his last great commission: "Go ye into all the world, and preach the gospel to every creature."

This universal offer of the gospel to every creature under heaven is enough to show that the atonement made by Christ was in its nature and value sufficient for all mankind, though it does not in fact save all. Hence, Paul could say to the Corinthians, "The love of Christ constraineth us; because we thus judge, that if one died for all, then were all dead: and that he died for all, that they which live should not henceforth live unto themselves, but unto him who died for them and rose again."

We need not discuss in these pages that deeper question of the theological schools and systems, What was God's design or purpose in making the atonement, as it regards those who are not saved by it? It is not for man to solve the secret counsels of God. We know that God has eternal decrees, and that he does not work without a purpose. But we should be slow to dogmatize or to formulate doctrines as to what the divine intentions are. "For who hath known the mind of the Lord, or who hath been his counselor to teach him wisdom?" Secret things belong to God, and things that are revealed belong to us and to our children. The part of wisdom is to accept the facts as God has revealed them, and leave the solution of them to a more perfect state of knowledge.

Many minds have been troubled with these deep and unsolved problems. But it should be borne in mind that on this particular point of the extent of the atonement there is a perfect analogy between it and other dealings of God. God makes the sun to shine on the evil and the good, and sends rain alike on the just and the unjust. His providential bounty is far wider than the good of his chosen people. Nor is his wider care vain and useless because men do not gratefully accept, but perish while receiving it. So also the ordinary operations of the Holy Ghost extend far beyond those who are called and saved by his effectual agency. Men strive against the Holy Ghost and resist his influences, and so perish in their sins. But we do not conclude that all those ordinary influences of the Spirit, which we know to be felt by the unsaved as well as by the saved, have been a failure because they have not ended in bringing lost men to glory. The providential work of God, exerted over all the world, and over the lost not less than the saved, is no failure. The spiritual work of the Holy Ghost, exerted as widely as the gospel has been preached and the Bible has been read, over the impenitent and the incorrigible, has been no failure even when it did not save. Why, then, should any man think that God's purpose in the atoning work of Christ is a failure even in the case of those to whom it has been freely offered by God, and by them freely rejected?

CHAPTER XII.

THE RESURRECTION OF CHRIST.

NEXT to the death of Christ, and not less important to the gospel plan of salvation, is the fact of his resurrection from the dead. It has generally been regarded as the keystone to the arch or the corner-stone to the temple of the Christian evidences. Christianity is not more a religion of doctrines and precepts than it is of facts—historical and well-attested facts. Four of the facts stand out with great prominence—the incarnation, the death, the resurrection and the ascension of Christ. These may be looked upon as the four cardinal points in the whole compass of Christian truth. With these Christianity as a system of salvation stands or falls. These constitute the deep and solid basis of its temple, for they all relate to Him who is the "only foundation," the true "Rock of Ages," and who declared, "Upon this rock I will build my church, and the gates of hell shall not prevail against it."

We have but to turn to the pages of the New Testament to see what prominence the apostles assigned to the resurrection of Christ. They declare themselves to be the witnesses of the great fact, and they appeal to others still living when they wrote to confirm their testimony. In the fifteenth chapter of his First Epistle to the Corinthian church, Paul associates the resurrection of Christ with his death as being the fundamental fact of the gospel which he had preached: "I delivered unto you first of all that which also I received, how that Christ died for our sins according to the Scriptures, and that he was buried, and that he rose again the third day according to the Scriptures." After instancing the infallible proofs of this resurrection—namely, that after being dead and buried he was seen at different times alive by Paul himself, by his fellow-apostles and by his brethren to the number of five hundred at once—he says, "Now is Christ risen from the dead, and become the first-fruits of them that slept."

From this whole chapter it is evident that the apostle Paul regarded the historical fact of Christ's resurrection as established beyond all controversy, in precisely the same way as was the fact of his death. Well he might; for had he not on the way to Damascus seen the risen Lord? and had not that appearance been the very means of his conversion? How could he ever doubt it again? and how could Thomas, who had once doubted, but was convinced by the sight of the pierced side and the nail-prints in the hands and feet of the Lord who stood before him inviting him to examine and believe? But Paul here presents this great fact not only as fully established on evidence, but as forming an essential part of the gospel itself; for it is the proof and the guarantee of the doctrine of the general resurrection: "Now is Christ risen from the dead and become the first-fruits of them that slept. For since by man came death, by man came also the resurrection of the dead. For as in Adam all die, even so in Christ shall all be made alive. But every man in his own order, Christ the first-fruits, afterward they that are Christ's at his coming."

In the opening chapter of his Epistle to the Romans, Paul tells us that "Jesus Christ was declared to be the Son of God with power, according to the Spirit of holiness by the resurrection from the dead;" which is equivalent to saying that the resurrection from the dead was the full, complete and convincing demonstration to men that he was what he claimed to be, the Son of God. It was the perfect vindication of all his Messianic claims. It was the proof that what he had asserted so often in life, had reiterated before the Sanhedrim at his trial, and had died affirming, was true—namely, that he was the Son of God. And it was the one complete demonstration to men and angels that the great work of mediation, suffering and death for which he had come into the world had been accepted, approved and ratified in heaven.

All this and more did the resurrection from the dead signify and seal. It placed for ever the significant and authoritative seal of the divine approval upon all that Christ had done on earth, upon all that he had promised to do in heaven. No greater event ever occurred in the annals of man. The unbarring of the rocky sepulchre and the release of its prisoner under the dawning light of that third day fulfilled all the grand prophetic hopes of the past, and opened a new world of power and beauty and triumph for the future. It was the final and conclusive evidence that Christianity is the one divine, final and universal religion for men. It was the proof to the Church that its great Founder was not a dead but a living Saviour—no longer under humiliation and shame, but exalted to universal and eternal dominion in earth and heaven. In that exaltation and glory of the third day his Church arose with him to newness of life, and the world itself awoke from the long sleep of ages to new hopes and a nobler destiny. The resurrection of Christ was the first triumph of the Church, and became the pledge of the last. The resurrection of Christ was the spiritual renovation of the world.

Accordingly, in the preaching of the apostles, and for many centuries in the pulpit of the early Church, no theme was more prominent than the resurrection of Christ. They told the story of the cross, but with it they told, with joy unspeakable and full of glory, the story of the opened sepulchre and the risen, ascended Lord. No story ever gained a hearing from such uncounted multitudes, or sent a thrill of gladness and wonder so deep and abiding into believing hearts. It was the very breath of inspiration for hundreds of years to the apostolic and primitive Church. It was the glad theme of Peter and his fellow-apostles on the day of Pentecost, when, reasoning out of the Old-Testament Scriptures, they spoke of David as foreseeing the resurrection of Christ, that "his soul was not left in the grave, nor did his flesh see corruption," and said, "This Jesus, whom ye slew with wicked hands, hath God raised up, whereof we all are witnesses. Therefore, being by the right hand of God exalted, and having received of the Father the promise of the Holy Ghost, he hath shed forth this which ye now see and hear." So also when the apostle Paul stood on Mars' Hill before the sages and skeptics of Athens, he preached this great fact of the resurrection with such prominence and power that Luke records it as the preaching "of Jesus and the resurrection." In like manner we find him doing the same thing before King Agrippa when, appealing to the king's knowledge of the Scriptures, he cried, "Why should it be thought a thing incredible with you that God should raise the dead?" (Acts ii. 32 and xvii. 28).

Probably no one doctrine of Christianity has been more frequently and more fiercely assailed by its enemies than this fundamental fact of the resurrection of its great Founder. But the opposition, begun in the early centuries and renewed from age to age, has only led to the fuller vindication of the truth. From the discussion of the subject by Athenagoras, the Athenian philosopher, and Justin Martyr, in the second century, down to the sifting examinations of Gilbert West on the *Resurrection* and Bishop Sherlock's *Trial of the Witnesses*, and in many treatises of the present day, the whole evidence has undergone an investigation which has placed the doctrine on an impregnable basis. It is felt by all fair and candid men that the historical fact of the resurrection is so attested by competent witnesses, and so confirmed by a thousand concurring circumstances, that we could as easily overthrow all human history as invalidate it.

That God should raise the dead is a proposition not incredible to those who, like King Agrippa, believed that there is a God, and that the Scriptures are a revelation from him; because in his infinite power we have an adequate cause, and in the Scriptures a sufficient reason, why a phenomenon so extraordinary should occur.

The resurrection of Christ is, without controversy, a great miracle and a great mystery; but then it is a miracle ascribed to the power of God, which explains everything else and justifies everything else in the Bible. It does not stand alone. It is no isolated act of God, it is no accidental event out of harmony with the plans and purposes of Jehovah. It is the great central fact of a whole sublime system, which must be judged in the light of its surroundings, its antecedents and its grand results. It is far more credible that Christ should have risen from the dead by divine power than that the antecedent life of Christ should be a fable and the whole Bible a stupendous imposture.

When the angel at the vacant sepulchre on the morning of the third day said to the disciples, "He is not here, he is risen from the dead; come see the place where the Lord lay," he only announced a fact which Christ himself had often predicted, and which placed the final seal of truth upon his own divine mission. Some twelve or fifteen times, as we find in the gospel records, had he spoken of his approaching death, and told his disciples with more or less distinctness that he must rise from the dead: "I, if I be lifted up, will draw all men unto me." They did not, while he was with them, comprehend the full import of his words, and they were slow to believe the glad tidings even after he had risen. But they were all at last convinced by proofs which were irresistible: for almost as many times as he had predicted his resurrection did he appear in person to some one or more of their number during the forty days between his rising from the dead and his ascension to heaven.

His resurrection involved first the complete verification of all the words he had spoken as our great Teacher. To the apostles, and to all others who were witnesses of the facts, no proof could have been more overwhelming than this of the resurrection, that Christ came from God, and went to God, and was God. And there is no indication in all the New Testament, after the first doubts of Thomas were removed, that any one of them ever doubted again.

Then, further, the resurrection, followed by the glorious ascension to heaven, was the perfect demonstration that all power in heaven and earth, as he said, had been committed to his hands. To him had now been given the keys of death and hell, for now most assuredly had he conquered both death and hell. By the resurrection it was proclaimed to all men: "I am he that liveth and was dead, and behold, I am alive for evermore, Amen; and have the keys of death and hell" (Rev. i. 18).

In his rising was also involved the final and glorious resurrection of all his followers. He had conquered, not for himself alone, but for all his people to the end of time. "Because I live," said he, "ye shall live also;" "He that liveth and believeth in me, though he were dead, yet shall he live;" "He that liveth and believeth in me shall never die;" "Be of good cheer, I have overcome the world;" "I am the resurrection and the life." Such were his momentous and inspiring words, the most wonderful and the most comforting to dying men that were ever uttered in human speech. What peace have they not given to troubled hearts! What light in adversity, what joy in bereavement, what strength in times of trial, what support and consolation in the dark valley of the shadow of death, have they not given to millions of our race! The old, the young, the poor, the rich, the unfortunate, the beautiful, have all alike found a solace here for life's woes, and an antidote in death, which nothing else has ever given.

CHAPTER XIII.

DIVINE PERSONALITY OF THE HOLY SPIRIT.

WE can have no better evidence for any religious truth than the teaching of Jesus Christ. With all devout Christian minds his word is the ultimate authority, and they have learned to rest upon it with implicit confidence. Recognizing him as the supreme Teacher in all things relating to God, because he came from God and went to God, and believing that he uttered the truth when he said, "We speak that we do know, and testify that we have seen," we rely upon all his utterances as containing the best and most certain information on these deep spiritual mysteries which it is possible for the human mind to gain while in this mortal state. In making this statement we feel that we have given a sufficient reason for our faith to every man who will admit that Jesus is what he claimed to be, a Teacher come from God, and the Son of God.

In attempting, therefore, however briefly, to set forth the doctrine of Scripture on that fundamental article of our Church creed, the personal agency and work of the Holy Ghost, it is obvious that we can adopt no method safer and more satisfactory than to plant our instructions first of all on the express teachings of Christ himself. Here, if anywhere, we should be willing to sit at his feet and learn of him, for it is unquestionably a subject on which he ought to know more than all the sons of men. On such a subject, whether regarding him as a revealer of new truths in the New Testament or as an expounder of old ones in the Old Testament, we are safe in following the lead of so infallible a guide.

In the parting discourses of our Lord to his disciples the night before he suffered, as recorded by John, we find him speaking of three distinct yet intimately associated personages, in language which cannot be attributed to any others, and which ascribes the highest divine intelligence, power and prerogative to each of the three alike. These are himself, the Father and the Comforter, or Holy Ghost. Taking his words in their plain and obvious import, we are compelled to feel as we read them that he does not more emphatically affirm his own distinct personality and his own supreme divinity than he affirms the personality and the divinity of the Father and of the Holy Ghost; for he speaks of all the three in precisely the same way, and he attributes to each a power, an intelligence and the function which can be ascribed to none but God.

The best way to see the force of this statement is to refer to the passages. In the fourteenth chapter of the Gospel by John he speaks of the Father and of the Comforter as absent and unseen, but he requires the disciples to believe in their personality and love even as they do in his own. He is about to ascend to the absent, unseen Father, and he will in a little while send the absent, unseen Comforter. He had spoken of himself as the Mediator between them and the Father, saying, "I am the way, and the truth, and the life; no man cometh unto the Father but by me." Then, referring to the loss they were about to sustain in his own near departure, he says, "I will pray the Father, and he shall give you another Comforter, that he may abide with you for ever; even the Spirit of truth; whom the world cannot receive, because it seeth him not, neither knoweth him; but ye know him; for he dwelleth with you, and shall be in you. I will not leave you comfortless; I will come to you."

Further on he is still more specific as to the character, relations and office of this coming One, whom he is soon to send, and whom the Father will send in his name. He says, "But the Comforter, which is the Holy Ghost, whom the Father will send in my name, he shall teach you all things, and bring all things to your remembrance, whatsoever I have said unto you." Still farther on he reiterates the great promise: "But when the Comforter is come, whom I will send unto you from the Father, even the Spirit of truth, which proceedeth from the Father, he shall testify of me. . . . It is expedient for you that I go away; for if I go not away, the Comforter will not come unto you. . . . And when he is come, he will reprove the world of sin, of righteousness, and of judgment; of sin, because they believe not on me; of righteousness, because

I go to my Father, and ye see me no more; of judgment, because the prince of this world is judged." Then, again, as if unwilling to leave this important revelation, he adds with increasing emphasis, "I have yet many things to say unto you, but ye cannot bear them now. Howbeit when he, the Spirit of truth, is come, he will guide you into all truth: for he shall not speak of himself; but whatsoever he shall hear, that shall he speak; and he will show you things to come. He shall glorify me: for he shall receive of mine, and shall show it unto you."

Now, if these more than thrice-repeated words of our Lord, uttered under the most impressive of all circumstances, as a perpetual legacy of inspiration and hope for his Church, do not distinctly teach the existence and the personality and the divine agency and work of the Holy Ghost—as distinctly, indeed, as they teach the existence and attributes of the Father and of Christ himself—it would be difficult to say what they teach or to say how such things can be taught.

These revelations, if they stood alone, would be sufficient to establish the ancient creed of the Church: "I believe in God the Father almighty, Maker of heaven and earth. I believe in Jesus Christ, his only Son, our Lord. I believe in the Holy Ghost." But they are far from standing alone. They are in full accordance with his antecedent teaching, as when he warned his hearers of that blasphemy against the Holy Ghost which is a sin that "hath no forgiveness, in this life or that which is to come." They are in full harmony with his final commission after rising from the dead, when he said to his apostles, "Go ye into all the world, and preach the gospel to every creature, baptizing them in the name of the Father and of the Son and of the Holy Ghost." They are in full accord with the fulfilled promise and the mighty manifestations of the day of Pentecost, when that divine Comforter descended upon the assembled Church with supernatural gifts, and sat, like cloven tongues of fire, upon each inspired apostle. They are in full accord with the recorded fact of the conversion of many thousands of unbelievers and enemies on and after that great day, as well as with all the signs and wonders and mighty works wrought by the apostles in his name, as they proclaimed the death and resurrection of their Master over all the nations of the ancient world, with a wisdom and power which neither Greeks nor Jews nor conquering Romans could gainsay or resist. The whole history of the early Church, recorded in the Acts of the Apostles, and a hundred passages scattered through all the New-Testament Epistles, each opening or closing with a sublime doxology of praise addressed to God the Father and the Son and the Holy Ghost, bear witness to two great facts—namely, that the incarnate Son of God had risen from the dead and gone to heaven, and that the Holy Ghost, the Comforter, the Spirit of truth, according to his promise, had descended from heaven in a baptism of fire, and had gone forth with the heralds of the gospel amongst all nations.

The man who can read the New Testament without seeing these things, or read the story of the triumphs of the gospel during the first three centuries, and, in fact, all subsequent centuries, and not see them, is as blind to all the great truths of the history as were the Jews when they crucified the Lord of glory. There is, in truth, no clue to this marvelous history, and no key to the problem of Christianity, short of the recognition of this fundamental and distinguishing doctrine of the Church— namely, that the Holy Ghost is God; that he is the Third Person of the adorable Trinity; that he exercises a perpetual agency in the Church; that he always and everywhere accompanies the proclamation of the gospel; and that his great beneficent function is to apply the truth of God to the sons of men in their conversion, regeneration and sanctification.

It is of deep significance that Christ appointed two, and only two, sacraments to be observed by his Church to the end of the world—the one setting forth his own great work of redemption from sin; the other, the Spirit's equally essential work of sanctification from sin. In the sacrament of the Lord's Supper, which is the Lord's passover, we celebrate the Lord's death till he come, thus symbolizing his sacrificial death upon the cross for our redemption and justification before God. In the other holy sacrament, the water of baptism, we celebrate and symbolize that other great work essential to our salvation, the work of the divine Spirit upon our heart and character, by which we are engrafted into Christ, enlightened in the knowledge of God, made willing and enabled to embrace Christ as a Saviour, regenerated in the spirit and temper of the mind, and gradually purified from sin. Such is the office and such the work of the Holy Ghost.

We can never appreciate too highly the presence, influence and agency of this divine Comforter. He is the direct Author of all efficient saving influences in the preaching of the gospel and the reading of the word of God. He who imparted grace to holy men of old when they "spake as they were moved by the Holy Ghost" imparts grace now and consolation to the soul of every *true* believer, from the date of his effectual calling to the hour at which his work here is done and he enters into rest. All right thoughts, all holy resolutions, all good works in the Church and in the life of the Christian, proceed from him. We can have no saving conversions from the world, no spiritual growth in the Church, no divine power in the pulpit, no blessed revivals in the work of the ministry, except as they come, in answer to prayer, from the presence of the Holy Ghost.

It is one of the greatest doctrines of Christianity, and certainly one of its supreme blessings, that it has revealed to us this divine Agent of good as Christ's own Vicar in the Church. It is not an absent but an ever-present and working Deity that is thus made known to us, at all times ready to hear us and to help us.

By nothing, probably, is Christianity more completely differentiated from all other religions than by the existence and presence of the Holy Spirit. It is a source of power to the Church and to the individual believer which the world does not recognize, and which human philosophy does not attempt to explain.

Nevertheless, the doctrine stands as one of the clearest revelations of the Bible. It is one, too, which is attested by the experience of the children of God in all ages of the Church. It is a most blessed assurance, for which every human heart should be profoundly thankful, that when our great Redeemer finished his work of sacrifice on earth, and ascended to his heavenly throne, he did not leave his Church here to work out her destiny alone, or the individual believer to work out his salvation alone. He said to each, "Lo, I am with you alway, even unto the end of the world;" and he sent the Comforter to fulfill the promise. In all the blessed influences of that divine Spirit, always and everywhere present in the bosom of the Church and in the heart of the Christian, we have the perpetual demonstration that the great promise of this new dispensation is unceasingly verified.

CHAPTER XIV.

THE LAW OF GOD.

"OF law," says Richard Hooker in the first book of the *Ecclesiastical Polity*—" of law there can be no less acknowledged than that her seat is the bosom of God, her voice the harmony of the world; all things in heaven and earth do her homage, the very least as feeling her care, and the greatest as not exempted from her power." If this famous impersonation holds true of all law, both physical and moral, natural and revealed, it is pre-eminently true of that divine moral law which is made known to us in the word of God, and which is to us the transcript of the divine character and the exponent of the divine will. There is nothing which brings us more directly up to the sublime conception of an almighty presiding Deity, holding sway over all worlds and all creatures, animate and inanimate, than the subject of law. The reign of law is the reign of God. Any right conception of man as under law is a conception of man as under a lawgiver. Any conception of law as a binding force and rule of life is a conception of an infinite God, who has right and power thus to bind and to govern; for it is the conception of an infinite Creator, who has the most perfect and indefeasible of all rights to govern the creatures of his power.

Now, it is a primal revelation of the Bible from beginning to end that God is in all and through all and over all, blessed for ever; that the whole universe is under law to him—that kind of law which we call physical or natural, as suited to its nature; and that man himself, as an intellectual and moral being like all other intelligent beings, is under the binding force of that kind of law which we call intellectual and moral. While God himself as Lawgiver is the seat and source of all law, physical and natural, rational and moral, as Hooker says, no creatures, whether great or small, animate or inanimate, are exempted from its binding authority. For in obedience to its high mandate is the peace, the harmony, the well-being alike of the individual creature and of the universe.

Certainly there can be no more august conception of law and order for the universe than this universal and omnipotent reign of law, and of an infinite God above the law, imposing and executing it. This is the Bible doctrine of law. It is the force of an intelligent, omnipotent will directing and controlling all things for his own glory and the good of his creatures.

In the Scriptures the word "law" is used to express the divine will in various applications. First it is applied to the whole revealed law of God contained in Scripture, as when the psalmist says, "Thy law is the truth;" "Oh, how I love thy law!" "Open thou mine eyes, that I may behold wondrous things out of thy law;" "The law of the Lord is perfect, converting the soul; the commandment of the Lord is pure, enlightening the eyes;" "His delight is in the law of the Lord, and in his law doth he meditate day and night."

In a narrower sense it is applied to a part of the word of God, as to the Old Testament when distinguished from the New, or to the Pentateuch as distinguished from the Prophets: "The law was given by Moses, but grace and truth came by Jesus Christ" (John i. 17). In the Sermon on the Mount, Christ said, "Think not that I am come to destroy the law or the prophets: I am not come to destroy, but to fulfill. For verily I say unto you, Till heaven and earth pass, one jot or one tittle shall in no wise pass from the law till all be fulfilled."

But the more frequent use of the term in Scripture, especially in the New-Testament Epistles, is that in which it refers to the Decalogue, or law of Ten Commandments, revealed from heaven on Mount Sinai, accompanied at the same time with many other laws, ceremonial and civil, for the worship of God and the government of the Jewish nation. These all together formed the Mosaic or Levitical code, intended, so far as they were ceremonial and national, for the Israelitish people alone, and so far as they were moral for the Church of God and for all mankind. The grand essential principles of this wider moral law, intended for all mankind and for all ages, are contained in the Ten Commandments. They are of universal obligation, and they constitute the basis of the civil jurisprudence of all civilized Christian nations, as they do also of all ecclesiastical law.

Nothing could exceed the solemnity and the awful grandeur in which this moral law was proclaimed by the voice of the Almighty to the assembled hosts of Israel at Sinai. The occasion was worthy of the great moral code of right and justice which was thenceforward to bind all civilized men together as brothers and all civilized states to the throne of God. It was, in fact, but the republication and the re-enforcement of that original moral law which from the first had been written by God's own finger on the moral constitution of man, but which till then had been neglected, and in part obliterated from the heart, by reason of the universal apostasy. Such a law needed to be revived and enforced by more solemn sanctions than it had ever been before. This was done, once for all, at Mount Sinai. This is the law of which the apostle Paul, referring to the solemnity of its proclamation, says, "It was ordained by angels in the hand of a mediator" (Gal. iii. 19).

It would be a grievous mistake to suppose that the moral law of God, all of whose requirements are holy, just and good, has been abrogated or its claims lowered by the gospel. Everything in the Bible is against such a position. The personal example of Christ is against it. His expositions of the law in his Sermon on the Mount, and all his instructions elsewhere, are against it. All the teachings of his inspired apostles in the New Testament are against it. Christ declares with great emphasis that he did not come to annul but to fulfill the law. There can be no higher confirmation of the law as good, no stronger vindication of its divine authority, than the fact that Christ did fulfill it to the last jot and tittle, perfectly obeying all its precepts and paying all its penalties for his redeemed people. Both by his life and by his teaching he illustrated the binding authority of the law, the extent and spirituality of its requirements and the equity of all its precepts and penalties.

The apostle Paul, who discusses the law more fully than any other New-Testament writer, shows clearly that by the deeds of law—that is, by works of personal righteousness—no flesh can be justified, because all men are sinners, and as such have violated the law. The law has no power to save those whom it condemns. It cannot both condemn and save. But it condemns every sin and every sinner. It failed *as a method of salvation* on the first breach of the law. The law makes no provision for its own violation, and has no remedy against transgression. It requires, and can require, nothing less than perfect unfailing obedience. Such obedience no human being except Christ ever rendered. Therefore, by the law as a method or means of salvation no soul can be saved; for all have sinned and come short of the glory of God. But what the law cannot do for us Christ has done.

The Decalogue is usually divided into two parts—the one, consisting of four commandments, relating to the worship of God and reverence for his name and his Sabbath; the other, consisting of six, all relating to our fellow-men, beginning with our parents. The six commandments of this second table of the law all pertain to the three most important interests of human society—that is, of man as connected with his fellow-man, life and property. All these, lying at the foundation of social well-being and individual happiness, are most sacredly guarded by the Decalogue. All its requirements, of each table alike, whether relating to God or to man, are enjoined as duties owed directly to God. Any breach of them in any particular is prohibited as a sin against God.

It is easy to see at a glance that this all-comprehensive law is no ephemeral thing. It was intended for all mankind to the end of the world. It is the most ancient and the most wonderful of all written human codes. Well might an inspired apostle say that it was "ordained unto life." It has stood the test of time; it has borne the closest scrutiny of all Christian ages. There is not one provision in it which does not meet some one or other of the deepest necessities of our moral and social nature. There is not one requirement of it which human experience has not demonstrated to be for man's highest intellectual, moral and national good. It contains alike the elements of a nation's greatness and of the happiness of every human being.

This divine law is one of the great things of the Bible. The devout psalmist felt its preciousness when he sang its praises in every one of the hundred and seventy-six verses of the beautiful one hundred and nineteenth Psalm, and when in another he celebrated it, saying, "He established a testimony in Jacob, and appointed a law in Israel, which he commanded our fathers, that they should make them known to their children; that the generation to come might know them, even the children which should be born, who should arise and declare them to their children; that they might set their hope in God, and not forget the works of God, but keep his commandments" (Psalm lxxviii. 5–7).

Instead of repealing or in any way disparaging this glorious and blessed law, it is the high distinction of Christianity that through its great Founder and his inspired apostles, Christianity has but incorporated and reaffirmed the divine law in all its requirements and prohibitions, giving a broader sweep to its precepts, an added sanction to its authority and a deeper tone to its heart-searching spirituality. The New Testament has given us the key to its interpretation when it tells us that "love is the fulfilling of the law." There is no true obedience to this law without love to the Lawgiver.

The extent and the spirituality of the Decalogue were seen from the beginning in its final command against covetousness. When the law said, "Thou shalt not covet," it reached the heart, the whole heart. Moses himself had set this spirituality of the law in a clear light when he said, "Hear, O Israel: The Lord our God is one Lord: and thou shalt love the Lord thy God with all thine heart, and with all thy soul, and with all thy might. And these words, which I command thee this day, shall be in thine heart: and thou shalt teach them diligently unto thy children, and shalt talk of them when thou sittest in thine house, and when thou walkest by the way, and when thou liest down, and when thou risest up. And thou shalt bind them for a sign upon thine hand, and they shall be as frontlets between thine eyes. And thou shalt write them upon the posts of thine house and upon thy gates" (Deut. vi. 4-9).

In like manner, the great Teacher set the seal of his own divine authority to this law, and revealed the deep spiritual import of all its requirements, when he said, "Thou shalt love the Lord thy God with all thy heart, and with all thy soul, and with all thy mind. This is the first and great commandment. And the second is like unto it, Thou shalt love thy neighbor as thyself. On these two commandments hang all the law and the prophets" (Matt. xxii. 37-39).

In the Epistle to the Galatians the apostle Paul, after discussing the gospel method of salvation through Christ, and showing that no soul can be saved by the righteousness of the law, raises the question as to the proper use or ends of the law: "Wherefore, then, serveth the law?" He answers by saying that the "law was added because of transgression" until Christ should come, and that the "law is our schoolmaster to bring us to Christ, that we might be justified by faith." In the light of this passage and others it is easy to point out three important ends or purposes contemplated, and, in fact, secured, by the law of God.

The first reason for its enactment was that it might be a perpetual vindication of truth and justice, and a perfect standard of right to men. Before the proclamation of law at Mount Sinai the world had fallen into utter apostasy and alienation from God. The reign of idolatry had become universal. The light of reason and the original law written on the conscience had proved insufficient as a guide to truth, unavailing as a standard of right, inoperative as a rule of conduct. All flesh had lost the knowledge of God and corrupted its way. Professing themselves to be wise, men became fools, and their foolish hearts were darkened more and more. Then was the law re-enacted, proclaimed from heaven—as the apostle says, "added because of transgression." And there it stands on the sacred pages, more enduring than the original tables of stone, for the reading of all mankind—a perfect moral code, condemning the wrong, enforcing the right, for all time, with the awful authority of God's own voice.

A second great object of the law is that which St. Paul points out when he says, "The law was our schoolmaster to bring us to Christ, that we might be justified by faith." Not only did the ceremonial law continually point to Christ by its types and symbols, but also this moral law by all its inflexible precepts. By requiring perfect obedience, which no sinner has rendered, or can render in his own strength, it continually points the way to One who has fulfilled all its claims, and made salvation possible to them that believe. "By the law," says Paul, "is the knowledge of sin. I was alive without the law once, but when the commandment came, sin revived and I died." It is only when a man is convinced of sin and guilt by a clear apprehension of the law of God, and of his own imperfection and impotence under that conviction, that he is led at last to look away from himself and fly to Christ as a Saviour. This purpose of the law is just as important to-day under the gospel dispensation as it ever was under the old. It is as much needed now in preaching the gospel as it was in the time of Paul or of Moses.

There is no effectual preaching of the gospel which is not grounded on the law of God, and which does not perpetually reiterate its claims. A gospel without law is really no gospel. It is a mistake and a delusion. The law of God is a perpetual instructor, ever pointing to the cross and preparing the soul to believe in Christ. The law condemns, and by condemning shuts us up to faith in Christ, who is the end of the law for righteousness to every one that believeth. Thus, as the apostle Paul writes in the third chapter of his Epistle to the Galatians, "Christ hath redeemed us from the curse of the law, being made a curse for us." St. Paul also sets this matter in a clear light in the eighth chapter of the Epistle to the Romans: "For what the law could not do, in that it was weak through the flesh, God, sending his own Son in the likeness of sinful flesh, and for sin, condemned sin in the flesh, that the righteousness of the law might be fulfilled in us, who walk not after the flesh, but after the Spirit."

The third important office of the law is that it might serve as a perpetual rule of practical duty to the people of God. It not only bears its testimony against all unrighteousness from generation to generation, and so maintains the truth of God before a world lying in wickedness, but it is, and will be to the end of time, a divine instructor to the Church in all the duties of practical godliness. The Church of Christ can no more dispense with the law than it can with the gospel. Both are of God, and both necessary to produce the grand result of holy living. If there is no salvation without the gospel, there is no morality without the law. The true gospel salvation is a new life in Christ, pervaded and controlled by law. "Do we then make void the law through faith?" asks the apostle. "God forbid; yea, we establish the law." There is no point which he more carefully guards against than that of abrogating the law of God. When he shows that it is no method of justification, it is only to show that it is for ever binding on the conscience of the saved sinner as his infallible rule of life. Every precept of the gospel is but a reiteration and development of the precepts of the Decalogue, and every prohibition but a new and more detailed statement of the things condemned by it. Christianity is a religion of peace on earth and good-will among men, because it is pre-eminently a religion of law; and its fundamental law is the Decalogue—the same through all time, the same for the individual man, for the social community, for the nation and for the world.

CHAPTER XV.

THE FORGIVENESS OF SINS.

NOTHING can be more distinctly characteristic of the gospel as a system of religion than to say it is a remedy for sin. Sin is the deep and fearful malady of our nature, for the removal of which God in infinite mercy, with infinite wisdom and at infinite cost, provides a remedy in the incarnation and sacrificial death of his Son. This voluntary immolation of the Incarnate One on the cross, in the place of sinners and for the help of sinners, constitutes essentially the plan of salvation, and makes the gospel a message of glad tidings from God to the men of all nations and all times. We have no one idea in the Bible —nor, indeed, anywhere else — more significant, more important, more universally acceptable, more supremely glorious, than this great idea of divine interposition for the remedy, the remission, the removal of sin. No candid man can read the Scriptures with the desire to understand their deep spiritual import without feeling that this long cry of deliverance from sin, this earnest conviction that God in Christ has appeared and wrought out remission and deliverance on the cross, is the never-dying keynote of the book from Genesis to Revelation.

What else did Christ say, and what less could he mean, when, after having died and risen again, and when about to ascend to heaven, he inaugurated his kingdom for the spiritual conquest of the world, saying to his followers, "Thus it is written, and thus it behoved Christ to suffer, and to rise from the dead the third day; and that repentance and remission of sins should be preached in his name among all nations, beginning at Jerusalem"? (Luke xxiv. 46, 47). The gospel would bring no salvation to man if it did not come preaching the forgiveness of sins, revealing God in Christ as a sin-pardoning God, who has found an adequate ransom and opened a way of deliverance by which he can consistently remit the sin and save the sinner. This is the one thing which every soul of Adam's fallen race most needs, and this the great redemption which is offered to every soul through Jesus Christ. Thus, to the weary, heavy-laden sinner, deeply conscious of guilt, the gospel preaches peace through Jesus Christ, because it comes as God's own remedy for sin, proclaiming forgiveness by the blood of the cross. We need not wonder, therefore, that in the earliest of all our Christian symbols, the Apostles' Creed, amongst its twelve essential articles of faith should be found this great and comprehensive doctrine of the system: "I believe in the forgiveness of sins." Our divine Master had already taught it, and formulated it to stand for ever, when he put it into his form of prayer in the Sermon on the Mount, "Forgive us our debts as we forgive our debtors," and when he uttered in it his dying cry upon the cross, "Father, forgive them, for they know not what they do."

The forgiveness of sins, as stated in this clause of the Creed, must be taken in the widest sense. It includes all that is done for us in the pardon, the removal and the conquest of sin by the three Persons of the adorable Trinity. God the Father in his sovereignty, or God in Christ doing whatever the Father does, forgives sin, for none but God can forgive sin. But Christ as Mediator, by his sacrificial death on the cross satisfying the demands of God's violated law, has rendered it possible for God to forgive sin, thus removing the first great barrier in the way of our salvation by taking away the guilt and penalty of sin.

Still, the plan of salvation would not be complete without another essential work. In order to pardon our sins and to justify us before God the objective work—the work without us, the work of sacrifice and death—had to be wrought by Christ. But in order to remove the pollution and power of sin within us the subjective work—the work *in* us— of regeneration and sanctification was equally necessary for our salvation. And this is accomplished for us by the indwelling agency of the Holy Ghost, whose divine office it is to reveal Christ to our souls, to apply to us the benefits of Christ's redemption, to quicken our sinful nature by his regenerating power, to subdue the love of sin and enable us to live a new spiritual and holy life.

Thus are the children of God delivered from the curse, the bondage and the pollution of sin— first, from its penalty and condemnation, through the redemptive work of Christ, so as to be pardoned and restored to God's favor in the act of justification; and, secondly, from its indwelling and ruling power, through the influence of the Holy Spirit in the work of regeneration and sanctification, preparing them for a life of holiness here and of glory hereafter. This, in brief, is the full, completed salvation of the gospel, which Christ first wrought out on the cross, then secured for all his people by the coming of the promised Comforter, and then, as he left the world, commanded his apostles to preach in his name among all nations, to the end of time.

All this is comprehended in the remedy for sin, "the propitiation in his blood," "the remission," "the reconciliation," "the atonement," "the redemption," as it is variously set forth in the Scriptures, and summed up in the one expressive word, "gospel." All this is included in the one great doctrine of the forgiveness of sins as formulated in what is called the Apostles' Creed.

There are, indeed, many passages of Scripture in which the doctrine is presented in the same broad and comprehensive terms; as, for example, in the Old Testament, when David says, "There is forgiveness with thee, that thou mayest be feared" (Psalm cxxx.); "As far as the east is from the west, so far hath he removed our transgressions from us" (Psalm ciii.); and also in the New Testament, when Paul says, "In whom we have redemption through his blood, the forgiveness of sins, according to the riches of his grace" (Eph. i. 7); and when John the Baptist says of Christ, "Behold the Lamb of God, that taketh away the sin of the world" (John i. 29).

It is plain that we cannot preach the gospel of Christ without preaching this fundamental doctrine of the great atonement, the pardon, the forgiveness, the remission of sins. Men do sometimes contrive to do what they call "preaching the gospel" without having anything to say about either sin or redemption. But this is mere child's play: it is worse; it is trifling with the Scriptures; it is making light of God's message to ruined men. No man ever did or ever can truly preach the gospel without earnestly grappling with the great doctrines of sin, guilt, redemption, atonement and remission of sin through the blood of Christ and the agency of the Holy Ghost. The message of God to men is essentially a message of mercy, love and forgiveness through the sacrificial atoning death of his Son and the work of his Spirit.

Yes, forgiveness of sin through the death of the cross is the one great word, the one great idea, which lies nearest to the heart of the gospel, nearest to the heart of the Scriptures and to the heart of God himself, and nearest also to the human heart. There is no theme for the pulpit deeper, wider, more essential, more attractive, more fraught with present and eternal interests, than this. Woe unto him—yea, unutterable loss and shame to him—

who pretends to minister at God's altar and to proclaim Christ's message to dying men, and does not preach it! Of what avail is his learning, his eloquence, or that beautiful empty nothing which he calls a "gospel," if it contain no remedy for sin, no assurance of forgiveness from God through Him who alone has power to take away the sin of the world?

The forgiveness of sins through the vicarious and atoning death of Christ is the great theme which is discussed in almost every one of Paul's Epistles. It is certainly the prominent theme in his Epistles to the Hebrews and the Romans, and scarcely less so in the Epistles to the Galatians, the Ephesians and the Colossians. He shows in all these, and with great fullness in the two larger treatises, that all men by nature are in a state of guilt and condemnation before God in consequence of sin—that all men are in fact dead in trespasses and sins, alienated from God by wicked works, impotent to save themselves from the dread consequences of transgression, and as such without God and without hope for the future. In this sad condition God himself provides a plan of salvation, a ransom, a deliverance, a complete redemption, through the death of his incarnate Son, who takes the place of the sinner, under the violated law, bears the curse for him on the cross, pays all sin's penalties and satisfies every claim of divine justice. This is the gospel as proclaimed by Paul through all his Epistles—the gospel of God's free and abounding grace, provided and offered to all men without money and without price, through the atonement of Christ. By his incarnation standing as our substitute under the law, by his life of sinless obedience fulfilling all the precepts of that law, and by the infinite merits of his atoning death paying its penalties, he takes away our sins; for he is the Lamb of God that was revealed from heaven to bear and to take away the sins of the world. He who knew no sin was made a sin-offering for us; he who was originally above law came under it for our sake, that he might redeem us from its curse by being made a curse for us. Thus "Christ became the end of the law for righteousness to every one that believeth."

Paul brings out in strong light this fundamental doctrine of atonement in the third chapter of the Epistle to the Romans when he says, "We are justified freely by his grace, through the redemption that is in Christ Jesus: whom God hath set forth to be a propitiation through faith in his blood, to declare his righteousness for the remission of sins that are past, through the forbearance of God; to declare, I say, at this time, his righteousness: that he might be just, and the justifier of him which believeth in Jesus."

It is said that the poet Cowper, in one of his seasons of deep melancholy, despairing of his salvation and driven almost to madness, chanced to read this passage, when the whole scheme of God's gratuitous salvation through Christ flashed upon his mind with such convincing power and beauty that he was satisfied and made to rejoice in hope. With similar effect the same great truth was revealed to another gifted mind by the reading of a passage of like import in the first chapter of the First Epistle of John. In the memoir of the young and once wayward Captain Hedley Vickars it is stated that while waiting for a young companion in worldly pleasure, he opened a Bible which was lying in the room, and his eye fell upon the words, "The blood of Jesus Christ his Son cleanseth us from all sin." Deeply conscious of his own sins and exceedingly unhappy in them, he read and re-read the words, asking himself, "Is this true? Is it true for me? Can I believe it? Yes, I believe it, and by the help of God I will from this day give my life to his service." He did so. It was the turning-point of his destiny. From that hour he was a new man, and until his heroic death in the trenches at Sebastopol he was as remarkable for his consistent Christian character as before he had been for his youthful folly.

The deepest want of the human soul, when convinced of its sinfulness and impotence, is that of a divine Helper able and willing to save. It is precisely this want which is met and satisfied in the gospel of Jesus Christ. In him the weary, heavy-laden sinner, tossed about with many a doubt and many a fear, at last finds a Friend and a Brother, an almighty arm on which he can lean, and a rest which the world can neither give nor take away. A divine Saviour in human form, one having power to forgive sin, is what we all need and what the believing soul finds in Christ. This is the great central truth of our common salvation. It is after

Paul has presented this gospel of salvation in all its fullness, and discussed it in all its divine and human relations, that he rises to that grand and joyful climax of thanksgiving at the close of the eleventh chapter of the Epistle to the Romans: "Oh, the depth of the riches both of the wisdom and knowledge of God! How unsearchable are his judgments, and his ways past finding out! For who hath known the mind of the Lord? and who hath been his counselor? or who hath first given to him, and it shall be recompensed to him again? For of him and through him and to him are all things, to whom be glory for ever. Amen." How well, too, does this great mystery of redemption through the blood of Christ, which fills the apostle of the Gentiles with such wonder and adoration, accord with that other doxology of the Apocalypse given by the beloved St. John: "Unto him that loved us, and washed us from our sins in his own blood, and hath made us kings and priests unto God and his Father; to him be glory and dominion for ever and ever. Amen!"

CHAPTER XVI.

THE GRACE THAT SAVES.

THERE is no doctrine more prominent on all the sacred pages, especially those of the New Testament, than that of salvation by grace. It is of grace because it is of God, of grace because not of ourselves, not accomplished by our own strength, not dependent on our own merits. The chief expounder of the doctrine is the apostle Paul. "By grace are ye saved, through faith," writes he to the Ephesians, "and that not of yourselves, it is the gift of God; not of works, lest any man should boast." That is to say, our salvation is of grace, and the faith which puts us in possession of it is also of grace, being the gift of God wrought within us by the operation of the Holy Ghost. Speaking of the gospel method of salvation in contrast with that of legal works, he says to the Romans, "Ye are not under the law, but under grace;" "Moreover, the law entered that the offence might abound. But where sin abounded, grace did much more abound, that as sin hath reigned unto death, even so might grace reign through righteousness unto eternal life, by Jesus Christ our Lord." And he tells them, further, that this salvation through Christ, which is not of works or human merits at all, "is of faith, that it might be of grace."

Speaking of the gospel, he says in the Epistle to Titus, "The grace of God that bringeth salvation hath appeared unto all men." In the Epistle to the Ephesians he traces that gospel to its primal source when he writes, "In whom [Christ Jesus] we have redemption through his blood, the forgiveness of sins, according to the riches of his grace." With the same thought in view — salvation by grace, contrasted with works of human merit — the apostle John says, "The law was given by Moses, but grace and truth came by Jesus Christ." In like manner the apostle Peter sums up the whole gospel in the closing verses of his First Epistle, when he writes, "Testifying that this is the true grace of God wherein ye stand." No one can read the New Testament without seeing that the gospel of Jesus Christ is preeminently a gospel of grace, and that it requires faith as the essential condition of salvation because it is a gospel of grace. It is faith in Christ that saves us; it is faith in Christ that justifies us before God; and faith itself is a grace of God.

What, precisely, are we to understand by the term *grace*, which occurs so frequently in the New Testament?

It is used in several closely-related senses. It denotes, first, that everlasting love or favor of God which prompted him to provide salvation for us in the gospel, and which is the source of all the spiritual blessing we get from him. In this sense it is applied to each Person of the Godhead, Father,

Son and Holy Ghost alike. Thus, Peter speaks of the Father as the "God of all grace, who hath called us unto his eternal glory, by Christ Jesus" (1 Pet. v. 10). Of Christ, Paul says to the Corinthians, "Ye know the grace of our Lord Jesus Christ, that though he was rich, yet for your sakes he became poor, that ye through his poverty might be rich" (2 Cor. viii. 9). In like manner the Holy Ghost, who is called by our Saviour the Spirit of truth, is called by Paul, in the Epistle to the Hebrews, "the Spirit of grace," and it is his office to produce all gracious affections in the hearts of men (Heb. x. 29).

In a second sense, the word "grace" is constantly used, as we have seen in some of the passages already cited, for the gospel itself, which is the result and the manifestation to men of that divine good-will and favor from which it sprung. Then, again, the term "grace" is frequently used to denote that beneficent and effectual influence which comes from God or Christ or the Holy Spirit in the work of our personal salvation. This is its import wherever the saving operations of the Holy Ghost in converting the soul are referred to. In this sense of a divine influence or agency in our hearts, working for our spiritual good, the word is used by Paul when he says, "By grace are ye saved, through faith; and that not of yourselves, it is the gift of God;" which is equivalent to saying we are saved by the gracious and effectual operation of God's Spirit in our hearts, producing saving faith. This is its most frequent signification both in biblical and in theological language. So, in accordance with this use of the word, all those fruits of the Spirit which are produced in the heart and character of the Christian believer, such as faith, love, hope, joy, patience, repentance for sin and perseverance in holiness, are denominated "grace" or the "graces of the Spirit;" as when Peter says, "Grow in grace and in the knowledge of our Lord and Saviour Jesus Christ."

From this it is easy to see how much is implied in the term "grace," and how it is that grace saves us. Well might Paul say, "By the grace of God I am what I am: and his grace which was bestowed upon me was not in vain; but I labored more abundantly than they all: yet not I, but the grace of God which was with me" (1 Cor. xv. 10). So, also, when recounting the triumphs of God's grace among the Gentiles through these abundant labors, he says to the Galatians (i. 24), "and they glorified God in me." Thus the apostle John describes the exceeding riches of the gospel as a gospel of grace, or divine saving influence, when he says, "Of his fullness have all we received, and grace for grace;" that is, grace answering to grace from first to last (John i. 16). It is grace that saves, because it is grace that provides and offers salvation to the sinful, the unworthy, the helpless; and it is the same grace that applies it and makes it effectual. It is grace that saves us, because it is grace that justifies, it is grace that sanctifies, grace that glorifies. It is grace that begins the work, and grace that completes it. Salvation is not in part; it is perfect, complete, glorious; and it is so because it is of God. It has human means and agencies and co-workers; but its prime efficiency and its all-sufficiency is of God, who worketh in us both to will and to do of his good pleasure.

In the light of these passages, and of many others like them, we can clearly understand how a sinner believing in Jesus is justified before God, and also why faith holds such prominence in the gospel as the justifying and saving act. Faith in Christ is the bond of connection which unites the soul with the righteousness of Christ; and, as this righteousness meets and satisfies the demands of the law of God in our behalf, the faith which puts us in possession of it at once justifies and saves, and is properly called "saving faith." "Faith in Jesus Christ," says the Westminster Shorter Catechism, "is a saving grace, whereby we receive and rest upon him alone for salvation, as he is offered to us in the gospel." And this office of faith, as the bond of connection between the soul and Christ, is in exact accordance with the definition of justification given in the same Catechism: "Justification is an act of God's free grace, wherein he pardoneth all our sins, and accepteth us as righteous in his sight, only for the righteousness of Christ, imputed to us, and received by faith alone."

Now, when we look into the Scriptures it is easy to see the relation in which both grace and faith stand to our justification, and consequently to our salvation. In order to be saved we must be justified; there is no salvation without justification. But it is God who justifies, or pronounces the soul that was under condemnation just in the sight of the law. It is his free and sovereign act. But it is an act of grace, and an act performed on the ground of what Christ has done for him who believes in Jesus. Hence the same Scriptures that tell us we are justified by grace declare also that we are justified by faith. Paul says to the Romans (viii. 1, 2), "Being justified by faith, we have peace with God through our Lord Jesus Christ; by whom also we have access by faith into this grace wherein we stand, and rejoice in hope of the glory of God." But he says in the same Epistle (iii. 24–26), "Being justified freely by his grace, through the redemption that is in Christ Jesus, whom God hath set forth to be a propitiation through faith in his blood, to declare his righteousness, that God might be just and the justifier of him which believeth in Jesus." And in the Epistle to Titus he says, "That being justified by his grace, we should be made heirs, according to the hope of eternal life." It is plain, then, that justification by faith is the same as justification by grace, and it is *by faith*, as Paul says, that it might be *of grace*. Otherwise, if salvation were of works, "grace would be no more grace." Thus we have the great doctrine of the Lutheran Reformation and of all evangelical churches—justification by faith, which is clearly the doctrine of Paul in all his Epistles, and, as Paul shows in his letter to the Romans, the doctrine of the Old-Testament Scriptures, as it is written, "The just shall live by faith."

It is not without reason that faith in Christ holds this pre-eminence as the justifying and saving grace. While it is the free, rational act of man, it is at the same time the gift of God. It is always wrought in the soul of the believer by the enlightening and quickening power of the Spirit of God. Faith justifies and saves, because under the gospel scheme of salvation it has been appointed of God to fulfill this essential function. No other grace could take its place without throwing the gospel scheme of salvation out of harmony as a gospel of divine mercy for the guilty and of life for the perishing. Faith justifies and saves, because it is the one act which receives Christ, rests upon Christ, brings the soul into contact with Christ, secures the righteousness of Christ, and finally assimilates the character of the believer to the divine character of Christ. No other grace does or could do this. Faith in Jesus does all this. Most assuredly, the grace which does this is entitled to the distinction of being called the justifying, saving grace of the gospel.

Faith is not only thus essential as the bond of union with Christ and the medium of our justification with God, but it has an essential bearing upon the exercise of all the other Christian graces. Without faith, we are told, it is impossible to please God. But it is equally impossible to grow in the virtues of Christian character without faith. In all these our strength and progress will be in proportion to our faith. We repent of sin best at the cross. We repent of sin in proportion as we believe in the mercy of God in Christ. We love God best as his love to us is revealed by a strong faith in Christ. We learn to persevere in good works as faith brings to our view the glorious recompense of reward in Christ. We rejoice in hope of the glory of God in proportion as our faith is strongly anchored to the things within the veil and to Christ the Rock of Ages. In fact, we believe in God according to the measure of our faith in Christ. We are not only justified by faith, but sanctified by faith. It is our faith that brings all the precious promises and restraining influences and constraining motives of the word of God to bear upon us in daily life. Thus the great work of sanctification is carried forward in our hearts. But for this primal grace of faith, implanted by God's Spirit within us at the beginning of our pilgrimage and perpetually renewed, all other motives, influences and virtues of the Christian life would be inoperative or impossible.

While, therefore, faith justly holds that place of pre-eminence in vital Christianity which nothing else can hold, it is not for a moment to be forgotten that faith does not stand alone in the Christian scheme. It is indispensable, but it is not all. It is a vital part, but not the whole, of godliness. It does not stand without good works. While the gospel excludes good works *as the ground or method* of our justification before God, peremptorily telling us that no soul can be saved in that way, the same gospel demands a life of good works from every believer, and tells us plainly that no faith is valid without such works. One important New-Testament Epistle, that of James, is largely devoted to the inculcation of good works as the rule of Christian life and the very proof of a true faith. A true faith in Christ, instead of being opposed to good works, must always produce them as its legitimate fruit. Faith in Christ is the very soul of vital godliness, of human charity, of pure and elevated morality. "Faith without works is dead, being alone." It is no living faith; it is only a pretence or a delusion.

CHAPTER XVII.

THE OFFICES OF FAITH.

IN the trio of permanently abiding graces—faith, hope and charity—mentioned by Paul in his first letter to the Corinthians, he tells us that the greatest is charity—that is, love. Love, according to the Scriptures, is the fulfilling of the divine law. In the Christian believer it is that element of character which more than any other brings the soul into the likeness of God as a God of love. It is that crowning grace which rounds out and completes the Christian character, and thus prepares the soul for heaven. Being thus in man the most perfect reflection of the divine excellence and the very exponent of what the soul is to become in heaven, Christian love is well entitled to the encomium which the apostle bestows upon it in calling it the greatest of the graces.

At the same time, it is not to be denied that faith holds the primal and pre-eminent place in the Christian system and in all true Christian experience. Some of our ablest writers have recently called attention to the prominence of faith in the gospel scheme of salvation. In an important sense it may be said to be the very life and soul of Christianity. There is, in fact, nothing in Christianity more vital, more distinctive and more characteristic than faith. It is one of its fundamental facts and one of its deepest experiences. It would be easy to point out the reason why faith holds such pre-eminence in all the Scriptures, in all saving grace and in all practical godliness, but our purpose at present is not so much to vindicate this high estimate of faith as to point out, in the light of Scripture, some of the essential functions which faith performs, or rather the offices which it holds. In this, perhaps more than in any other, way we shall be led to see the pre-eminence of faith.

In the first place, faith is everywhere presented in Scripture as the *justifying* grace. It is God that justifies, for justification is always an act of God's free and sovereign grace. But then God justifies through faith on the ground of the merits and righteousness of Christ, received by faith alone. By faith the soul of the believer lays hold upon Christ, and is so united to him in that act as to be at once delivered from the condemning sentence of God's law, restored to the divine favor and entitled to all the benefits of Christ's redemption. This is a distinction attributed to no other grace except faith. God is the justifier of him that believeth on Jesus. "Therefore," says Paul, "being justified by faith, we have peace with God through our Lord Jesus Christ."

Paul tells us that Abraham believed God and it was counted unto him for righteousness. By this justifying faith in God, Abraham became the father of the faithful, the great model and type of all true believers. In order to be saved we must be justified, and in order to be justified we must believe in God, or, as it is expressed in the New Testament, must believe on Him whom God has appointed to be our Mediator, the Lord Jesus Christ. Thus Christ says, "Ye believe in God, believe also in me." In the Westminster Shorter Catechism this act of faith, as the one medium of our justification and the prime condition of our salvation, is expressed in the most brief and emphatic terms: "Faith in Jesus Christ is a saving grace, whereby we receive and rest upon him alone for salvation." Every Bible-reader knows with what earnest and unceasing reiteration the doctrine of faith is pressed upon us by Paul and all the other New-Testament writers. The great object of saving faith is Christ himself, and the essential element of a true faith is trust in God, trust in Christ.

In the next place, faith, more than any other, is the *sanctifying* or purifying grace of the Christian life. This function is assigned to it by Paul in his address before King Agrippa when recounting the commission he had received from Jesus Christ as the apostle of the Gentiles. He says that Christ had sent him to the Gentiles "to open their eyes, and to turn them from darkness to light, and from the power of Satan unto God, that they may receive forgiveness of sins, and inheritance among them which are sanctified by faith that is in me" (Acts xxvi. 18). The same prominence is ascribed to it by Peter in the council at Jerusalem when he tells how God had given to the Gentiles the Holy Ghost, "and put no difference between us and them, purifying their hearts by faith" (Acts xv. 8, 9).

Now, it is the distinctive office of the Holy Ghost to sanctify the soul, even as it is that of God the Father to justify. But in each case alike faith is the essential medium and condition both of the justification and of the sanctification. It is easy to see how this must be so. In his intercessory prayer Christ says, "Sanctify them through thy truth: thy word is truth," and, in his second letter to the Thessalonians, Paul gives thanks to "God, who had from the beginning chosen them to salvation, through sanctification of the Spirit and belief of the truth." These and other passages show that under the influence of the Holy Ghost the word or truth of God becomes the essential means of sanctification. But then the word of God can produce no sanctifying or purifying effect except so far as it is believed. Without faith it would be a dead letter. It is just as necessary that we should believe the truth in order to be sanctified as that we should believe in Christ in order to be justified. Hence the prime necessity of faith to the human soul as its great sanctifying or purifying exercise. If we have no faith, we can have no holiness. Faith is the substance of things hoped for and the evidence of things not seen. It alone can supply the influences and bring to bear upon us the motives from the word of God which will prompt us to holy life. Our growth in grace and our sanctification will be great or small in exact proportion to our faith.

Faith brings before our minds all the grand, inspiring doctrines of the word of God, the things unseen and eternal of the life to come, and specially the elevating influence of the character and example of Christ. Thus faith sanctifies and purifies the heart. "He that hath this hope in him," says John, "purifieth himself, even as he is pure."

In the third place, faith is the *working* grace of all Christian experience. It is the active principle, the impelling power, in all true religious life. There is such a thing as a dead faith, a faith without works, mentioned by the apostle James. But a true and living faith must work, cannot cease to work. It is the mainspring in the whole machinery of subjective theology, of practical godliness. It holds the same relation to the Christianity of the gospel that the mainspring of the watch holds to all other parts. It is that without which not a single wheel within or index-finger without can go. Its office is to start, to impel and to regulate the whole inward and outward movement.

No one can read such a passage as the eleventh chapter of the Epistle to the Hebrews without seeing the force of these remarks. There everything in the life of the Old-Testament saints—all energetic service, all heroic zeal for God, all self-denial and patient endurance unto death for conscience' sake—is attributed to faith as the grand impelling power of the Christian profession. It is not that other graces are ignored, but it is that this one grace, when it takes possession of the soul, sets all the rest in motion and sustains the believer in every service and under every trial. "According to your faith be it unto you," said Jesus. And so we read of the old believers that "through faith they subdued kingdoms, wrought righteousness, obtained promises, stopped the mouths of lions, quenched the violence of fire, waxed valiant in fight, out of weakness were made strong." In his letter to the Galatians, Paul not only affirms faith to be the working grace, but also shows how it works: "For in Christ Jesus neither circumcision availeth anything, nor uncircumcision, but faith which worketh by love" (Gal. v. 6).

Once more, faith is the *overcoming* and *victorious* grace. John has always been distinguished as the beloved disciple and the very apostle of love, love being the keynote of all his writings. But it is the venerable John who says, "Whatsoever is born of God overcometh the world: and this is the victory that overcometh the world, even our faith." When our Saviour had eaten his last passover with his disciples and was about to leave them, he said, "In the world ye shall have tribulation; but be of good cheer, I have overcome the world." By grace his disciples are all enabled sooner or later to do the same thing. When he overcame he overcame for his people; they all share in his victory. But it is by faith that they do so. By faith they are united to him and justified; by faith they are assimilated to him in character and sanctified; by faith they work for him and with him in all appointed service; and by faith at last they conquer all his and their enemies —the flesh, the world and the devil. By faith they fight the good fight, and by faith they win the victory. "To him that overcometh," said Christ, "will I grant to sit with me in my throne, even as I also overcame and am set down with my Father in his throne." Now, if faith, through the operation of the Holy Ghost, can do all this for the believer—justify the soul, purify the heart, energize and consecrate the life and overcome the world—clearly it deserves the high distinction accorded to it in the word of God. From all these important offices of faith we see the force of Paul's definition of it—" Faith is the substance of things hoped for, the evidence of things not seen"—and also of his strong statement, that " without faith it is impossible to please God; for he that cometh to God must believe that he is, and that he is a rewarder of them that diligently seek him" (Heb. xi. 1, 6).

CHAPTER XVIII.

REPENTANCE UNTO LIFE.

IT is to be feared that in the pulpit ministrations of our times the doctrine of repentance does not hold the prominent place which it held in former days, and which it certainly holds in the Scriptures. In some of the fashionable metropolitan pulpits, and with most of the itinerant revivalists and lay evangelists, there has been a strong tendency to simplify and popularize the gospel by making everything converge on a single definite point—namely, the act of faith which accepts and appropriates Christ. The result is, in some cases, that little more than a half gospel is preached, and the act of faith is so exalted that the law of God sinks away from the public view, and many minds, in their estimate of the essential importance of faith, lose sight altogether of the equally essential duty of repentance.

It must be plain on a moment's reflection—at least to every attentive Bible-reader—that there can be no salvation without repentance, any more than without faith. The one is as prominent in the Scriptures and as essential to our salvation as the other. We are all by nature sinners, "dead in trespasses and sins." We can never be delivered from sin and live anew to God except as penitents and believers. It is just as necessary that we should turn to God by repentance in order to live the new regenerated life as that we should take refuge by faith in Christ as our only Saviour. The two exercises go together as equal and essential factors of that gospel which is to deliver us from sin; and they can never be dissociated without pulling asunder what God has for ever joined together in the gospel plan of salvation, and what has always been found thus together in the experience of every penitent, believing sinner. Repentance is the tear of sorrow which trembles in the eye of the sin-burdened believer as he looks up to God through the cross of Jesus Christ.

This indissoluble co-relation of the essential graces of faith and repentance is well stated by Dr. Charles Hodge in the opening of his chapter on "Repentance" in his work *The Way of Life:* "Clearly as the Scriptures teach that whosoever believes shall be saved, they teach no less clearly that except we repent we shall all perish. These graces are not only alike indispensable, but they cannot exist separately. Repentance is a turning from sin unto God through Jesus Christ, and faith is the acceptance of Christ in order to return to God. Repentance is the act of a believer, and faith is the act of a penitent. So that whoever believes repents, and whoever repents believes."

We have only to turn to the New Testament to see what prominence is there given to the duty of repentance. We cannot preach the gospel of Christ in reality without also preaching this duty. When Christ first appeared he signalized his own public ministry by proclaiming it, saying, "The time is fulfilled and the kingdom of God is at hand: repent ye, and believe the gospel." His forerunner, John the Baptist, had done the same thing in the wilderness of Judea and on the banks of the Jordan when he preached the baptism of repentance for the remission of sins, and cried, "Repent ye, for the kingdom of heaven is at hand." So also our Saviour, when he had finished his redeeming work on earth and was about to ascend to heaven, ordained that "repentance and remission of sins should be preached in his name among all nations, beginning at Jerusalem." And precisely this we find his apostles doing on the day of Pentecost when they preached Jesus to the assembled multitudes, saying, "Repent and be baptized, every one of you, in the name of Jesus Christ, for the remission of sins, and ye shall receive the gift of the Holy Ghost."

So essential was repentance in the preaching of the apostles that we find it sometimes spoken of, like faith itself, as the very sum and substance of the gospel; as, for example, in the twelfth chapter of the Acts, when Peter preached to the household of the Roman centurion: "When they heard these things they held their peace, and glorified God, saying, Then hath God also to the Gentiles granted repentance unto life." In like manner, repentance and faith are associated as comprising the sum and essence of the whole gospel; as when Paul says to the Ephesian elders at Miletus, in the twentieth chapter of the Acts, "I have kept back nothing that was profitable unto you, but have showed you and have taught you publicly and from house to house, testifying both to the Jews, and also to the Greeks, repentance toward God and faith toward our Lord Jesus Christ."

In this important passage we see repentance and faith conjoined as the virtual fulfilling of all duty under the gospel, each alike indispensable as a part of the divine testimony. The object of the one grace is God—a merciful, reconciled and sin-pardoning God and Father, ready to hear the prayer, accept the penitence and blot out the sin of the believing penitent for the sake of Christ; the object of the other, the loving, compassionate, sin-atoning Son of God, willing to receive and save the soul of every humble, penitent believer who will thus come unto God through him and rest on him alone for grace and salvation. This is the true scriptural conception of evangelical repentance—a grace which stands with one hand uplifted to God in prayer, and with the other stretched out to Christ in loving, trustful obedience.

No better definition of evangelical repentance can be given than that of the Shorter Catechism. It is beautiful and complete, in both its simplicity and its usefulness: "Repentance unto life is a saving grace whereby a sinner, out of a true sense of his sin, and apprehension of the mercy of God in Christ, doth, with grief and hatred of his sin, turn from it unto God, with full purpose of, and endeavor after, new obedience."

Here are all the essential elements of genuine repentance, each particular word embodying a deep spiritual truth, a true sense of sin as offensive to God and condemned by his holy law, and a view of the great mercy of God as revealed in Christ Jesus dying for sinners, leading the soul to return to God with grief and abhorrence of sin as an evil and bitter thing, and at the same time with a full purpose, desire and determination, by God's help, to live a new and holy life. This is scriptural repentance; but, analyzed to the bottom, this is also saving faith, for no soul thus repents and turns to God except in the exercise of a saving faith, resting on God's promise of pardoning mercy through the atoning death of his Son.

God commands all men everywhere to repent. No duty of the gospel is more urgent, more universal. How can the Christian ministry fulfill its high calling of God if it ceases to ring out the command to repent? The author just named closes his fine chapter with these stirring words: "This call to repentance commonly follows men from the cradle to the grave. It is one of the first sounds which wakes the infant's ear; it is one of the last which falls on the failing senses of the dying sinner. Everything in this world is vocal with the voice of mercy. All joy and all sorrow are calls to return unto God, with whom are the issues of life. Every opening grave, every church, every page of the Bible, is an admonition or an invitation. Every serious thought or anxious foreboding is the voice of God saying, 'Turn ye, for why will ye die?' It is through all these admonitions that men force their way to death. They perish because they deliberately reject salvation."

CHAPTER XIX.

THE NEW BIRTH.

THE topic is an old one, and perhaps not so much discussed in our pulpits and in our current religious literature as it ought to be, and as it was in former times. If it is not the "article of a standing or a falling Church," it is at all events the point from which dates the beginning of every true religious life and the inner spiritual growth of every efficient Christian Church. It belongs to what we call the subjective, practical theology, as distinguished from the historical and the objective. It relates essentially to that incipient life which begins within us under the operation of the Holy Ghost when the soul of the believer is made alive to Christ, and is enabled to accept the great redemption which he purchased for us on the cross. In experimental godliness nothing can be more vital, more important.

The change which marks the beginning of this new and higher life of the soul is set forth in Scripture with great distinctness — not only by many explicit statements, but under many strong metaphors and analogies drawn from the material world and from our present human life. "Marvel not," said Christ to a teacher in Israel, " that I said unto thee, Ye must be born again," or, as it is more properly rendered, "born from above." "That which is born of the flesh is flesh, and that which is born of the Spirit is spirit. Verily, verily, I say unto thee, Except a man be born again (born of water and of the Spirit), he cannot see the kingdom of God. Art thou a master of Israel and knowest not these things? We speak that we do know and testify that we have received." Certainly there is no teaching in all the Scriptures more emphatic and unmistakable than are these words of the divine Witness.

The change of heart and life thus emphasized by Christ as the one thing needful to an introduction into the kingdom of God is described as a new or second birth, a regeneration, a new creation, a transition from light to darkness, a quickening, an awaking from sleep, a resurrection from the dead. All these and other strong analogies used in Scripture imply a change of life and character so radical and complete that those who have felt it may be said to have passed from a death of sin to a life of holiness. They were blind, but now see; old things have passed away, all things have become new; the natural man has become a spiritual man, and henceforth walks in "newness of life." The believer in Christ may not be able to explain this change, to tell precisely how or where it began, but of its reality there can be no doubt, and the whole subsequent life proves it.

Indeed, all the explanation that needs to be given is that it is a change of state as it regards the soul, and a transformation of its character and purpose which results in a new and higher life—which, in fact, marks the beginning of such a life. The Scriptures assure us that our natural condition is one of sinful depravity, of alienation from God, of aversion to holiness and propensity to evil, and that this condition must be changed before we can see God's face in peace. Without this change no man can be admitted to the presence of God in heaven, and no man could be happy there without it were he admitted. The holiness of God, the requirements of his service, the employments of heaven, the sad derangement of the human soul in its natural state,—all combine to confirm the great necessity proclaimed by Christ when he said, "Ye must be born again."

The sacred writers always ascribe this change of heart to the power of God and to the grace of God. It is wrought within us by the special agency of the Holy Ghost, whose office it is to apply the redemption of Christ to our souls and to regenerate our sinful nature. By his divine influence, working when and how he pleases, we are convinced of sin and brought to repent of it, restored to God, and led to exercise saving faith in Jesus Christ. A new purpose, a new habit, a new principle of spiritual life, is implanted within our minds, and this we call the grace or power of God, because it is from God, and not from man or from ourselves.

Nothing can be more explicit than the teaching of Scripture as to the divine authorship of this new life and this new principle of grace. It is affirmed in a hundred passages. Let one suffice: "But as many as received him, to them gave he power to become the sons of God, even to them that believe on his name, which were born, not of blood, nor of the will of the flesh, nor of the will of man, but of God" (John i. 12, 13).

Evidently, it is not in the power of human nature, dead as it is in trespasses and sins, to regenerate itself. It can no more raise itself from this death of sin than it could create itself. We might as soon expect a stone to lift itself. The power of this new spiritual creation must come from above. Whether we regard the soul as passive or as active in this beginning of new life, it is manifest that the germ of life must be from without, that the incipient and all-efficient agency must be that of God, and not of man. This is only equivalent to saying that the new birth is more than natural; it is supernatural, it is wrought by the mighty operation of the Spirit of God.

Human means and agencies may combine, and often do combine, as the Scriptures abundantly teach, in the production of this change. The written or preached word of God has its important influence on the mind; the minister of the gospel, the Christian teacher, the Christian parent, the religious book, each in turn or all together, may contribute their influential share in bringing a soul to God. Last of all, the sinner himself, however passive at first, and even resistant to divine grace, is made willing in the day of God's power, and becomes wide awake with all his active powers in the work of his conversion. For in this as in other things God works by means and through the appointed human methods and agencies. Still, over and above all human powers stands the grand essential gospel truth that the soul of every Christian believer is born again—not of man, not of itself, but of God. Without this supernatural divine influence there can be no new creation, no beginning of spiritual life, no birth into the kingdom of God—at least, for adult sinners. And even in the case of infants, saved as they are by the blood and imputed righteousness of Christ, it has been held by many sound divines, including Calvin, that they too are regenerated and sanctified by the operation of the Holy Ghost.

The salvation of the soul must necessarily include the double agency and the double work of the Son of God and the Spirit of God, the one delivering us from the guilt and condemnation of sin, and the other from the power and pollution of sin. We can no more be saved without the "washing of regeneration and renewing of the Holy Ghost," recreating and purifying our sinful nature within, than we can be saved without the shedding of the blood of Christ and his redemptive work, delivering us from the curse of God's violated law. Thus is our salvation made complete in Christ under the regenerating, sanctifying and saving influence of the Holy Ghost, raising us from the deadness of sin and enabling us to walk in the new spiritual life of God's children.

CHAPTER XX.

THE CONDITIONS OF SALVATION.

THE salvation of the gospel, so far as it is objective—that is to say, external to ourselves—is a finished thing absolutely complete in itself. In this view of it there can be no conditions; it is a fact accomplished. But as something connected with our own human agency it proposes certain terms to be complied with and means to be used and things to be done by us which are properly called the conditions of salvation, because without them we cannot be saved. Though God may work these things within us by his Spirit and help us by his grace to do them, still, in some way or other, our personal activity, both intellectual and moral, must be employed. Doubtless, God can save, and does save, infants without any personal agency of their own, but there is nothing in the Bible to warrant the belief that he ever saves rational adult minds without the putting forth of their consenting and working activities. While, therefore, we are saved by God and saved by grace, we are not saved except on the terms and conditions laid down in the gospel.

"What must I do to be saved?" No problem can be more important than this earnest question of the

Philippian jailer. It is the very turning-point of the soul's life both here and hereafter. In its solution every human being has the deepest of all interests at stake. We need not wonder that rational men feel an undying solicitude to find the proper answer, and crowd in multitudes to hear any preacher or lecturer who discusses it. It may without doubt be called the most vital question propounded in the Bible or anywhere else. The answer given on that occasion by an inspired apostle was brief, but it was decisive, and it was satisfactory to the inquirer: "Believe on the Lord Jesus Christ, and thou shalt be saved." This makes faith in Jesus Christ the one essential condition of salvation. But this in no way contradicts other equally explicit passages of Scripture which speak of repentance or conversion or confession of Christ or regeneration as a condition of salvation. This assurance of Paul to the Philippian jailer, that to believe in Christ Jesus brought salvation to him and his house, was not inconsistent with the declaration of the apostle Peter on the day of Pentecost to the conscience-stricken sinners of Jerusalem when they asked a similar question: "Men and brethren, what shall we do?" and received the answer, "Repent and be baptized, every one of you, in the name of Jesus Christ, for the remission of sins, and ye shall receive the gift of the Holy Ghost."

Such repentance for the remission of sins and baptism in the name of Jesus Christ as clearly implied faith in Jesus Christ on the part of these penitents as the faith of the Philippian jailer implied repentance for sin and baptism on his part. For how could these crucifiers of the Lord of glory repent of their sin in having once rejected him without now believing him to be the Lord of glory? and how could they be baptized in his name for the remission of sins without now believing on that name, and thus believing in his saving power? Thus we see that according to the gospel preached by Paul and all the apostles, instead of faith standing alone as the condition of salvation, repentance for sin must accompany the faith and stand with it as equally essential to salvation. Each grace implies the other and is never possessed without it. The one is always implied in the other. There is no saving faith possible without a true repentance of sin, and there is no evangelical repentance possible without saving faith in Jesus Christ.

This is evident when we consider what the salvation of the gospel is, and what it demands. The gospel is God's remedy to deliver men from sin. It is not salvation in sin, but salvation from sin. It professes to save men not only from the wrath of God and from the penalties of sin in the life to come, but from the reigning power and pollution of sin in the present life. If faith in Christ did not make men repent and turn from sin and do works meet for repentance in the present life, it would be a nullity, a dead letter; it would fail of all the great ends of salvation; in a word, it would be no salvation. Hence the indispensable necessity of repentance, and of all good works flowing from it. Never did Christ speak more emphatically than when he preached the gospel of repentance and said, "Except ye repent ye shall all likewise perish." In answering the question, then, "What must I do to be saved?" we see that it is impossible to separate repentance from saving faith in Christ, because repentance is the turning unto God from sin, and no man who does not repent of sin and turn from it can believe savingly in Christ as a Saviour from sin. Repentance, therefore, is as truly a condition—*sine qua non*—of salvation as is faith. Faith in Christ saves the believing penitent—that is, the penitent believer.

It is instructive to notice in how many varying forms the conditions or terms of salvation are stated in the New Testament, all of which, however, imply the same thing. Thus our Saviour said to Nicodemus, "Marvel not that I said unto you, Ye must be born again. Except a man be born of water and of the Spirit, he cannot see the kingdom of God." Here regeneration, or the being born of God, implying a change of heart and a new nature, is made as indispensable to salvation as are faith and repentance. But there is no inconsistency between this act of the Holy Ghost which makes us new creatures in Christ Jesus and our own exercise of faith and repentance under God's regenerating act; for He who performs the one thereby imparts to the soul that saving grace which enables it to comply with the terms of the gospel and fulfill the conditions on man's side by repenting and believing. So that, while we cannot be saved without repentance and faith, we cannot be saved without that regenerating agency of God's Spirit by which we pass from death unto life and are enabled to repent of sin and believe in Christ. There is not only no inconsistency here between the divine and the human agency in our salvation, but there is a perfect agreement, as Paul has so clearly expressed: "Work out your own salvation with fear and trembling; for it is God that worketh in you both to will and to do of his good pleasure."

Again, the terms of salvation are stated in another form by Paul in the Epistle to the Romans: "The word is nigh thee, even in thy mouth and in thy heart, that is, the word of faith which we preach, that if thou shalt confess with thy mouth the Lord Jesus, and shalt believe in thine heart that God hath raised him from the dead, thou shalt be saved. For with the heart man believeth unto righteousness, and with the mouth confession is made unto salvation." But these are not new conditions. To make outward confession with the mouth before men of that faith in Jesus Christ which is felt in the heart is virtually to renounce a life of sin, to take up the cross and follow Christ with "full purpose of, and endeavor after, new obedience," and thus to fulfill the conditions of salvation. And so, in another passage, the same apostle sums up the requirements of the gospel in this twofold statement where he speaks of "testifying both to the Jews and Greeks repentance toward God and faith toward our Lord Jesus Christ."

Faith is unquestionably the justifying act of the soul. As such it is the prime condition of salvation. We are justified by faith without the deeds of the law. He that believeth shall be saved, and he that believeth not shall be damned. "This," said Christ, "is the work of

God, that ye believe on him whom he hath sent." But it is a great mistake to represent faith as standing alone. "Faith," says the apostle James, "being alone and without works, is dead." It cannot save any man when it is divorced from good works. Any profession of faith which is not accompanied by repentance and does not produce good works is a profession without principle. Jesus Christ himself was holy, and his gospel demands a holy life in all his followers. It is a perversion of all the teachings of Christ and his inspired apostles, and an utter misrepresentation of Christianity, to say that the gospel does not require a life of ceaseless warfare against sin and of pure, unselfish morality. What is called character and good conduct, where there is no faith and no repentance, will not save us; but it is certain we cannot be saved on mere professions of faith without character and good conduct. We are justified by faith in Christ, but then it must be a living faith justified by good works, and not a dead faith without any good works to justify it.

If a justifying faith in Jesus, accompanied by repentance, be, as it certainly is, the essential condition of salvation, it is equally clear that a life of evangelical obedience in all good works is the essential condition, as well as proof, of such a faith; and we deceive ourselves when we claim to possess the faith without the corresponding evidence of a holy life. Thus we must explain all those passages of Scripture which require obedience to Christ's commands, submission to his will and faithful continuance in well-doing in order to be saved. Christ said, "Whosoever doth not bear his cross and come after me cannot be my disciple;" and, "Whosoever he be of you that forsaketh not all that he hath cannot be my disciple" (Luke xiv. 27, 33). When the young ruler came with the question, "What must I do to inherit eternal life?" he was first told to keep the commandments, and, after protesting that he had kept all these from his youth up, Jesus said, "One thing thou lackest. Go thy way, sell whatsoever thou hast, and give to the poor, and thou shalt have treasure in heaven, and come, take up thy cross and follow me."

Still further, there are passages which require that the soul must submit to God and obey the gospel in order to be saved: there is no salvation possible to those who rebel and refuse to obey the gospel. So also our Saviour says, "He that shall endure unto the end, the same shall be saved," where salvation is made to depend on faithful continuance in well-doing. Thus, too, our Lord closed his Sermon on the Mount, saying, "He that heareth these sayings of mine, and doeth them, shall be likened to a wise man who built his house upon the rock." But these are not new conditions of salvation, differing from what is implied in those already stated. All these and other forms of requirement are necessarily involved in repentance, faith and a holy life. We must be holy, we must turn from sin and bring forth the fruits of righteousness in all well-doing as long as we live. But it is precisely when and as we repent and believe in Christ that we are inclined and enabled to do all these things. For no man ever obeys the gospel, submits to God, keeps his commands, renounces the world and follows Christ, who does not exercise a true repentance and a saving faith.

Although the gospel comes to us thus restricted in its application by terms or conditions which must be complied with, it is easy to see that the terms are the very lowest which would be compatible with salvation from sin. The terms are neither difficult nor unreasonable. What better could we ask God to do for us than to save us from sin and hell on the exercise of faith in Christ, repentance of sin, and a new life of holiness and virtue? If God is holy and heaven holy, what less could we desire than to have our sinful nature so regenerated and changed that we can enjoy the presence of God in heaven? If holiness is better than sin, what less could we ask of God than to give us that repentance which will turn us effectually from a life of sin to a life of holiness? If God be entitled to the soul's confidence and homage, and Christ be worthy of implicit faith and love, what less could we desire in the scheme of salvation than to be required to exercise such a faith in God and in the Son? "Ye believe in God, believe also in me." We must see that, from the very nature of things, there is not only no salvation without these equitable conditions, but that there ought to be none.

Still further, no candid man can fail to see that this gospel of faith and repentance and holy living is offered to all men freely, and offered without any price to pay or merits to plead on their part. It is both free and gratuitous. The evangelical prophet Isaiah portrays this offer of salvation in glowing terms: "Ho, every one that thirsteth, come ye to the waters, and he that hath no money; come ye, buy and eat; yea, come, buy wine and milk without money and without price."

The Son of God stood and cried on the last great day of the feast at Jerusalem, "If any man thirst, let him come unto me and drink." The last proclamation of the Apocalypse is, "The Spirit and the Bride say, Come. And let him that heareth say, Come. And let him that is athirst come. And whosoever will, let him take the water of life freely."

CHAPTER XXI.

THE CHRISTIAN PROFESSION.

THE divine Founder of Christianity has made it incumbent on every one who would be his disciple to profess his name before men. This is, in fact, the outward act which from the beginning has drawn the line of distinction between his disciples and all other men. It is not the only, or even the chief, line of distinction, but then it is one which has its importance, and which cannot be safely set aside. The duty of professing Christ is as reasonable as it is explicit. "Them that honor me I will honor" is a principle of action the justness of which all men acknowledge. The Author of Christianity demands our grateful homage. He has assuredly done enough for us, and has enough of intrinsic excellence in himself, to entitle him to receive it. To confess his name before men is to honor him, and to honor him is not only to render a service which is due, but to give the most fitting expression to every generous prompting of a loyal, grateful heart. The question with every true and loving disciple is not one of duty merely, but of highest privilege. It is not so much why he is bound to render the service, but how he could possibly withhold it.

There is perhaps no act of duty enjoined upon his followers by our blessed Lord which he has laid down in more emphatic terms than this duty of confessing him before men.

In the tenth chapter of the Gospel by Matthew, on the occasion of calling and sending forth his twelve apostles, our Saviour uttered these impressive words: "Whosoever, therefore, shall confess me before men, him will I confess also before my Father which is in heaven. But whosoever shall deny me before men, him will I also deny before my Father which is in heaven." In the twelfth chapter of the Gospel by Luke the same important statement is given in its twofold form, and in the very same words except the added clause that this confession or denial shall be "before the angels of God." Then, again, we have substantially the same great alternative of duty performed or neglected, presented in similar terms by both Mark and Luke: "Whosoever will come after me, let him deny himself, and take up his cross and follow me. For whosoever will save his life shall lose it; but whosoever shall lose his life for my sake and the gospel's, the same shall save it. For what shall it profit a man if he shall gain the whole world and lose his own soul? Or what shall a man give in exchange for his soul? Whosoever, therefore, shall be ashamed of me and of my words, in this adulterous and sinful generation, of him also shall the Son of man be ashamed, when he cometh in the glory of his Father with the holy angels."

With these weighty words before us, four times reiterated in the Gospel narratives, can we say that any duty is more imperative in the Christian pilgrimage than that of confessing Christ? How can any man think it safe to ignore or defer so plain a precept, delivered under conditions so solemn and so vital? If Christ in these words has not made a Christian profession indispensable to his favor and indispensable to any claim of discipleship, it would be difficult to say what is indispensable. This is still further evident when we turn to such a passage as that of Paul in the tenth chapter of the Epistle to the Romans, where the duty of confession, like faith itself, is made a condition of salvation: "If thou shalt confess with thy mouth the Lord Jesus, and shalt believe in thine heart that God hath raised him from the dead, thou shalt be saved. For with the heart man believeth unto righteousness; and with the mouth confession is made unto salvation."

Seeing, therefore, that the duty of confessing Christ is so clearly taught in the Scriptures and is so essential to Christian character, it becomes a matter of the utmost importance to consider how the obligation is to be discharged. With the apostles, at their first calling, it was simply to follow Christ from place to place, to become a learner in his school of instruction, and to obey his directions. Afterward it meant much more. Endowed with power from on high by the descent of the Holy Ghost, these chosen apostles were commissioned to preach his gospel among all nations, beginning at Jerusalem, and at last, as confessors of and martyrs for the truth, they laid down their lives for his sake. Hundreds and thousands since that day have been called to confess and honor him at a similar sacrifice.

But what are we to understand now by a true profession of Christ? There are three several applications of the term, implying three different ways in which the service is to be rendered.

The first is in the act of a formal separation from the world and a voluntary union with the Christian Church, by what is known as a public profession of religion. No candid man can read the New Testament without seeing that Jesus Christ came to establish a kingdom in the world which is not of the world, but entirely separated from it. This is his Church, consisting of his own followers, his true disciples, who in every age have formed a peculiar people distinct from the world, the little flock to whom he said, "Fear not, for it is your Father's good pleasure to give you the kingdom." From the beginning till now it has been made the perpetual law of his kingdom, binding on all his true children in every land and nation, that those who love and honor him should attest their allegiance by coming out from the world and attaching themselves to his person, to his cause and to his people by a public and voluntary act of consecration. This they ought to do, if they are his, by the highest of all obligations; this they are bound to do, whenever they have the opportunity, by the most sacred of all ties. In the light of the New Testament, it is impossible to see how any man or woman having the opportunity and failing thus to profess Christ can have any claim to be called his disciple.

A second way in which a true confession of Christ before men is exemplified and attested is by a faithful attendance on the appointed ordinances of his worship, particularly in the two sacraments of baptism and the Lord's Supper. "Ye are my friends," said he, "if ye do whatsoever I command you." There is certainly no truer way of honoring him before men and of proving our allegiance to him than by a faithful, conscientious observance of his statutes. Be they many or few, great or small, his commandments were given to be kept. They are not grievous, but right and honorable; in the keeping of them there is great reward; and the little here is as true a test of the disciple's friendship and obedience as the great. It is a lifelong profession of Christ before the world when we observe his Sabbaths, respect his sanctuary, attend upon the worship of his house, identify ourselves with all the interests of his kingdom, give our time and substance to maintain and extend his cause, and remember all his commandments to do them.

This is especially true with respect to the two sacraments of the Church. He has required every disciple to be baptized in his name, with that of the Father and the Holy Ghost. This is the first outward badge of discipleship; this is the very door of initiation into his kingdom. It was a part of the great commission given as he left the world: "Baptizing them in the name of the Father, and of the Son, and of the Holy Ghost;" "He that believeth and is baptized shall be saved." What injunction was ever given to men with more sacred and endearing sanctions than that which requires every believer to come to the Lord's table and commemorate his death? "This do in remembrance of me;" "As oft as ye eat this bread and drink this cup ye do show the Lord's death till he come." Can any man or woman who has never once done this, but has gone through life having many opportunities, yet habitually neglecting it, claim to be his disciple?

A third essential attestation and exemplification of a true Christian profession is that of a consistent Christian character, a life spent in the practice of good works and charity, a faithful continuance in well-doing even to the end. This, and this alone, can complete the picture of the full stature of a perfect man in Christ Jesus. The full requirement of Christ is nothing less than to take up our cross daily and follow him. We must be like Christ himself—like him in all holy living; like him in character and conduct; like him in self-denial and charity; like him in word and deed; like him in the spirit and temper of our minds—in order to vindicate our Christian profession before the world: "By this shall all men know that ye are my disciples, if ye have love one to another." Then only is our Christian profession a living power for Christ before the world, when by faithful continuance in well-doing we grow into his likeness, and so become living epistles known and read of all men.

CHAPTER XXII.

CONSECRATION TO CHRIST.

AS Christ Jesus is the central figure in theology, holding relatively to all lesser truths the place which the sun holds among the planets, even so is he the central attraction in all Christian experience. It is not without a deep significance that he holds this supreme place in the scheme of salvation and in the hearts of his redeemed people. It is the one thing which makes vital Christianity so attractive to a believing soul, and so productive of holy and blessed influences over life and character. If we consider who Christ Jesus was, what he became and what he now is, we shall not wonder why he holds this seat of pre-eminence in the Church on earth, amongst the heavenly hosts, and in the deepest experience of every believing heart. "Chiefest among ten thousand, and altogether lovely," he holds the throne in our hearts and the throne in heaven because he alone is worthy to fill it.

In assuming the vows of a worthy Christian profession and in entering upon the high and sacred obligations of a religious life, no one thing is of more vital importance than the soul's attitude of service toward Jesus Christ. It is an attitude of complete surrender at his feet and of eager, joyful obedience in his service.

It is the attitude in which we may suppose the once doubting Thomas to have stood at the hour when every demand for evidence had been met and every doubt had vanished, and he exclaimed in devout homage, "My Lord and my God!" It is the attitude which without doubt the once persecuting Saul of Tarsus was brought to occupy when, smitten to the earth by the exceeding glory of that Saviour whom he was persecuting, he cried out with a new and hitherto unknown consecration, "Lord, what wilt thou have me to do?"

Now, there is everything in the life, sufferings, character and attributes of our adorable Redeemer to entitle him to the supreme homage of the human soul. It was one part of the great mystery of godliness that man's Redeemer should become his brother; that He who should stoop from heaven to save us should not only come into the world a God confessed, but should become God manifest in the flesh—the God incarnate, clothed in the veil of our mortality, a brother-man, "tempted in all points like as we are, yet without sin." He blended the two natures perfectly and gloriously in the one person of Immanuel. Had there been about him more of Godhead and less of humanity, we could not have loved him with that pure and sympathetic touch of human kindness which we now feel. Had there been more of humanity and less of the supreme Godhead overshadowing him, we could not have worshiped him with that elevated and unstinted adoration which now swells the believer's unconditional loyalty and love. The more we shall study the purposes and the conditions of this mystery of mysteries—the incarnate Godhead of Jesus Christ—the more we shall feel that it is the great thing of the Christian system, that it is unlike all other things known to man, and that it is in all respects just what it ought to be on the assumption that the Bible and its method of salvation are from God.

It hath pleased the Father that in him all fullness should dwell, the brightness of the divine glory and the express image of his person. He hath made the Captain of our salvation perfect—that is, *complete*—through suffering. He is a perfect Mediator, possessing at once every attribute of the divine and of the human nature. As man he is a sympathizing, loving friend and brother who has descended to our low estate and has promised never to leave or forsake us, being "touched with the feeling of our infirmities." As God he is "the same yesterday and to-day and for ever," able to save unto the uttermost all who come unto God through him. As such he is both a Saviour and a Sovereign, the King of kings and Lord of lords, having a right to the entire allegiance of our souls as one who has redeemed us from sin and death and hell, and "who ever liveth to make intercession for us."

In the light of these truths we see how equitable is the requirement, how essential the duty and how high the privilege, of yielding the soul's entire and unreserved homage at the feet of Jesus, and that at the name of Jesus every knee should bow. Hence the gospel requires nothing less, and it ought to require nothing less, than the whole-hearted consecration of time, talent, labor, life itself, in his service, on the part of every believer. Can we believe that the Master whom we profess to love and serve is what he claims to be, Immanuel — that he has bought us with his blood, called us into his kingdom, delivered us from sin and hell, and given us a sure title to eternal life in heaven—and then think of honoring him before men with a miserable lip-service of neglect and coldness— think of withholding the true service of a heart and life baptized with his Spirit and consecrated to his work?

It is obvious that no outward profession of religion, no mere church connection, is of any avail without a living Christ in the heart and in the life. Christ the power of God and the wisdom of God unto salvation must be in the creed and also in the heart of the believer. He, and he alone, can transform the character and christianize the life. Genuine Christianity is more than a true creed, more than an orthodox profession: it is a living, soul-transforming experience of grace, and a daily practice of self-denial and good works out of love toward the person of Christ and a conscientious obedience to all his commands. No formalist, no hypocrite, no mere theorizer, can ever fulfill its high requirements. No man can serve two masters: he must be all for Christ, or he will be found against him.

To one wishing to enter upon such a life, and so to fulfill the law of Christ, we may say that three things are essential. Supposing him to have been born of the Spirit and to have accepted Christ as the Saviour and Sovereign of his soul, in order to live this higher spiritual life there are three things which he must make up his mind, by God's help, not to neglect.

First, he must hold communion with Christ in the

daily reading and study of his written word. He must establish and maintain unceasing intercourse with Christ through the appointed medium of prayer.

Then he must go forth in the daily intercourse of life and business to work for Christ, to do something for his cause, something to honor his name, something to help his brethren and to persuade his fellow-men to be reconciled to God through him. There are a thousand influences which a soul fully consecrated to Christ can exert, and a thousand things which willing hands can do in his service, besides preaching the gospel, or teaching a Sabbath-school, or going far hence to proclaim Christ among the heathen. A truly consecrated life, like that of George Müller or of David Livingstone or of Alexander Duff, will indeed often demand of the young disciple that he should renounce earthly honors and pleasures and relinquish worldly pursuits, even of lawful business, that he may give his whole life to the ministry of the gospel at home or in pagan lands.

But these are not the only fields or the only pursuits in which a consecrated life of service is needed. He demands the same sort of consecrated service from every one of his professed followers — from every member of the Church militant. There is work for all and a place for all, but no true effectual work will be done without this missionary spirit of a consecrated life. No acceptable work ever has been done except in the spirit of the great apostle of the Gentiles when he cried, " Lord, what wilt thou have me to do?" It is recorded among the incidents of the gospel history that our Lord once had need of a colt. It was a small, menial service, and yet an honorable service, which was required of "the ass's colt." Is there a single member in the Church to-day, however humble, who is not as valuable as the colt, and of whom it might not be said, for some particular service, "The Lord hath need of him"? If not, let the young man or the young woman, or perchance the older disciple, respond to the summons in the spirit of a consecrated service: "Lord, here am I; send me."

Blessed be God, this spirit of consecration is not confined to the learned and the great. The humblest disciple in his lowly sphere of duty, and the most shrinking of Sabbath-school teachers seeking to win her little pupils for Christ, may possess it as truly as may the honored foreign missionary who has given up all for his divine Master. But in our times, when there is so much work to be done for the Lord on every hand and so few to do it, when the harvest-fields are so white and the reapers so inadequate, when the world is so full of need and the Church herself so worldly, when God by his providence and Christ by his gospel are calling so loudly for more laborers and a higher consecration, is it not amazing that there are not more to say, "Lord, I am ready—consecrated to the work or for the sacrifice"?

How, then, shall this baptism of consecrated zeal be obtained? We have already indicated the process and pointed out the means. All experience proves, and all the saints of God join in the testimony, that there is no other way except through the three essential conditions already named. To begin with, there must be a living faith and a full purpose of heart to live this life. Then we must commune with Christ daily in his written word—must commune with him without ceasing in the secret place of private prayer—and then, as we go forth each day or hour to our appointed occupations, we must go in that earnest working spirit which practices what it preaches and what it prays, saying, " Lord, what wilt thou have me to do? Lord, what can I do for thee and for thy cause to-day?" All life will thus become a work for Christ, all work an earnest prayer, all prayerful, earnest toil a song of joy. The hands will labor and the heart will sing :

> " I am thine, O Lord! I have heard thy voice,
> And it told thy love to me;
> But I long to rise in the arms of faith,
> And be closer drawn to thee.

> " Consecrate me now to thy service, Lord,
> By the power of grace divine ;
> Let my soul look up with a steadfast hope,
> And my will be lost in thine."

M

CHAPTER XXIII.

THE SPIRITUAL LIFE.

WHATEVER differences of opinion may exist as to the value of creeds and systems of doctrine, all evangelical churches profess to hold that spirituality is essential in the Christian life. To divest religion of this attribute is to rob it of all saving power. A church without spirituality is a dead or dying church. A professing Christian who has no spirituality in his experience, no spirituality in his daily life, has but a name to live, while his heart is far from God. A minister of the gospel who has no spirituality in his preaching may attract the multitude by his gifts of eloquence or by his learning, but in the end his ministry will be as barren of lasting good as sounding brass or a tinkling cymbal. God is a Spirit, and they who worship at his altars or proclaim his word must do it in spirit and in truth. Christianity is nothing except as it is a spiritual religion; and the soul has not made the first real advance in the divine life except so far as by prayerful experience it has attained to that condition which the Scriptures describe as the spiritual mind.

Let us not deceive ourselves, for God is not mocked and cannot be imposed upon: "Whatsoever a man soweth, that shall he also reap. For he that soweth to his flesh, shall of the flesh reap corruption: but he that soweth to the Spirit, shall of the Spirit reap life everlasting" (Gal. vi. 7, 8). Christianity is more than a name; religion is more than church-membership; the vital experience of the soul is more than zeal for orthodoxy, or genteel conformity to conventional propriety on the Sabbath, or fiery championship of a party in the Church. All history shows that we may have respectable formalists and heartless professors in the Church, just as easily as we have time-servers and partisans and ambitious aspirants for place and power in the public service of the State.

Nothing can be plainer in all the teachings of Christ and his apostles, as seen in almost every page of the New Testament, than that spirituality is the very essence of vital godliness; that there is no true religious experience, no true Christian life, without it; that the "kingdom of heaven is within us;" that it does not consist in meat and drink or any mere outward service, but in "righteousness and peace and joy in the Holy Ghost."

In illustration of this essential requirement and condition of true Christian life we might quote a large part of the Scriptures, not only of the New Testament, but also of the Psalms and of the prophets. Let us instance one brief but most emphatic statement of the apostle Paul in the eighth chapter of the Epistle to the Romans: "For they that are after the flesh do mind the things of the flesh; but they that are after the Spirit, the things of the Spirit. For to be carnally minded is death; but to be spiritually minded is life and peace: because the carnal mind is enmity against

God: for it is not subject to the law of God, neither indeed can be. So then they that are in the flesh cannot please God. But ye are not in the flesh, but in the Spirit, if so be that the Spirit of God dwell in you. Now, if any man have not the Spirit of Christ, he is none of his. And if Christ be in you, the body is dead because of sin; but the Spirit is life because of righteousness. . . . Therefore, brethren, we are debtors, not to the flesh, to live after the flesh. For if ye live after the flesh, ye shall die: but if ye through the Spirit do mortify the deeds of the body, ye shall live. For as many as are led by the Spirit of God, they are the sons of God."

In all the Scriptures is there anything more essential to salvation and to growth in Christian character than the great doctrine of spiritual life so forcibly presented in these verses? They tell us what the true life of God in the soul is, how it is sustained and by what agency it is wrought within us. It is a life of holiness, of resistance to sin, of conquest over the world, the flesh and the devil, through Jesus Christ and the Holy Ghost. It is a ceaseless spiritual warfare against corruption within us and against evil without us and around us. It is a new spiritual life as distinguished from the old life of the natural man, which is carnal and earthly. It is a spiritual heavenly life drawing its influences and motives from above as distinguished from that life of sin and folly which unregenerate men live in the world. It is a spiritual life consisting in a gradual conformity of the soul to the holy law of God, and of likeness to the pure and elevated character of Christ, by which all God's regenerate children are delivered more and more from the power of indwelling sin and have more and more in themselves the mind and the Spirit of Christ. It is a spiritual and Godlike life, wrought in every believer by the mighty power, the indwelling abiding energy, of the Holy Ghost, enabling the soul to resist evil, to overcome temptation, and to triumph at last over every fleshly, worldly and satanic foe. There is nothing in Christianity more vital, more precious, more glorious—not even Christ's own work of sacrifice and death upon the cross—than this work of the Holy Ghost within the soul of the believer enabling him to live the spiritual life. We are saved by the death of Christ, and, with equal truth, we are saved by the indwelling agency of the Spirit of God.

One of the strongest tendencies of human nature, even when partially sanctified by the gospel, is to depart from a pure, simple, spiritual faith in Christ and to take refuge in an empty outward profession, in the observance of rites and ordinances, the exaltation of the letter above the spirit, the external above the internal. We know how completely the Jews had sacrificed the spirit to the letter and made void every principle of the law of God by their traditions at the time when Christ appeared. We know also how the Roman Catholic and other ritualistic churches have done the same thing, teaching for doctrines the commandments of men, and finally subverting every spiritual element of the gospel. The Reformation of the sixteenth century restored the gospel and kindled anew the flame of spiritual devotion among all Protestant churches, but toward the close of the seventeenth century these churches and their ministers had so declined in spirituality that Richard Baxter wrote his famous book *The Reformed Pastor* mainly to break the reign of worldliness and call the secularized clergy to a higher spiritual life. It was only the great revivals under Whitefield and the Wesleys, about the middle of the following century, that saved spiritual religion. By these revivals God rolled away the reproach of a dead formalism from the British and American churches, and set that high standard of spiritual evangelism which has held its predominant influence to the present time.

It is to be feared that just now there are indications in all the great evangelical churches, especially of our own country, that a reaction has again set in toward secularism and worldly conformity and the mere externals of religious observance, which is not only lowering the spiritual tone of the pulpit, but sending its deadening influence down through the ranks of the rising ministry and the lives of all Christians. No greater calamity can befall the Church of God in our day or in any day. To lose the true spiritual life from the ministry and members of the Church is to lose the greatest power God ever gives to them. It is to lose the presence and the agency of the Spirit of God; and to lose these is in the end to subvert the truth and destroy the saving power of the gospel. God save us from an ambitious, mercenary ministry and a secularized, mammon-worshiping and world-conforming Church!

CHAPTER XXIV.

RELIGION AS A LIVING POWER.

IT is only as it moulds the character and controls the life that religion becomes a living power. As a mere system of dogmas, unfelt and unpracticed, it is to all intents and purposes a dead letter. In the dry light of dogma alone it might deserve the indifference or contempt which its enemies sometimes show for it. In proportion, however, as its doctrines are cordially embraced, intelligently understood and reduced to practice in daily life, religion becomes a vital and ever-present reality amongst men, winning the admiration of the good and commanding the respect even of its enemies. Viewed in this truer aspect, it is far more of a reality in our Christian society than superficial observers are apt to think. In fact, it may be questioned whether there is any other reality in the world so potential and so vital.

Let us notice for a moment some of the manifestations of this living and controlling power of evangelical religion. We shall find them not in one Church alone, not in one class of Christians alone, but in all true Christian churches, among all sincere men and women of every name who have in any way come under the influence of Bible Christianity. We shall find that Christianity has its strongholds in society and gives daily manifestations of its power which it would be well for the skeptical rejecters of its claims to consider. There are several of these indications of vital influence which are exceedingly striking as showing the degree in which Christianity has won its way to the hearts of men and triumphed in our modern society.

The first of these is seen in the worship of the Christian congregation. Whenever and wherever a congregation of Christian worshipers, large or small, is assembled on the Sabbath-day, in city, town or country, there is the ocular demonstration of what Christianity is doing for men, there is the standing monument of the progress which it has made across the ages and over the earth. What is it that everywhere simultaneously draws these multitudes and holds together these attentive, interested and devout worshipers? Is it any feeble or inadequate power that has done this so long, and is still doing it, in every part of Christendom? If on any given Sabbath we could see all the Christian congregations in the world assembled in their places of sacred worship, with their solemn ordinances of prayer, of praise to God, of reading and expounding the Scriptures, and of the proclamation of the gospel according to the last command of Christ, what an idea would this vision give us of that influence which has gone out over the earth and is perpetually controlling the thoughts, the purposes, the plans of life and the actions of living men! None but the divine mind is adequate to grasp this vision, to measure this influence, to understand the power of this agency. And yet nothing less than this is the influence and the agency which Christianity is exerting in every land under heaven where the gospel is preached, the Sabbath observed and the public worship of the congregation established. Can anything less than a great and vital power accomplish a result like this? No man can dispute the fact that it is accomplished, but the fact itself is a perpetual demonstration that the religion of Christ is not a mere dogma, not an abstract idea, not a dead letter, but a living reality amongst men.

A second indication of the living power of Christianity perhaps even more potential than the foregoing is seen in the home-circle. The religion of Christ has its private not less than its public sanctuaries. Its influence in the great congregation is that of assembled multitudes actuated by the same spirit and combined for a definite object, the worship of God. But this is an influence exerted for the most part only one day in seven, sending its impulse through the week. But the religion of Christ covers all the duties of man and throws its salutary power over all days alike. Thus it erects its sanctuary in every household, it establishes its morning and evening worship at every family altar. It becomes a daily instructor and guide to the youth of each particular home-circle, it makes the family a training-school for Christ and for the Church, and it sheds over all the duties of life the fragrance of religious worship, the blessed influence of parental precept and example. Once a day at least, and for the most part twice, God's venerated book is read in the hearing of the household group, the voice of beseeching prayer is lifted heavenward, and the sacred hymn with its notes of thanksgiving and praise gives unction to the sweet hour of prayer. We do not say that this picture of social devotion is realized in every family circle, but it is in many, in different parts of the land. This, at any rate, is the type and model of family worship which the gospel aims to exemplify, and does exemplify in the degree to which Christian parents live up to their high vocation.

Now, can any one fail to see that here is a strong influence exerted over the character and the actions of Christian families which is as salutary and powerful as that which goes out from the weekly ministrations of the great congregation? It is, in fact, when we divide the great congregation into its constituent elements— the Christian families—and trace the public influences of the one through all the more private influences of the other, that religion may be said to exert its greatest power and to reach the very citadel of its strength. The triumph of Christianity is never more complete than when it is found to establish and control the Christian homes of the people. All that is done and said in the great congregation is for the express purpose of moulding the lives of the people in their Christian homes. These are the well-springs of gospel influence; these are the very hiding-places of its power.

A third illustration of the living power of Christianity, still wider than either of those we have mentioned, is found in the inner life of the individual. There are thousands of persons belonging to no Christian congregation, having no Christian home of their own, and perhaps attending no house of God on the Sabbath, to whom, nevertheless, Christianity is a living power. They feel its influence in their deepest experience; it comes home to them as a sweet remembrance of the past, as a hope of relief for the future, and as a consolation in the present. Sooner or later this experience comes home to almost every man. It comes with special power in the dark days of adversity, in the sad hour of bereavement, in the privations of penury and want, in the gloom of sickness, in the approaches of old age and infirmity, in the bitter waters of death. At such seasons of trial what can a man do without religion? He may shake off all concern about it in times of health and prosperity, but the deepest experience of his soul will cry out for it long before he reaches the end of life, or, if not before, certainly at the end.

Will any one tell us that to this numerous class outside of our churches and our Christian homes religion is not a vital reality, the gospel of Christ is not a living power? In ten thousand such cases it is felt to be a living power, and the dying man, though no professor of religion, flies to it as his only refuge and his greatest privilege. It is not only the Christian who bears witness to the fact that the gospel of Christ is the power of God and the wisdom of God unto salvation: every man reared in a Christian land has felt its power through life as a restraint on sinful passion, and most men have borne witness to its truth at the dying hour.

The living power of religion finds another still more striking illustration. It is seen in the godly lives of the faithful few who live nearest the cross and hold daily communion with God. It is the privilege of all Christ's disciples to ascend to this higher plane and breathe this purer air of holy living, but comparatively few attain it. The gospel, however, to-day as in all former ages, back to the apostles, shows what it can do in the transformation of character by appealing to its living witnesses of this higher type. They may be few in number—here and there a disciple among many professing Christians, here and there a true man of God in the ministry or eldership of the churches—but, wherever they are found, they have power with God. And they never fail to leave their deep spiritual impress on the community around them—it may be, on the very age in which they live. One such minister, or even private Christian, is equal in holy influence to a thousand sleeping disciples or worldly-minded professionalists in the pulpit. These faithful ones are the true workers, and the true types of Christianity. They give us the real measure of the advance which the gospel is making in all lands. Out of this class come nearly all our foreign missionaries, both men and women—the Judsons and the Harriet Newells who carry the glad tidings of salvation to the heathen. In this class are found our best Sabbath-school workers and our indefatigable evangelists among the poor and the perishing.

To this class belong the godly men and women who in the churches sustain the hands of the pastor and are never absent from the prayer-meeting. These are the praying ones, who live the religion they profess, and who, if needful, would stand ready to die for it; and if the Lord should come at midnight or in the morning, they would be found faithfully waiting and watching at the post of duty. "These are my witnesses, saith the Lord." They are the light of the world and the salt of the earth. Before Christianity is condemned let it be tried by this class of its disciples.

That Christianity is a living power for good among men and nations, the most civilized as well as the most ignorant, it is too late now to deny or question. Even Mr. Froude, who disputes its divine origin, has said, "So far as philosophy can see, there may be nothing in the materials of Christianity which is necessarily and certainly supernatural. And yet Christianity exists, and has existed, and has been the most powerful spiritual force which has ever been felt among mankind."

CHAPTER XXV.

CHRISTIAN LIFE A MINISTRY OF LOVE.

A VOLUME might be filled with precepts from the Bible illustrating the sentiment that Christian life was designed to be a perpetual ministry of love. Love is the crowning grace of the Christian code of ethics, and Christian experience is never at the full until it reaches this perfection. God is love; Christ the Incarnate is love; the Holy Ghost is the Spirit of love. The disciple in this school is one whose highest lesson is to become assimilated to the character of his divine Teachers in all the offices of love. His life is a ministry of love in the double sense that it is prompted by love and that its ends are love. It springs from love at the root, and it produces love as its ripened fruit. Its very law of existence is ceaseless activity in doing good to others, in communicating blessing to all within its reach. "To do good and communicate," says the apostle of the Gentiles, "forget not, for with such sacrifices God is well pleased;" "And let us not be weary in well-doing, for in due season we shall reap if we faint not;" "As, therefore, we have opportunity, let us do good unto all men, especially unto them who are of the household of faith;" "And remember the words of the Lord Jesus, how he said, It is more blessed to give than to receive;" "Ye have the poor with you always, and whensoever ye will ye may do them good."

Such a ministry of love was that of Christ himself, illustrating the great law of beneficence for all his followers. Such a ministry was that of Paul and of each of the chosen apostles, teaching us by their untiring labors, their heroic zeal and their deep compassion for the perishing how to work and how to suffer for Christ and our fellow-men. It is the glory of Christianity that through all its centuries it has been adorned by a long list of faithful men and women who, inspired by the example of the great Founder, have exhibited this ministry of love in their own lives. "What noble women the Christians have!" was the encomium given by a pagan philosopher of the early centuries; and it has been justified by a "great cloud of witnesses" in every century, who have learned at the cross how to make life beautiful and sublime by the practice of beneficence and the lustre of good deeds. The world itself does homage to the majesty of Christian character when that character is fashioned according to the pattern of the divine Master and is illustrated in the walks of daily life by saintly men and women who count no sacrifice—not even that of life itself—too dear to rescue the fallen.

Among the things pointed out by Christ in proof that his religion was from heaven and he the Messiah of the prophets was his benevolent regard for the poor. "Go and shew John again," said he, "those things which ye do hear and see: the blind receive their sight, and the lame walk, the lepers are cleansed, and the deaf hear, the dead are raised up, and the poor have the gospel preached to them." When he entered upon his public ministry in the synagogue at Nazareth, he said, "The Spirit of the Lord is upon me, because he hath anointed me to preach the gospel to the poor. He hath sent me to heal the broken-hearted, to preach deliverance to the captives, and recovering of sight to the blind, to set at liberty them that are bruised, to preach the acceptable year of the Lord." No religion in the world has so exalted the virtue of benevolence and shown so tender a care for the poor as Christianity. There has been known amongst men no friend for the poor like the gospel. This deep and yearning compassion for the poor was not only inaugurated, but exemplified to the full, in the life, labors and instructions of the divine Founder, and it has been illustrated in the life and character of all true followers just in proportion to the degree in which they have possessed his spirit and imitated his example.

The lesson of charity, of benevolent, self-sacrificing zeal for the helpless, is enjoined in a thousand passages, and it has been exhibited in ten thousand examples. There is no one point on which the teaching of Christ and his inspired apostles is more emphatic. The gospel does not more explicitly require holiness in the hearts of its disciples than it requires zealous and ceaseless endeavor in their lives in doing good to others. If a man feels no interest in his suffering fellow-men, puts forth no helping hand to the poor and perishing, it matters not what pretensions to piety he may make or in what Church he may fold his arms of self-complacent ease, he is no true disciple of Christ. He has none of his spirit; he lacks the most essential evidence and the most Christlike virtue of Christianity.

Now, he who has learned how to make life a perpetual ministry of love to those around him has learned the great secret both of usefulness and of happiness. It is in this school and in this service that the question is answered, " Is life worth living?" When life becomes a blessing to all within its sphere of influence, and gives its possessor the consciousness of God's approval and the approbation of all good men, then, assuredly, it is worth living. It is the aim of the gospel to make every life thus blest of God and man. It is in this school of Jesus Christ and in this work of doing good to men that life becomes a ministry of love and human character rises to its noblest type. In this service it is the privilege of every disciple of Jesus Christ, even the humblest, to make his life beautiful in its sentiments of good-will, its acts of kindness, its sacrifices of love and toil. Is there any exemption from this law of beneficence? Is there any one too lowly to exercise this sublime virtue of extending a helping hand or a sympathizing word to those who are ready to perish? The widow's two mites are sublime in their exhibition of the spirit of Christ, and the cup of cold water given in the Master's name may be eloquent as a delineation of Christian character. Make life a ministry of love, and it will always be worth living.

The law of Christ requires that we should be faithful in that which is least, that we should use the one talent committed to our trust as diligently as we would use the ten. The command to every disciple is, " Freely ye have received, freely give;" " Occupy till I come;"

"Go work to-day in my vineyard." The great law of the kingdom reaches down to every member of it; it is, "Do good unto all men as ye have opportunity." Here is the extent of the law—*unto all men;* and here is the only limit to its application—*as ye have opportunity.* Nothing could be wider, nothing could be more equitable. If there is a soul in the world that has no opportunity, not even to give two mites, or the cup of cold water, or the word of good cheer, or the prayer of faith, that soul is exempt from the binding force of the law; but even that soul ought to be ready for the good deed when the opportunity comes. If there is a soul in the Church so unlike the good Samaritan as to have no neighbors, either Jew or Gentile, among the "all men" of this command, that soul may stand before Christ at the day of judgment and say, "I had no suffering brother-man to whom I could give the two mites or the cup of cold water. I pray thee have me excused."

It was for a little act of love, a last memorial of affection and sympathy, that our Saviour spoke the word of encomium to a faithful disciple when she had broken her precious alabaster box to anoint his head and his feet: "She hath done what she could." What a witness to the world it would be if the whole brotherhood of disciples would exemplify in their daily action that single text of James, "Pure religion and undefiled before God and the Father is this: to visit the fatherless and the widows in their affliction, and to keep himself unspotted from the world"!

CHAPTER XXVI.

THE GOLDEN RULE.

NO precept of Christ has been more applauded than the one known as the Golden Rule, uttered first in his Sermon on the Mount: "Therefore all things whatsoever ye would that men should do to you, do ye even so to them; for this is the law and the prophets." It has commended itself to the judgment of mankind as true and wholesome doctrine, as the very essence of that ethical system of justice and beneficence which we find illustrated alike in the teachings and in the actions of the Founder of Christianity. It is said that the sternly-just Roman emperor Alexander Severus so admired the sentiment that he had it inscribed on the walls of his chamber, often quoted it in giving judgment, and held both Christ and his disciples in great honor on account of it.

Some scholars and critics of recent times have maintained that the doctrine here enunciated is not original with Jesus Christ. They tell us it has been found elsewhere in ancient writings, both Jewish and pagan. Some find it in the Talmud among the maxims of Hillel, a famous doctor of the Jewish law, who says: "What is disagreeable to thyself, do not thus to another"—a wise negative precept unquestionably, but certainly very far short of the broad, positive injunction of Christ. Others tell us that something like it has been discovered in the writings of Isocrates and other Greek philosophers, and also in the teachings of Confucius, Buddha and other ancient sages and religious founders of the Orient. Very likely; it would be rather singular if a sentiment so deeply founded in the elemental principles of justice and humanity should have entirely escaped observation and utterance on the part of all the world's greatest thinkers—at least, in some negative or partial application of it. As Adam Clarke well remarks, " it seems as if God had written it upon the hearts of all men, for sayings of this kind may be found among all nations, Jewish, Christian and heathen."

It is to be observed, however, that our Saviour does not claim originality for the rule he announced. The opposite is implied on the very face of the passage; for, having stated the doctrine in its broad, positive and emphatic terms, he adds, " For this is the law and the prophets," precisely as he does in so many other instances where he appeals to the Old-Testament Scriptures in vindication of his own sublime instructions. It is equivalent to saying, " This all-comprehensive requirement of duty to your fellow-men which I here reaffirm and enjoin is the very sum, substance and spirit of all the precepts of the second table of the Decalogue, and all the precepts affirmed by the prophets of God as taught in that law." As all the precepts of the first table relating to God are fulfilled in one comprehensive summary, " Thou shalt love the Lord thy God with all thy heart and soul and mind and strength," so all the duties of this second table relating to man are fulfilled in one similar word, "Thou shalt love thy neighbor as thyself," or, as it is here expressed, in doing to others as ye would that they should do to you. To do this is to catch the very spirit of the old law, which is love—love to one's neighbor, love to all men. To do this is to secure the very end aimed at by the law and the Lawgiver—namely, to secure that reign of amity and peace and good-will among men heralded in the glad tidings of Christ's gospel.

The idea suggested by some learned men—that Christ borrowed this Golden Rule either from the Jewish rabbins or from the writings of Oriental pagan philosophers—seems far-fetched and groundless. Such an origin is not only without proof, but is contradicted by the obvious fact that Christ himself gives the sentiment its true origin in the Scriptures and in the law of God. Why trace to Confucius, to Menu, to Buddha, to Isocrates, to the Jewish doctors, or to any other human authority, a maxim which the great Teacher himself tells us is the essential principle and the all-pervading spirit of at least six commandments of that law which Moses and Israel heard from God's own voice on Mount Sinai? The learned critics might as well tell us that his new commandment, "To love one another," is not of scriptural but of pagan origin. The connection in which the passage stands in the Sermon on the Mount shows clearly that our Saviour intended it as a brief compendium of all the duties demanded in the second table of the Decalogue, and of the true spirit required in the discharge of those duties; for he is there expounding those duties in their deep spiritual import against the perverted interpretations of the Pharisees, who had made void the law by their traditions. The whole matter is set in a clear light by the following comment of the apostle Paul in the thirteenth chapter of the Epistle to the Romans: "Render therefore to all their dues: tribute to whom tribute is due; custom to whom custom; fear to whom fear; honor to whom honor. Owe no man any thing, but to love one another; for he that loveth another hath fulfilled the law. For this, Thou shalt not commit adultery, Thou shalt not kill, Thou shalt not steal, Thou shalt not bear false witness, Thou shalt not covet; and if there be any other commandment, it is briefly comprehended in this saying, namely, Thou shalt love thy neighbor as thyself. Love worketh no ill to his neighbor: therefore love is the fulfilling of the law."

God himself is love, and the only obedience which can satisfy and fulfill any precept of the divine law, whether to God or to man, is the obedience prompted by love. In the last analysis every law of God is a law of love. The Golden Rule is but the comprehensive statement of this sublime principle in its application to the duties we owe our fellow-men. Instead of teaching, as did the Pharisees, that we are to treat our fellow-men *as they treat us*, which would be to establish our own self-interest as the prime rule of action, our Saviour teaches that we are in "all things whatsoever we do" to consider the feelings, the rights and the welfare of others—that is, to treat them *as we would have them treat us*, which is to enthrone the principle of good-will and beneficence as the rule of action. No law ever was promulgated more just, equitable, reasonable and beneficent than this. It is the fundamental law of Christian ethics; it is the basis of all true moral conduct between man and man. Christ did more than simply announce it. Others may have done that much. The glory of the teaching of Christ is that with the announcement he gave the world in his own life and character a practical and perfect exemplification of the rule which he enjoined. He taught the lesson and he showed the way.

He had taught the lessons of mercy and good-will in some of his most striking parables; he had said, "If ye forgive not men their trespasses, neither will your heavenly Father forgive you." He had indeed for ever incorporated the lesson of reciprocity and forgiveness into the daily prayers of his worship, making it thereby a perpetual law of his kingdom: "Forgive us our sins; for we also forgive every one that is indebted to us." But it was because he more impressively than all other teachers had showed the way in his own life of benevolence and death of self-sacrifice for others that the lesson has had such power over the hearts of men, and has become so precious and imperishable a remembrance to all his followers. All intelligent men feel that this is the essence of the religion of Christ; all good men instinctively do homage to the principle as one that must be true. Even the cultured skeptic can join the prayer,

"Teach me to feel another's woe,
To hide another's fault;
That mercy I to others show,
That mercy show to me."

CHAPTER XXVII.

THE NEW COMMANDMENT.

"A NEW commandment I give unto you, That ye love one another: as I have loved you, that ye also love one another. By this shall all men know that ye are my disciples, if ye have love one to another" (John xiii. 34, 35). The command is new, not in the essential principle of it, *love*, which he had taught before as the very sum of the moral law, but in the *extent, motive* or *example* of it, which is that ye my disciples should do to one another as I your Lord and Master have done to you. The key to the interpretation is in the clause, "As I have loved you, that ye also love one another." He had just said, "I have given you an example, that ye should do as I have done to you." He had just illustrated the measure of his own love in the menial service of washing their feet, and in telling them, further, that it was a love even unto death: "The good Shepherd giveth his life for the sheep." It was new also in being now enjoined as the very badge and test of all true discipleship: "By this shall all men know that ye are my disciples, if ye have love one to another."

The apostle John, who in his Gospel has recorded these impressive words and the circumstances in which they were uttered, evidently refers to the same thing in the second chapter of his First Epistle: "Brethren, I write no new commandment unto you, but an old commandment which ye had from the beginning: The old commandment is the word which ye have heard from the beginning. Again, a new commandment I write unto you, which thing is true in him and in you." Here the context shows that it is this highest form of brotherly love, as illustrated in the example of Christ, which constitutes the essential feature of the new commandment. For this is the thing, he says, this living illustration of it in Christ and his disciples, which is "true in him and in you." The commandment is at once both old and new. It is old as to the essence of it, which is love, for the moral law always requires love and could be fulfilled only by love; but it is new as to the form and expression of it, being perfectly illustrated and fulfilled only in Christ, and in his disciples just so far as they imitate Christ and are like Christ.

The word "love" had not indeed been used in the Decalogue in the commands of either table. The precepts of the Decalogue, being mostly negative prohibitions of wrong-doing, had not been expressed in the positive form of love's high requirements. But the thing itself had always been there, as we see from Deut. vi. 5 : "Thou shalt love the Lord thy God with all thine heart, and with all thy soul, and with all thy might." There could be no true obedience, no acceptable fulfillment of any command, without love to God or to man. This is plain from Christ's own exposition of the Decalogue as given in Matt. xxii. 37–40 : "Thou shalt love the Lord thy God with all thy heart, and with all thy soul, and with all thy mind. This is the first and great commandment. And the second is like unto it; Thou shalt love thy neighbor as thyself. On these two commandments hang all the law and the prophets." The apostle James also refers to this condensed statement of the law by Christ in the second chapter of his general Epistle, where he calls it the law of liberty and the royal law. He says, "If ye fulfill the royal law according to the scripture, Thou shalt love thy neighbor as thyself, ye do well: but if ye have respect to persons, ye commit sin, and are convinced of the law as transgressors."

If we put all these passages together, we shall see how perfect is the agreement of Scripture, and how the old commandment given by Moses in the Decalogue, and interpreted by Christ as the law of love to God and love to man, becomes the all-comprehensive new commandment of the New-Testament Church, illustrated by the living example of Christ himself, and requiring the most intense self-sacrificing love in his name to the whole brotherhood of his disciples, and universal good-will to our fellow-men as neighbors and brothers. We shall see, too, with what wonderful comprehensiveness of application and with what depth of spiritual import our Saviour summed up the whole of this new and old commandment when, in his Sermon on the Mount, he expounded the second table of the Decalogue and gave the Golden Rule for all the Church and all the world: "Therefore, all things whatsoever ye would that men should do to you, do ye even so to them: for this is the law and the prophets."

It is to be feared that the great law of love and

brotherhood, so enforced by Christ and so exemplified in his own life, is far too much ignored in the ministrations of the pulpit, and far too much neglected in the daily life of his disciples. How seldom do we hear a sermon on the Golden Rule or on the new commandment! Have Christians forgotten that such passages are in the Bible, and that they stand among the most emphatic words of the Saviour? The writer cannot recollect having heard a sermon for many years on either text. In looking recently over many volumes of sermons in his own library, from preachers of different denominations, he was surprised that he could find but one published sermon on either subject. This was by Dr. Chalmers, on the text in Matt. vii. 12, entitled "The Great Christian Law of Reciprocity between Man and Man," a fine practical discussion of the theme. If our divine Master should come back to his Church, would he not have "somewhat against us," to find his ministers and churches thus forgetting or putting in the background precepts so precious to him and so essential to all true life and godliness?

Still further, an interpretation is sometimes put upon this law of love which virtually reverses it. Christ requires us to love one another even as he loves us, and not only to love our fellow-Christians as being his disciples, but to love all men, even our enemies, with the love of kindness and good-will. We are commanded to do good unto all, especially to those who are of the household of faith; for all men are our neighbors, according to his teaching, and all Christians are our brethren. Are we living up to this law? It has certainly been enjoined, and it has never been repealed. But many professing Christians act as if the Golden Rule ran thus: " Do unto others what they do to you; treat them as they treat you." In most cases those who adopt this low, selfish rule do not even live up to their own interpretation. They do not, in fact, treat their fellow-men or their fellow-Christians half so well as they are treated. It is of the nature of selfishness to aim low in morals and then to fall even lower than it aims.

A man is not often better than his principles. If his moral principles are lax and selfish, there is nothing to elevate his character. If he begins by injuring those who injure him, speaking evil of those who speak evil of him, he will end by failing to return good even for the good he receives. His low moral aim will lead him to construe and measure the good conduct of others by his own selfish standard of action. What a blessed thing it is that Christ has given us a perfect moral code, a pure and spiritual standard of action, the highest and the purest ever propounded to man! He only will attain to true excellence who adopts this lofty standard of right and aims at it perpetually in his daily life. All others fall short and miss the mark. Though the Christian man may be all his life approaching and never quite attaining this perfect standard of the Golden Rule and the new commandment, still he will approximate it more and more, and in the end rise immeasurably higher than the man who has no higher law than the wretched selfishness of his own heart.

CHAPTER XXVIII.

THE MORALITY OF THE GOSPEL.

THE Bible is neither a poem of beautiful sentiments nor a dry creed of arbitrary dogmas. It does not exclude either extreme, but the main body of its truth lies between. It has enough of sentiment to make it attractive, and enough of dogma to give it divine authority; but its chief merit is that it sets forth a complete salvation as it regards our relation to God, and a pure, practical morality as it regards our duties to man. It is a book of religion in the highest sense of the term—the only true, universal and ultimate religion. At the same time, it gives us a complete code of practical ethics, the highest and best the world has ever seen.

It is worthy of notice that the nearest approach to a definition of religion to be found in the Scriptures is one which includes both ideas and makes it at once a life of charity and an experience of piety, the charity being set in the foreground as the ocular demonstration of the inward piety. "Pure religion and undefiled before God and the Father," writes James, "is this, To visit the fatherless and widows in their affliction, and to keep himself unspotted from the world" (James i. 27). Could we have a finer illustration of the fact that Christianity is a gospel of charity not less than of piety—a great code of pure, practical morality among men not less than a divine revelation of those truths which are unto salvation? How perfectly, too, does this text of the New Testament, both in its ideas and in the order of their statement, harmonize with a similar summary of duties given by the ancient prophet!—"He hath showed thee, O man, what is good; and what doth the Lord require of thee, but to do justly, and to love mercy, and to walk humbly with thy God?" (Mic. vi. 8).

In forming an estimate of the elevated morality required by the gospel, we are always compelled to distinguish between the ideal Christianity of the New Testament and the actual Christianity existing around us in the Church. Christianity has always been better than the lives of its professed followers. The morality of the gospel, as taught by Christ and illustrated in his own character, or even as taught and illustrated by his inspired apostles, has always been a purer and nobler thing than that which has passed for Christian morality in the conduct of multitudes who have professed his name. Men and women have been found in the Church of every age, and such are still found, who, like the early Christians, have in some good degree attained to this nobler type of New-Testament morality; for they have felt that the law of love, as expounded by Christ in his Sermon on the Mount and summed up in the Golden Rule, was binding on them, and they have aimed to live up to it. When, therefore, we judge of the pure, elevated morality required by Christianity, we must take the measure of it, not from the worldly-minded or the half-hearted or the backsliding or the selfish and ambitious classes of professing church-members, but we must either judge by the lives of the faithful few who have walked worthily of their high calling, or else we must go directly to the original standard contained in the New Testament. This is the law and the testimony to which Christianity always appeals, and by which it is willing to be tested.

If, now, we turn to the New Testament to ascertain what Christian morality is and what are its high requirements, we find three principal illustrations of it, each forming a distinct line of argument, and all together a perfect demonstration of its immeasurable superiority over every other code of ethics known amongst men. The first is seen in the explicit teachings of Christ the Master, and of all his inspired apostles as they exemplified and confirmed his injunctions. These are what continually appear in all the New-Testament commands, precepts, statutes, ordinances, both for worship and for conduct. It is quite too much overlooked that a large part of Christ's teachings, a large part of the New-Testament Epistles, and hence a large part of the gospel, come to us in the form of law or precepts enjoining a life of holy and active obedience. The gospel, on every page of it, requires obedience to the law of Christ, and Christ, in every sermon and in every parable, requires obedience to the pure and holy law of God. The whole Sermon on the Mount, running through three chapters of Matthew's Gospel, is an exemplification of the point. The command is clear and unmistakable: "Except your righteousness shall exceed the righteousness of the scribes and Pharisees, ye shall in no case enter into the kingdom of heaven;" "Be ye, therefore, perfect, even as your Father which is in heaven is perfect;" "All things whatsoever ye would that men should do to you, do ye even so to them: for this is the law and the prophets." This memorable discourse, which comes to us like a new and enlarged proclamation of the law of God, covers all our duties to God and to man. He closes it with the solemn declaration of life and salvation, not to him who hears and professes his name before men, but to him that "heareth and doeth these sayings of mine:" "For not every one that saith unto me, Lord, Lord, shall enter into the kingdom of heaven; but he that doeth the will of my Father who is in heaven."

If we look into any of the Epistles of his inspired apostles, we find the same inculcation of divine law and high Christlike morality. They enjoin every precept which he enjoined and call upon his followers continually to remember his commandments and do them. In no single instance do they ever reverse or attempt to abrogate or modify this code of absolute perfection, this Christlike morality, demanding the purity of the whole heart and the whole life. The apostle Peter, writing to the Christian believers everywhere scattered abroad in his time, takes up the very words of his divine Master, and says, "As obedient children, not fashioning yourselves according to the former lusts in your ignorance: but as he who hath called you is holy, so be ye holy in all manner of conversation; because it is written, Be ye holy; for I am holy." His two General Epistles are largely taken up with the inculcation of the great practical principles of that high and pure morality which had been taught by Christ, and which the great Gentile world, with all its philosophy and with all its culture, had neither practiced nor known.

Grandly, too, in its contrast with the best Greek and Roman paganism of the day, is the superior excellence of this gospel morality brought before us in all the writings of Paul. Some of his Epistles, as those to the Romans and the Hebrews, are largely taken up in unfolding the doctrinal system of the gospel; but even these, like all the rest, contain in their closing chapters clear and powerful elucidations of the whole practical code of Christian ethics. There is not one great principle of virtue and morality, as between the Christian and his brother-Christian, and as between man and his fellow-man, in every sphere and relation of life, from the household altar to the throne of government, which is not unfolded and enforced in these writings of Paul. The same may be said of the other New-Testament Epistles, brief though they be. What a summary of duty, for example, is given in the first chapter of the Second General Epistle of Peter!—"Giving all diligence, add to your faith, virtue" (energy, fortitude, courage); "and to virtue, knowledge; and to knowledge, temperance; and to temperance, patience; and to patience, godliness; and to godliness, brotherly-kindness; and to brotherly-kindness, charity. For if these things be in you, and abound, they make you that ye shall neither be barren nor unfruitful in the knowledge of our Lord Jesus Christ."

The high, inflexible, and yet loving, morality enjoined by Paul is seen in a hundred such passages as the following: "We exhort, you, brethren, warn them that are unruly, comfort the feeble-minded, support the weak, be patient toward all men. See that none render evil for evil unto any man; but ever follow that which is good, both among yourselves, and to all men. . . . Abstain from all appearance of evil. And the very God of peace sanctify you wholly; and I pray God your whole spirit, and soul, and body, be preserved blameless unto the coming of our Lord Jesus Christ" (1 Thess. v. 14, 15, 22, 23); "Finally, brethren, whatsoever things are true, whatsoever things are honest, whatsoever things are just, whatsoever things are pure, whatsoever things are lovely, whatsoever things are of good report; if there be any virtue, and if there be any praise, think on these things" (Phil. iv. 8).

We have not space now to develop, but simply to indicate, the other proofs of the superior excellence of the morality inculcated in the gospel. The one is seen in those peculiar virtues—such as beneficence, charity and self-denial—which Christianity has exalted among men, and the other is seen in the actual practice of these and all the associated virtues in the lives of Christ and his apostles; for not only did they teach this exalted, unselfish morality in all their public instructions, but Christ Jesus lived and acted it before men in absolute perfection, and his apostles, by his grace, were enabled, in an eminent degree, to imitate the divine example.

The superior excellence of the Christian code is seen in its benevolent and philanthropic spirit. It breathes universal good-will to men and proclaims peace to all nations. From the first it broke over the traditional conventionalities of race and nation and social rank, and embraced the whole world. It did what no school of ancient philosophy and no system of political government had ever done: it recognized the equality of men and preached a morality for the poor as well as for the rich. It inaugurated a new and noble class of virtues. It raised humility, self-denial, benevolence, charity, philanthropy, and their kindred virtues, to a place of prominence which they had never before held, and to a place which they now hold in the estimation of all civilized Christian nations simply because Christ and his apostles had so exalted them.

The spirit of individual self-sacrifice for the good of others, of beneficent endeavor to rescue the poor and the perishing, and of a philanthropy as wide as the world, which to-day so exalts Christianity in the eyes of those pagan nations to whom the heroic missionary has carried the gospel, breathes forth in all the teachings of Christ, and in fact constitutes the essential principle of that practical morality which he enjoined on all his followers. No man can read the gospel history without seeing this pure and elevated beneficence on every page. His system was a complete salvation which, in the song of the angels announcing the nativity, brought "glory to God in the highest;" but at the same time it was a pure beneficent code of practical ethics which should ultimately prevail over the selfishness of mankind, bringing peace on earth and good-will among men.

Another striking illustration of the superior excellence of the morality inculcated in the gospel is found in the power of its motives and sanctions. Many of the philosophers and sages of antiquity inculcated beautiful precepts, and some, like Socrates, Seneca, Cicero and the Antonines, partially exemplified them in their own lives. But their splendid systems of philosophy and their comparatively pure moral codes all failed as a rule of life, because they were enforced by no divine sanctions; they had no eternal basis of truth on which men could rely as a sufficient motive of duty. Just here is the point at which the gospel morality makes its appeal to the consciences of men with a power unknown to any other system. It is not only grounded on the truth of God as revealed in the moral law of God, but it constitutes an essential part of the truth itself. It has all the high and sacred sanctions of that divine religion of which it is a part; and these sanctions are drawn from the nature of God, the nature of man and the retributions of that eternal world to which we are destined. No sanctions can be higher, no motives more effective. All the precepts enjoined by Christ and reaffirmed by his apostles come to us with the authority of him "who spake as man never spake," and they come with the added practical demonstration that they were exemplified to the full in the life and character of the great Teacher, and also to some good degree in the lives and characters of commissioned apostles. The grand distinction of the Christian ethics is that the code not only comes to us with the high authority of our Creator and Christ our Saviour, but it comes illustrated and enforced in every particular by the perfect model life of the Incarnate One. And this great example set before us in the New Testament, as it was seen by his apostles, is continually appealed to by them as the pattern and the encouragement of our own conduct. This is an advantage which no other teacher ever can or ever could give his disciples.

Thus the apostle Peter, when exhorting his fellow-Christians to be patient and cheerful under all the tribulation and persecution man can inflict, appeals to this perfect example of Christ as at once their incentive to duty and their consolation: "Because Christ also suffered for us, leaving us an example, that ye should follow his steps: who did no sin, neither was guile found in his mouth: who, when he was reviled, reviled not again; when he suffered, he threatened not; but committed himself to him that judgeth righteously: who his ownself bare our sins on his own body on the tree, that we, being dead to sins, should live unto righteousness: by whose stripes ye were healed" (1 Pet. ii. 21–24). When practically expounding the law of Christ for the varied relations of life in his First Epistle, he asks, "Who is he that will harm you if ye be followers of that which is good?" and gives us this admirable summary of what is good: "Submit yourselves to every ordinance of man for the Lord's sake: whether it be to the king as supreme; or unto governors, as unto them that are sent by him for the punishment of evil-doers, and for the praise of them that do well. For so is the will of God, that with well-doing ye may put to silence the ignorance of foolish men: as free and not using your liberty for a cloak of maliciousness, but as the servants of God. Honor all men. Love the brotherhood. Fear God. Honor the king."

The scholars and the thinkers of our day are not a

little disposed to disparage Christianity as an ethical system. They often tell us of the stern, heroic virtues of old Greeks and Romans, and point to the grand characters produced under the Stoical philosophy and the pagan mythology. But, after all, what a narrow, selfish, bloody and vindictive morality it was! how dark, how hopeless, how unloving and unlovely! gods and men alike impelled by vindictive passions and ruled by blind, irrational, inexorable fate. Let any one read the old Greek poets to see the spirit and the practical working of such a morality and such a religion, or let him study it even as presented in its most attractive light in Thomas Noon Talford's tragedy of "Ion." What a contrast to the gentle, loving spirit of the gospel! What a relief to turn from those best achievements of classic paganism to the bright and joyous and beautiful precepts of Christ and his apostles!

CHAPTER XXIX.

PRAYER A DUTY AND A PRIVILEGE.

"AND he spake a parable unto them to this end, That men ought always to pray and not to faint."

It shows the estimate which was placed upon prayer by the Son of God that he made it the subject of one of his most beautiful parables. That estimate is sustained not only by his invariable instructions, but by the impressive fact that prayer was exemplified in the daily habit and practice of his own life. He taught his disciples to pray, he performed some of his mighty miracles in the exercise of prayer, and he at times retired to mountains and desert places where he spent the night in communion with God. If the incarnate and sinless Son of God while tabernacling for a season in this human state felt the need of prayer, and often withdrew from the society of men to hold intercourse with God, how irresistible is the argument of the parable that frail and sinful man ought always to pray and not to faint! Is there a need of the human soul more universal and more pressing in its demand than this deep need of prayer?

"Prayer," says Dr. Charles Hodge, "is the converse of the soul with God. Therein we manifest or express to him our reverence and love for his divine perfection, our gratitude for all his mercies, our penitence for our sins, our hope in his forgiving love, our submission to his authority, our confidence in his care, our desires for his favor and for the providential and spiritual blessings needed for ourselves and others." It is pre-eminently in the act of prayer that we worship God. Prayer is the appointed medium through which we approach him; and when we approach him in the exercise of humble, sincere, earnest and believing prayer, offered in the name of Jesus Christ, our worship is always acceptable. In this spirit the psalmist said, "It is good for me to draw near to God." "Whoso offereth praise glorifieth me," saith the Lord. In all the multitude of human actions which men perform in this life there is perhaps no one thing more intrinsically noble and acceptable to God than that act in which an earnest devout mind holds communion with its God in prayer.

Prayer is one of the general ordinances of divine worship which, like the day of sacred rest, was appointed for all time, and it has belonged alike to every dispensation of the Church. There has never been a period when the children of God did not love to call upon the Lord in prayer, and there has been no one distinction more characteristic of a sinner turning from the ways of sin unto God than to say of him, as was said of Saul of Tarsus at his conversion, "Behold, he prayeth." It is one of the doctrines of the Bible on which there has been little conflict of opinion among Christians, and almost no controversy. The infidels and skeptics of our day call in question both the utility and the necessity of prayer, but all the churches of Christendom, however they may differ on other points, stand as a unit on the creed that it is man's duty to pray, and that the fervent, effectual prayer of a righteous man availeth much. It will be long before mankind, even under the lead of distinguished modern scientists like Mr. Tyndall, can be shaken out of the belief that sincere and earnest prayer meets the divine approval and receives the divine blessing.

In every form of divine worship prayer holds a prominent place. In fact, there can be no acceptable worship without it. It is one of the divinely-appointed means of grace through which the soul draws near to God, and in which God bestows his blessing. It is alike essential to the secret worship of the individual when alone with God, to the evening and morning worship of the family, to the united worship of the social circle in the prayer-meeting, and to the more formal worship of the public assembly. In every place and under all circumstances it is an indispensable condition of all true Christian experience and of all steady growth in grace.

The simplest idea of prayer is that of petition or supplication to God for his help. It may be accompanied with other exercises, as adoration, praise, thanksgiving, but the essence of prayer is the asking of God for such things as we need. It takes in the whole range of human wants, both temporal and spiritual. Nothing is too great and nothing too small to be a fitting object of prayer. It is in this wide sense that the apostle Paul says, "Be careful for nothing, but in everything by prayer and supplication, with thanksgiving, let your requests be made known unto God." Thus our Saviour, in the Sermon on the Mount, expounds the law of prayer and shows us in what spirit and to what extent we should make known our requests to God: "Ask, and it shall be given you; seek, and ye shall find; knock, and it shall be opened unto you: for every one that asketh, receiveth; and he that seeketh, findeth; and to him that knocketh, it shall be opened." Then he illustrates and enforces this duty of prayer by appealing to the loving care of an earthly parent: "What man is there of you, whom if his son ask bread, will he give him a stone? or if he ask a fish, will he give him a serpent? If ye then, being evil, know how to give good gifts unto your children, how much more shall your Father which is in heaven give good things to them that ask him?"

On no subject are the Scriptures more richly instructive than on the duty of prayer. They give us every motive to encourage us to a life of prayer, and they set before us the conditions of successful prayer. They everywhere reveal God as loving to hear and to answer the cry of his children. They set before us many noble examples of prevailing prayer, as in the case of Abraham interceding for Lot in the doomed cities of the plain, Jacob wrestling all night with the angel, Moses pleading with God for the rebellious children of Israel, Hannah praying for the gift of a son, Elijah praying for rain, David crying for mercy after his great transgression, Hezekiah asking for restoration to health, Jeremiah and Daniel interceding for rulers and for their people, not to mention the many striking cases in the life of our blessed Lord and in the writings of his apostles. Paul tells us to "pray without ceasing," thus making it the daily duty of life, to be continued as long as we live. Writing to Timothy in his public character as a minister of God, he says, "I exhort therefore, that, first of all, supplications, prayers, intercessions, and giving of thanks be made for all men: for kings, and for all that are in authority; that we may lead a quiet and peaceable life in all godliness and honesty." James, referring to the history of Elijah, says, "He was a man subject to like passions as we are, and he prayed earnestly that it might not rain: and it rained not on the earth" (that is, the land of Israel) "by the space of three years and six months. And he prayed again, and the heaven gave rain, and the earth brought forth her fruit;" "The effectual fervent prayer of a righteous man availeth much;" "Is any among you afflicted? let him pray. . . . Is any sick among you? let him call for the elders of the church; and let them pray over him, anointing him with oil in the name of the Lord: and the prayer of faith shall save the sick."

The conditions of prevailing prayer—that is, of prayer which God will hear and answer—are very clearly laid down in many passages of Scripture. The first is that we should ask for things in accordance with his will and in deference to his will. God has not promised to give us everything we ask: it would not be wise for him to do so; it might not be for our good. No wise parent would do that. John says, in his First Epistle, "This is the confidence that we have in him, that if we ask any thing according to his will, he heareth us: and if we know that he hear us, whatsoever we ask, we know that we have the petitions that we desired of him." Even our exalted Saviour prayed this prayer of deference to his Father's will, when in Gethsemane he cried, "If it be possible, let this cup pass from me: nevertheless, not as I will, but as thou wilt."

The second condition is that we should pray in all honesty and sincerity of heart, desiring to know and to do God's will. God has not promised to hear the prayer of hypocrisy and deceit. David said, "If I regard iniquity in my heart, the Lord will not hear me;" and he adds, "But verily God hath heard me; he hath attended to the voice of my prayer." If, however, David had clung to his sins, unrepentant and persistent in them, there is no evidence that God would have answered his prayer. God will hear the persistent believing sinner, but it is when he is turning from iniquity and no longer cherishing it in his heart. The humble publican prayed this prayer of sincerity when he cried, "God be merciful to me a sinner;" and the penitent thief on the cross did the same when he said, "Lord, remember me when thou comest into thy kingdom."

A third condition of successful prayer is faith. Without faith it is impossible to please God, and without faith it is impossible to pray the effectual fervent prayer of the righteous man. The penitent publican and the penitent thief believed in the God to whom they prayed. It is the prayer of faith that prevails to heal the sick and to open the heavens. "According to your faith be it unto you," said our Saviour when he opened the eyes of the blind. The rule might be applied with equal propriety to those who pray: their prayers will be answered according to their faith and according to their earnest importunity in asking. On nothing were the instructions of our Lord more emphatic than on the duty of exercising strong faith in God. "All things," said he, "are possible to him that believeth." "O thou of little faith, wherefore didst thou doubt?" said he to Peter sinking in the waves. "If ye have faith as a grain of mustard-seed, ye shall say unto this mountain, Remove hence to yonder place; and it shall remove." So also says the apostle James, "If any of you lack wisdom, let him ask of God, that giveth to all men liberally, and upbraideth not; and it shall be given him. But let him ask in faith, nothing wavering. For he that wavereth is like a wave of the sea driven with the wind and tossed. For let not that man think that he shall receive any thing of the Lord. A double-minded man is unstable in all his ways."

Another important requisite of prevailing prayer is that it shall be offered in the name of Christ. It is the declared will of God that all men should honor the Son even as they honor the Father. It is through Christ the Mediator, and for his sake, that God has promised to confer all spiritual blessings on his people. They should therefore always approach him in the name of the well-beloved Son. When about to leave his disciples he said, with great emphasis, "Verily, verily, I say unto you, Whatsoever ye shall ask the Father in my name, he will give it you. Hitherto have ye asked nothing in my name. Ask and ye shall receive, that your joy may be full."

Prayer is to be regarded in the light of privilege not less than of duty. If all the deep wants of nature prompt us to it as an ever-pressing duty, all the precious promises of God invite us to it as one of the highest privileges we can enjoy in this life. What arithmetic can compute the amount of happiness conferred upon the suffering children of want and sorrow by this one blessed and inalienable privilege of bringing their cares and their distresses to the throne of grace in prayer? What a different thing life here without prayer would be to them from what it now is in the daily habit of prayer! To strike from a good man's life his daily intercourse with God, and with it the assurance that God's ear is always open to his cry, would be to rob him of that which has been his unfailing consolation in distress and leave him to utter desolation and darkness for the future.

The farther on we go in life the stronger is our conviction that we cannot live without prayer. The young and the worldly, it is true, in the eager chase of present pleasure or from the pressing calls of business, do continue for a season to get on without prayer; but even in their case the dark day of calamity sometimes suddenly falls upon their pathway and drives them sooner than they thought to the secret place of prayer. In the hour of calamity, and above all in the dread hour of death, there is no privilege like that of prayer. There is no more pressing want of the human soul than access by faith to a prayer-hearing and a prayer-answering God. In this supreme crisis no other helper can bring relief, no other friend whisper peace like that which comes to him who prays.

The children of God in every age of the Church have testified how great and how precious is the privilege of prayer. It has been the vital breath of their whole spiritual experience. It has been the power which has come down from God to sustain them under their conflicts with temptation as they have passed through the dark valley of humiliation and the shadow of death. It has been the strong influence which through all their pilgrimage has thrown an ever-brightening radiance of peace and hope over their lives. There is probably no one thing in which the Christian people of all ages, all countries and all churches have been more alike and more allied than in their estimate and their experience of the value of prayer.

It is a significant fact that one whole book of the Bible—that of the Psalms—consists largely of the rich experience of prayer. This experience, too, is as diversified as human life, running through all joy and all sorrow, the deepest adversity, the highest prosperity. Though written by a warrior-king nearly three thousand years ago, these wonderful psalms of praise and prayer are as deeply expressive of our Christian experience to-day as they were at first. The devout soul now in its approaches to God, whether in joy or in sorrow, in penitential supplication for mercy or in confession of sin or in joyful thanksgiving for blessings received, can find no other words so apt, so fresh, so admirable as the inspired words of the psalmist.

How many sin-burdened penitents have cried to God in the brief sententious utterances of the fifty-first psalm!—"Have mercy upon me, O God, according to thy loving-kindness: according unto the multitude of thy tender mercies blot out my transgressions." And how many grateful hearts rising from beds of sickness or after deep experiences of bereavement and sorrow have entered into all the exultant emotions of the one hundred and sixteenth psalm!—"I love the Lord, because he hath heard my voice and my supplications. Because he hath inclined his ear unto me, therefore will I call upon him as long as I live. The sorrows of death compassed me, and the pains of hell gat hold upon me: I found trouble and sorrow. Then called I upon the name of the Lord; O Lord, I beseech thee, deliver my soul. Gracious is the Lord, and righteous; yea, our God is merciful. The Lord preserveth the simple: I was brought low, and he helped me. Return unto thy rest, O my soul; for the Lord hath dealt bountifully with thee. For thou hast delivered my soul from death, mine eyes from tears, and my feet from falling. . . . What shall I render unto the Lord for all his benefits toward me? I will take the cup of salvation, and call upon the name of the Lord. I will pay my vows unto the Lord now in the presence of all his people, . . . in the courts of the Lord's house, in the midst of thee, O Jerusalem. Praise ye the Lord."

This is but one of the many similar instances of approach to God in distress, and of joyful deliverance in answer to prayer. How deep are the chords of sympathy which he touches in millions of praying hearts in passages like the following!—"In my distress I called upon the Lord, and cried unto my God: he heard my voice out of his temple, and my cry came before him, even unto his ears" (Psalm xviii. 6); "I sought the Lord, and he heard me, and delivered me from all my fears. They looked unto him, and were lightened:

and their faces were not ashamed. This poor man cried and the Lord heard him, and saved him out of all his troubles. The angel of the Lord encampeth round about them that fear him, and delivereth them. O taste and see that the Lord is good: blessed is the man that trusteth in him. O fear the Lord, ye his saints; for there is no want to them that fear him. The young lions do lack, and suffer hunger: but they that seek the Lord shall not want any good thing" (Psalm xxxiv. 4-10); "The righteous cry, and the Lord heareth, and delivereth them out of all their troubles" (Psalm xxxiv. 17); "Call upon me in the day of trouble: I will deliver thee, and thou shalt glorify me" (Psalm l. 15); "O thou that hearest prayer, unto thee shall all flesh come" (Psalm lxv. 2).

We have heard of the consolations of philosophy, and of the pure delights of a life of literature, and of all the sweet comforts which a home of elegance and a host of friends can bring to the possessor of wealth and power; but, after all, in times of bereavement and sorrow and calamity, commend us evermore to the book of God and to the place of prayer. We have seen the aged saint in her deep enjoyment of this unfailing source of comfort; we have seen the young and the beautiful, lying on the bed of pain and awaiting the hour of release with calm serenity, sustained and cheered by this consolation when all others had been cut off. Blessed is the soul that knows the value and has learned the true experience of a life of prayer.

CHAPTER XXX.

THE INSPIRED WORD OF GOD.

AS the sacred writers bear witness to their own inspiration and to the inspiration of one another, it may be useful to set here in the foreground a few of the proof-texts from the New Testament by which this important doctrine of the Christian faith is attested. If we admit Christ to be, as he claimed to be, the true Messiah and the true Son of God, invested with all divine authority, it is difficult to see how we could have any higher evidence for the doctrine of Scripture inspiration than this explicit testimony of Christ and his apostles. What he affirmed must be true, and what they affirmed must be true, because he was a true Teacher come from God, and they were teachers invested with authority by him and inspired with unerring wisdom by the Holy Ghost. There can be no uncertainty in this conclusion, and no escape from it if we admit the facts on which it rests.

The apostle Paul, writing to Timothy, says, "From a child thou hast known the holy scriptures, which are able to make thee wise unto salvation through faith which is in Christ Jesus. All scripture is given by inspiration of God" (that is, *theopneustic*, "God-inspired"), "and is profitable for doctrine, for reproof, for correction, for instruction in righteousness; that the man of God may be perfect, throughly furnished unto all good works" (2 Tim. iii. 15, 16). He opens his Epistle to the Hebrews saying, "God, who at sundry times and in divers manners spake in time past unto the fathers by the prophets, hath in these last days spoken unto us by his Son." To the Corinthians he writes claiming the very same kind of inspiration which he had ascribed to the fathers: "Now we have received, not the spirit of the world, but the Spirit which is of God; that we might know the things that are freely given to us of God. Which things also we speak, not in the words which man's wisdom teacheth, but which the Holy Ghost teacheth; comparing spiritual things with spiritual" (1 Cor. ii. 12, 13). In like manner, the apostle Peter, comparing the new with the older Scriptures, asserts the doctrine of divine inspiration in both in the following words: "We have also a more sure word of prophecy; whereunto ye do well that ye take heed, as unto a light that shineth in a dark place, until the day dawn, and the day-star arise in your hearts: knowing this first, that no prophecy of the scripture is of any private interpretation. For the prophecy came not in old time by the will of man: but holy men of God spake as they were moved by the Holy Ghost" (2 Pet. i. 19–21).

Now, these claims of divine inspiration by the apostles for themselves, and for all the Scriptures of the Old Testament and of the New, are in perfect accord with the words of Christ when he promised to send upon them the Comforter, which promise we know began to be fulfilled on the day of Pentecost. He said

"When the Comforter is come, whom I will send unto you from the Father, even the Spirit of truth, . . . he shall testify of me;" "He shall teach you all things and bring all things to your remembrance, whatsoever I have said unto you;" "He will guide you into all truth, . . . and he will show you things to come" (John xv. 26; xiv. 26; xvi. 13). Among the many references which he made during his public ministry to the Old-Testament Scriptures, two will be sufficient to cite here as showing his estimate of their divine authority and their infinite importance: "Search the scriptures; for in them ye think ye have eternal life: and they are they which testify of me" (John v. 39). On the occasion of meeting two of his disciples after the resurrection it is recorded that, "beginning at Moses, and all the prophets, he expounded unto them in all the scriptures the things concerning himself. . . . And he said unto them, These are the words which I spake unto you, while I was yet with you, that all things must be fulfilled which were written in the law of Moses, and in the prophets, and in the psalms, concerning me. Then opened he their understanding, that they might understand the scriptures, and said unto them, Thus it is written, and thus it behooved Christ to suffer, and to rise from the dead the third day: and that repentance and remission of sins should be preached in his name among all nations, beginning at Jerusalem. And ye are witnesses of these things. And behold, I send the promise of my Father upon you: but tarry ye in the city of Jerusalem, until ye be endued with power from on high" (Luke xxiv. 27, 44–49).

These, and other passages like them too numerous to be quoted here, justify the conclusion on which the Church has rested from the time of the apostles—that the Scriptures of the Old and New Testaments contain the true oracles of God. They consist of sixty-six writings of unequal size, written originally in the Hebrew and Greek languages by not less than forty different authors from Moses to John, extending through a period of fifteen centuries. But, though so varied in authorship, in size, and in the time and the place of composition, they all breathe the same pure and elevated religious spirit, utter the same sublime and wonderful truths, and all together contain a complete, compact and symmetrical system of moral and religious truth and duty adapted to all men of all ages, such as the world has nowhere else seen. No candid student of history can read them without feeling that their unity of spirit, of matter, and of purpose is perfect, and no intelligent and candid man can resist the conviction that one superintending and intelligent mind has pervaded and guided the pens of all the human writers. It would be as impossible to deny this all-pervading unity of design and end in the Bible as to deny it in the unwritten book of Nature.

The Bible, then, is God's record and God's testimony, given for the purpose of revealing his character, declaring his will and making known man's whole duty on points where the light of nature and of reason had proved an insufficient guide. It contains for us the knowledge of that truth which is unto salvation. It comes from God as a gospel of glad tidings to the perishing. It comes from God as the revelation of Jesus

Christ the Saviour of the world. It comes from God as the only infallible rule of duty, the only perfect standard of moral and religious truth. Being inspired of God, it is sufficient; and it is the only sufficient guide of life. As such it justifies the maxim of Protestantism: "The Bible, the whole Bible, and nothing but the Bible, the religion of Protestants." As such, Christianity has always accepted it; as such, all evangelical churches in the world accept it to-day, and are willing to stand or fall by it.

It is impossible to overestimate the value of the Bible. We may say with David, "Thy testimonies have I taken as an heritage for ever: for they are the rejoicing of my heart" (Psalm cxix. 111). This inspired word is one of God's three supreme gifts to man. He has given us his Son, to die for us; he has given us his Holy Spirit, to abide in us; and he has given us his sacred Book, containing the knowledge of himself and of his Son and of his Spirit. Thanks be unto God for all his unspeakable gifts!

The Bible is so unique and so wonderful in its origin, so original and so weighty in its communications, so pure and so elevated in its tone, so potential and so salutary in its influence upon human character—in a word, so utterly unlike all other books—that it can in no way be accounted for except on the ground of its divine authorship. Admit this supernatural origin, and all is plain; deny it, and the book remains the unsolved enigma and wonder of all literature. But by the potent and blessed influence which it has always exerted, and still exerts, over the human heart, the Bible is itself the standing demonstration of the truth of Christianity. In the Bible, Christianity may be said to carry its own open credentials of truth; for it cannot be that a book which reveals such truths and produces such results is founded on falsehood and sets forth a religion of falsehood. "By their fruits ye shall know them" is one of Christ's own maxims. It is a sound one, and by it Christianity and the Bible have been demonstrated a thousand times over to be of God.

The inestimable value of the Bible is seen not only in its being a perfect and infallible standard of truth and duty, but also in the important place which it holds among the appointed means of grace. It is in all spiritual things the guide of life. It is the nourisher and the sustainer of all true spiritual life. It is that on which the soul of the Christian perpetually feeds, and that by which Christian character is formed. Truth is unto godliness, and the Bible contains the truth. So our Saviour utters that comprehensive petition for his disciples, "Sanctify them through thy truth: thy word is truth." Thus David said, "Thy word have I hid in mine heart, that I might not sin against thee;" "Wherewithal shall a young man cleanse his way? By taking heed thereto according to thy word." Paul speaks of the strong meat of the word for them who are of full age, and Peter writes, "As new-born babes desire the sincere milk of the word, that ye may grow thereby." The word of God is the food of the soul—as needful for its spiritual life and growth as material bread is for the body. Hence it stands, with prayer, preaching, the sacraments and other ordinances of worship, among the regular means of grace by which men are brought into the Church of Christ and prepared for glory. Under the operation of the divine Spirit, we are enlightened, quickened, sanctified and saved by the word of God. It is by the preaching of the word under the appointed Christian ministry that sinners are converted to God, and his own children are edified, instructed and trained continually.

The word of God is "the sword of the Spirit;" and by that instrument, which is "quick and powerful, sharper than any two-edged sword, and a discerner of the thoughts and intents of the heart," the Holy Spirit makes efficacious his office in the conversion of men. It is by the same powerful instrument—the pure word of God—that the ministers of the gospel are enabled to win souls for Christ. There is no true spiritual work done in the Church except through the word of God. There is no growth in grace except through the knowledge of the word of God. Our salvation in Christ is intimately connected with the word. Practically, there is nothing in Christianity more essential to all growth, whether of the individual soul or of the whole Church, than the continual preaching of the word of God and the lifelong reading and study of the word of God.

"Unto them," says Paul, "were committed the oracles of God" (Rom. iii. 2). We do not yet sufficiently appreciate the inestimable value of the Scriptures as the oracles of the living God, our infallible standard of truth, our unerring guide in duty. This is indeed our priceless inheritance as Protestants, our fundamental distinction as Christians of the Reformation—the Bible, the whole Bible, and nothing but the Bible, to bind the conscience in matters of faith. By this high historic position, we are bound to bring everything to the law and to the testimony of God; and if we speak not according to this rule, it is because there is no truth in us. The one sufficient justification of this conceded supremacy of the Scriptures lies in the fact that they are *theopneustic*—that is, inspired of God. They are human as to their penmanship, but they are divine as to their authorship. The holy men of old who wrote them spake as they were moved by the Holy Ghost.

Men may differ about theories of inspiration—whether the writers themselves were inspired or only their thoughts were inspired, or their thoughts and words were all inspired. But, as to the fact itself of inspiration, and that a full inspiration, there ought to be no dispute. The fact is plain and patent on the very face of the book. The doctrine of the plenary inspiration of all the Scriptures, both of the Old Testament and of the New, rests ultimately on the authority of Christ and his apostles. The whole argument for it may be briefly summed up in one sentence: Christ claimed divine authority for all his own instructions, and then he promised divine authority and inspiration to his chosen apostles; which promise he verified by fulfillment on and after the day of Pentecost; and these apostles, thus inspired and authorized by Christ, claimed inspiration for themselves, and ascribed inspiration to the Old-Testament Scriptures and to one another; under which inspiration the books of the New Testament were written.

CHAPTER XXXI.

THE DAY OF REST AND OF WORSHIP.

EXPERIENCE and history prove that man needs a day of rest from secular toil in which to recuperate his exhausted powers — a day of worship in which to communicate with God and to prepare for heaven. In the same way, it has been abundantly demonstrated that one day in seven is the amount of time in each man's life and in the world's great cycle which is best adapted to secure the ends of rest and worship for the individual, without interfering with the legitimate demands of secular business and pleasure. In nothing, perhaps, has the religion of the Bible, both under its Jewish and its Christian dispensation, more highly commended itself to the approval of sages and statesmen and to the grateful admiration of earth's toiling millions than by this appointment of a sacred day of rest and worship. Its perpetually-recurring sabbatic rest is the perpetual demonstration that it is the friend of man and the benefactor of the world. It has been fittingly called the "pearl of days," "Heaven's antidote for the curse of labor." It is not less needed by the toiling body and the working brain as a day of respite than by the spiritual part of man. It brings repose to the wearied muscles, restoration to the overtaxed mind and divine refreshment to the troubled, fainting spirit.

Whether we regard the Sabbath from the standpoint of God's requirement, recalling the human soul from the too-absorbing pursuits of secular business and pleasure to seasons of meditation and prayer, or from the standpoint of our own physical and intellectual necessities, demanding rest and relaxation, the argument for such a day is equally decisive. The whole history of the world, both where the Sabbath has been observed and where it has not, only serves to illustrate the wisdom of God in its appointment and in the portion of time which it consecrates. Had more time been thus consecrated than one day in seven, it would have disturbed the economy of the working world by subtracting too much from needful labor. Had less been given for rest and worship, it would not have sufficed to relieve the toiling faculties and to conserve the great ends of moral education and religious worship.

Thus, Christianity has ordained and blessed a Sabbath, as did its predecessor, Judaism. In truth, the inauguration was in each case the same. The authority enacting the ordinance was the same; the divine Lawgiver was the same; the great moral, spiritual and physical ends contemplated were the same. The earlier Sabbath only prepared the way for the later, and transferred to it its own divine sanctions. The merely Jewish and local restrictions were set aside, and the time of observance changed by Christ and his inspired apostles from the closing to the opening day of the week. All else remained in its binding and universal obligation. That is to say, the Founder of Christianity, organizing his Church on a basis which should be as wide as the world and stand through all time, took this sacred day of rest—which had been ordained in Eden, which had been observed by patriarchs and prophets, which had been promulgated by God's own voice from Mount Sinai and written on tables of stone by his finger as one of the ten commandments of the moral law, and which had not been unknown among the statutes of many ancient nations—and incorporated it as the law of his own spiritual kingdom, making it, in fact, the very bond of connection between the old and the new, the one great link which should bind all dispensations together as having one Church, one Sabbath, one worship.

"The Sabbath was made for man, and not man for the Sabbath. Therefore the Son of man is Lord even of the Sabbath day." These words of Christ, so far from abrogating the Sabbath, as some have strangely imagined, only establish it on a wider basis. The Sabbath is something more than an exclusively Jewish national institute. It is not only of divine authority as binding the Jew, but of universal obligation as an institution needed by the race. He who ordained it at the beginning to commemorate the finished work of creation has authority to interpret its import, and a right to change it from the seventh to the first day of the week to commemorate the finished work of redemption. And that Lord of the Sabbath who both created and redeemed the world is Christ. As such he had authority over the Sabbath.

Rising from the narrow sepulchre to which the Jews in their ignorance and folly had consigned him, and having all power given to him in heaven and earth; through his apostles whom he invested with full power he changed the time of the sabbatic rest to the first day of the week, the day on which he rose from the dead, making it thenceforth the Lord's day. As such we find it observed by the apostles and Christians of the early Church, from that first day of his resurrection down through the New-Testament history, and down through all the centuries to the present day. The strong probability is that through eighteen centuries there has never been a single return of the first day of the week which has not been celebrated as the Sabbath of rest and worship by some portion of the Church. Thus the succession of Lord's days has been as complete from the beginning as has the succession of the Church.

The prophets of the Old-Testament dispensation had earnestly protested against a slavish and merely ceremonial observance of the Sabbath, and called the people to a higher and more spiritual keeping of it in works of benevolence and mercy. Isaiah had indicated the true spirit of the Sabbath worship when he said, "If thou turn away thy foot from the Sabbath, from doing thy pleasure on my holy day; and call the Sabbath a delight, the holy of the Lord, honorable; and shalt honor him, not doing thine own ways, nor finding thine own pleasure, nor speaking thine own words: then shalt thou delight thyself in the Lord; and I will cause thee to ride upon the high places of the earth, and feed thee with the heritage of Jacob thy father: for the mouth of the Lord hath spoken it" (Isaiah lviii. 13, 14). But it was reserved for our blessed Lord, both by his example and by his instructions, to set the law of the Sabbath in a clear light. The

Jewish doctors of his day were great sticklers for the letter of the law. They rigidly enforced its observance outwardly and violated it in the spirit. Our Saviour, much to their indignation, wrought some of his mighty miracles on the sacred day to show them that it was lawful to do good and to save life on the Sabbath. In this impressive way he taught us that true interpretation of the law which has prevailed in the Christian Church, and under which works of necessity and of mercy may be performed without any violation of the Sabbath. It was on one of these occasions that he uttered the weighty saying that he was Lord of the Sabbath, and that the day must be used for man's good and not for his injury.

It is impossible to overestimate the value of the Sabbath to man or its essential importance to religion. We can scarcely conceive of a greater blessing to society—to the individual member of it, to the families that compose it, to the nation in its aggregate of communities—than the Sabbath institute. It is the very feeder and preserver of all that is good in religion, that is dear in the home-circle, that is great and noble in the life and the character of nations. By no one thing is the advance of true civilization in the world more accurately measured than by the manner in which the day of sacred rest is observed. Under God, the Sabbath is the grand conservator of religion. It is difficult to see how Christianity could have made much headway amongst men or retained its hold upon the world without its sacred day of rest, of worship and of public instruction. Around this day cluster all true ideas and influences of religion, and by it they are promoted; for along with its sacred day Christianity has carried its sacred book, its house of divine worship, its spiritual instruction and its living ministry.

By all these divine institutions operating together as a great religious and educational agency, Christianity has thus far won its way over the minds of men, and has been able to retain its influence. By these it has trained the young and educated the people of every generation. It is easy to see that all the other agencies—the house of worship, the text-book of instruction, the living ministry and the ordinances of preaching and prayer—are able to perform their appointed work chiefly by reason of the time given them by the sacred day. To destroy the sacred day, therefore, or to relax its divine authority, would be in the end to lessen or to destroy the influence of all the other appointments, and so far to destroy Christianity itself.

Hence we conclude that the man who seeks to undermine the authority of the Sabbath and to destroy its hold upon the people is, whether aware of it or not, an enemy of Christianity and a subverter of the highest and best interests of his fellow-men. And that community or nation which by its legislation, by its public press or by the customs of its people tramples in the dust this sacred day is at war with the authority of God, at war with Christianity and the Church, at war with the peace and order of society, and at war with all true individual and national prosperity.

CHAPTER XXXII.

THE TWO SACRAMENTS.

WHILE Christianity is pre-eminently a spiritual religion, requiring the whole-hearted service of the inner man, it does not altogether reject the outward observance of rite and ceremony. On the contrary, it has established and enjoined amongst its ordinances of worship two important services, which are distinguished as holy sacraments and are to be observed to the end of the world. These are baptism and the Lord's Supper. They were each instituted by Christ, and it is his divine authority that gives them their sacred character and their perpetual obligation in his Church. They stand closely connected with the essential and distinctive doctrines of his religion. The one relates to his own sacrificial and redemptive work on the cross, the standing memorial of his death; the other, to the equally essential work of the Holy Ghost in the human heart, regenerating, sanctifying and cleansing from sin.

Baptism had indeed existed as a religious ordinance before the advent of Christ. The proselyte baptism had been known and practiced among the Jews for many centuries as one of the rites to be observed on the introduction of Gentiles into the commonwealth of

Israel; and John, the forerunner of Christ, had preached on the banks of the Jordan the baptism of repentance for the remission of sins to prepare the Jewish people for the inauguration of the Messiah's kingdom. But neither of these was distinctively Christian baptism. Christian baptism as instituted by Christ when he gave the great commission to preach the gospel among all nations, and as practiced by his apostles on and after the day of Pentecost, was indeed with water, as baptism had always been, but it was with a new and distinctive formula. It was in the name of the Father and of the Son and of the Holy Ghost. It was this added formula of the Trinity and this great command of Christ that properly inaugurated Christian baptism as the initiatory and perpetual ordinance of the Church and made it one of the holy sacraments. Thenceforward it signified and sealed precisely what circumcision from the time of Abraham had signified—namely, separation from the world, cleansing from sin, and ingrafting into Christ through the righteousness of faith. And thus, under the authorized action of the apostles of Christ as given in the New Testament, we find baptism substituted in the place of circumcision, the old Jewish rite ceasing to be observed and the Christian ordinance being universally adopted in the Church.

In like manner, the sacrament of the Lord's Supper, instituted by Christ in person on the evening before he suffered, thenceforth took the place of that paschal supper which had come down from the time of Moses and the Exodus. The Lord's Supper was not only thus engrafted by divine authority on the old Jewish festival which had so long commemorated deliverance from the bondage of Egypt, but it signified and sealed to the Christian believer in a higher and wider sense what the passover had signified and sealed—namely, redemption through the shed blood and the atoning righteousness of Christ.

Thus the two great sacraments of the older dispensations—one coming down from the Abrahamic and the other from the Mosaic dispensation—were changed and merged into the two corresponding sacraments of the Christian Church under this last and closing dispensation. Hence, in the language of the New-Testament writers, the Lord's Supper is "the Lord's passover," for Christ our Passover is sacrificed for us, and Christian baptism, which symbolizes "the washing of regeneration and renewing of the Holy Ghost," stands for that true circumcision of the heart in the spirit which is not of the letter nor outward in the flesh (Tit. iii. 5; Rom. ii. 29).

There is an eminent propriety in the appointment of two sacraments, and only two. The work of the Son of God redeeming us from death needed to be perpetually represented in a holy sacrament, and the work of the Spirit of God needed also to be represented in the Church by its appropriate sacrament. On these two divine agents and their work depended our complete salvation. It is fit, therefore, that the Church should to the end of time celebrate the two instituted rites which symbolize the joint agency of the second and the third Persons of the Trinity in our salvation. Nor could any symbols in nature have been found more strikingly appropriate for this end than those which have been chosen—namely, the water of baptism and the bread and wine of the Eucharist. Through the Old-Testament history water had always been used to represent cleansing from sin, and blood—the shedding, sprinkling and pouring out of blood—had always been used to represent atonement, redemption or the taking away of the guilt of sin. Thus we have water, still used in the baptism, and the bread and wine of the Supper, representing the broken body and the shed blood of Christ, the true Lamb of God that taketh away the sin of the world.

Nothing can be more simple, beautiful and appropriate than these two sacraments of the New Testament when they are observed in the way Christ has ordained them. They have been strangely distorted and perverted from their intention and mixed up with various superstitious observances in the Church of Rome and other communions. The Church of Rome has added five other alleged sacraments to the original two, and has so covered up the real design of baptism and the Lord's Supper by a mass of human traditions as to destroy their very significance and turn them into instruments of idolatry and priestcraft. But all evangelical Protestants stand agreed in observing the two appointed sacraments of Christ as the only ones binding on the conscience, because they are the only ones having any New-Testament authority.

There are several interesting aspects in which we may regard these holy sacraments. One has been already indicated. We may regard them as most significant symbols of Christ's great atoning work and the Spirit's sanctifying work. As such they touch the very centre of all saving truth and the heart of all true

Christian experience. There is plainly no vital Christianity without them. They contain in symbol the very essence of the gospel. They are designed by God and they are well adapted to keep alive in the remembrance of the Church and in the heart of every believing soul the great central facts and doctrines of our salvation. By their continued celebration they are a standing witness to the world of what Christ has done. They preach the gospel from age to age. They are to the Church the perpetual signs and seals of God's covenant.

The baptism in the name of Father, Son and Holy Ghost, as often as it is administered, proclaims this great mystery of the Godhead and calls for a holy consecrated life on the part of the recipient, whether child or adult. The pure water, whether applied by affusion or by enveloping the recipient by immersion, is the emblem of a new and holy life. Be it little or be it much, applied or received, the water is equally the sign and the seal of that only true baptism which is the inner baptism of the Holy Ghost. So, in the Lord's Supper, the bread and the wine are the spiritual symbols of the broken body and the shed blood of our Lord. Says Paul, "The cup of blessing which we bless, is it not the communion of the blood of Christ? The bread which we break, is it not the communion of the body of Christ? For we being many are one bread, and one body: for we are all partakers of that one bread" (1 Cor. x. 16, 17). In this sacred ordinance we see the deep spiritual import of our Saviour's words to the Jews when speaking of the manna which God gave to their fathers: "I am the living bread which came down from heaven; if any man eat of this bread he shall live for ever: and the bread that I will give is my flesh, which I will give for the life of the world. . . . Verily, verily, I say unto you, Except ye eat the flesh of the Son of man, and drink his blood, ye have no life in you. . . . For my flesh is meat indeed, and my blood is drink indeed. . . . It is the Spirit that quickeneth; the flesh profiteth nothing; the words that I speak unto you, they are spirit, and they are life" (John vi. 51-63).

In the next place, the sacraments are to be viewed in the light of Christ's most solemn and binding commands requiring implicit and perpetual observance on the part of his people. He has made it the sacred duty of all his disciples to be baptized—to recognize their allegiance to him and the separation from the world by this public act of baptism. The one command of the apostles on the day of Pentecost was, "Repent and be baptized, every one of you, in the name of Jesus Christ, for the remission of sins, and ye shall receive the gift of the Holy Ghost." This is the act of allegiance to Jesus Christ by which the believer publicly declares to the world that it is his purpose to render all other acts of obedience. Thus were three thousand baptized on the day of Pentecost and added to the Church; thus were the Roman centurion at Cæsarea, the Philippian jailer and Lydia baptized with their respective households, and so added to the Church.

No command of Christ was ever given under more impressive circumstances than that which requires his disciples to commemorate his death in the holy Supper: "Take, eat; this is my body, which is broken for you. This cup is the new testament in my blood."

"For," says Paul, "as oft as ye eat this bread and drink this cup, ye do show the Lord's death till he come." It is a tender, touching memorial of our absent Friend and Lord. It is a perpetual remembrance of him who gave his life for us. While it stands in its purity love can never die; and while love lives in the Christian heart this outward memorial and expression of it can never die. In all probability, since the Lord himself instituted it in the upper chamber at Jerusalem no single Lord's day has passed without witnessing this sacred celebration somewhere among his disciples.

The sacraments must also be regarded in the light of high and precious privileges. They stand among the most important of the varied means of grace which Christ has appointed in his Church for the spiritual growth of his believing people. This is especially true of the Lord's Supper, which, as being the memorial of the Lord's passion and the outward expression of communion and fellowship among his people, comes to us with influences peculiarly adapted to touch the heart of its recipient. It would be impossible to conceive of an institution better fitted to conserve the great end of keeping the love of Christ fresh and warm in the human heart than this extraordinary memorial Supper. It is a festival, not of nativity, but of death, and as such it stands out distinct from all the common celebrations of men. It was instituted by Christ in person under such peculiar circumstances that every solemn celebration of it brings distinctly before the minds of his followers all the touching scenes of that drama of patience and love which ended at the cross and the sepulchre; and the constant recurrence of this commemorative ordinance through the whole life of the Christian believer (in some churches on every Lord's day, in others every month, and at farthest several times a year) singles it out from all the other means of grace as a great and precious privilege.

CHAPTER XXXIII.

THE CHURCH OF CHRIST.

OUR survey of the fundamental principles of the Christian system would not be complete without some notice of the Church. Nothing is more clearly revealed in the Bible than the fact that in saving men Jesus Christ has founded a society or kingdom which he calls his Church. The topic is a fruitful one throughout the Scriptures, and the idea of such a kingdom formed among men and consecrated to the service and glory of Christ is scarcely ever absent from the sacred pages, especially those of the New Testament. He did not come to save men singly as isolated individuals of the human family, but to associate them together in this salvation in a community separated from the world, under new bonds of relationship to himself and to one another. This community he called the kingdom of God, the kingdom of heaven, his Church. Distinctly did he proclaim it when at the opening of his public ministry he preached, saying, "Repent, for the kingdom of heaven is at hand," and when on Peter's confession that he was the Messiah, "the Christ, the Son of the living God," he said, "Upon this rock" (this fundamental basis of his own acknowledged Godhead) "I will build my Church; and the gates of hell shall not prevail against it."

Isaiah, Daniel, Jeremiah, Zechariah, Malachi and other Old-Testament prophets had long before predicted his coming and this establishment of his kingdom. His sceptre should be a sceptre of righteousness and truth, his dominion as wide as the world and coextensive with time: "Of the increase of his government and peace there shall be no end, upon the throne of David, and upon his kingdom, to order it, and to establish it with judgment and with justice from henceforth even for ever" (Isa. ix. 7). Of this reign of truth and righteousness Daniel had spoken when it was revealed to him in vision that the God of heaven should set up a kingdom amongst all other kingdoms of the earth which should never be destroyed, but should stand fast for ever (Dan. ii. 44). When our blessed Lord stood before the bar of the Roman governor Pilate and was asked, "Art thou a king then?" he evidently had reference to these ancient predictions, now about to be fulfilled in the spiritual community of his universal Church, when he declared with deepest emphasis, "Thou sayest that I am a king. To this end was I born, and for this cause came I into the world, that I should bear witness unto the truth. Every one that is of the truth heareth my voice." "My kingdom is not of this world: if my kingdom were of this world, then would my servants fight, that I should not be delivered to the Jews: but now is my kingdom not from hence" (John xviii. 36, 37).

No one can read the Scriptures, either of the Old-Testament prophets or of the New-Testament apostles, without seeing how prominent is the conception of a society or community separated from the world as a distinct body, having its own laws, ordinances and institutions, both of government and of worship. This is the spiritual kingdom of God, the Church of Christ, called out from the world by special covenant as his peculiar people, to whom he has given the dispensations of his grace, the sacred oracles of Scripture, the ministry of reconciliation, the holy sacraments, and all other ordinances necessary for the preservation of his worship and the dissemination of his truth among men. It is designated in Scripture under various highly-appropriate names and titles. It is the "pillar and ground of the truth," "the house and family of God," the spiritual "temple of God," the "commonwealth of the saints" and "kingdom of God," "the body" of which Christ is the Head, the "fullness of him that filleth all things," the "Zion or city of God," and, in the Apocalypse, the "New Jerusalem" and the "Bride of the Lamb." In the Old Testament it is most frequently called the "congregation of Israel" or the "congregation of the Lord." By whatever name designated, it is always conceived of in Scripture as one body, one kingdom, one Church.

Whether in the Old Testament or in the New, whether under the Christian dispensation or under the three dispensations which preceded—the Adamic, the Abrahamic, the Mosaic—the Church of God is always one and the same Church. At any given period it may consist of a few members or of a membership scattered as wide as the earth, or it may consist of many local communions and separated denominations of Christians, but still, under all forms and orders and outward organization, this great spiritual body of which Christ is the Head is one Church, and not many. All are one in

Christ Jesus; all who by faith and practice are worthy to be members in any Church are by their high calling of God in Christ Jesus members of the one holy catholic, apostolic Church, which is the Church of patriarchs, prophets and apostles, the one true and only Church. In the Church, says Paul, there is neither Jew nor Greek, circumcision nor uncircumcision, barbarian, Scythian, bond nor free, but Christ is all and in all. This unity of the Spirit, unity of the true faith, unity of the common salvation, is, in fact, one of the essential attributes of the Church, even as spirituality of worship is another. Diversity of forms and of organizations no more breaks the oneness of the Church than diversity in nature breaks the unity of creation and the true order of the universe.

The oneness of the Church in Christ is a favorite theme with the apostle of the Gentiles. In his Epistles to the Romans and to the Galatians he argues at length to show that all true believers are the children of Abraham, and that the Church under all dispensations, consisting of true believers, is one and the same. He tells the Galatians that the gospel was preached before unto Abraham in the promise that in his seed (the Messiah) all nations would be blessed, and that the legal dispensation did not annul but confirmed that everlasting covenant made with Abraham according to which the same gospel was preached and the same Church reorganized on the day of Pentecost. Writing to the Romans, he says, "For as we have many members in one body, and all members have not the same office; so we being many are one body in Christ, and every one members one of another." To the Corinthians he says,

"Now there are diversities of gifts, but the same Spirit. And there are differences of administrations, but the same Lord. And there are diversities of operations; but it is the same God which worketh all in all." He exhorts the Ephesians to keep the unity of the Spirit in the bond of peace, saying, "There is one body, and one Spirit, even as ye are called in one hope of your calling; one Lord, one faith, one baptism, one God and Father of all, who is above all, and through all, and in you all."

Our blessed Lord himself had given the text of this far-reaching spiritual unity in his kingdom when in the intercessory prayer he said, "Neither pray I for these alone, but for them also which shall believe on me through their word; that they all may be one, as thou, Father, art in me, and I in thee, that they also may be one in us; that the world may believe that thou hast sent me. And the glory which thou gavest me, I have given them; that they may be one, even as we are one; I in them and thou in me, that they may be made perfect in one; and that the world may know that thou hast sent me, and hast loved them, as thou hast loved me."

The history of the Church is, in fact, coextensive with the history of redemption. It dates back to the garden of Eden and to the first promise of salvation by the Messiah, who as the coming One, the woman's seed, should bruise the serpent's head. From that small beginning of hope and promise, and from Abel's altar of faith and burnt sacrifice, the Church was gradually developed through the ages before and after the flood until the time of Abraham; then, with the added covenant and rite of circumcision, it was transmitted through other centuries down to the time of Moses, when a third significant symbol was added in the passover. And thus again, after a long interval of fifteen centuries had come and gone—when the Adamic dispensation with its burnt-offering had yielded to the Abrahamic with its covenant of circumcision, and this, again, to the Mosaic with its passover and its law—then, when the fullness of the time was complete, these three earlier dispensations all gave way to that which Christ himself inaugurated, the Christian dispensation. It is the last, the greatest and the best; and the others had but prepared the way for its coming.

It would be a great mistake to conceive of the Church as existing for the first time at the opening of the Christian dispensation. This fourth and last dispensation is indeed a new and better dispensation, having better promises, higher hopes and clearer light in its enlarged Scriptures. It is well styled the dispensation of the Spirit, from the outpouring of the Holy Ghost on the day of Pentecost. It is also appropriately called the gospel dispensation, from its grand commission of the ascended Saviour to preach the gospel among all nations, beginning at Jerusalem. But the Church itself was no new thing either at the ascension of Christ or at the day of Pentecost. It was almost as old as the creation. It had come down through all the ages and all the preceding dispensations from the very gates of Eden. It had come down with all its great hopes and exalted privileges, its miraculous interpositions and revelations of God, its altars of burntsacrifice, its holy tabernacle and temple-worship, its sacred books of life and salvation, its sublime moral and ceremonial laws, its preached gospel, its inspired prophets, its sacred bards, its sacraments of circumcision and the passover, its true faith, its pure gospel, its way of salvation and its devout believers.

To the Church thus enshrined in the sacred memories of four thousand years, thus filled with the gifts and the graces of the Holy Ghost on the day of Pentecost, and thus prepared for the conquest of the world, the risen and exalted Saviour gave his last great commission, and with it the ordinances, sacraments and office-bearers of this Christian dispensation. All these we have in the New Testament. They are commonly called his ascension gifts, in accordance with the Messianic prediction, quoted from the sixty-eighth psalm, by Paul, in the fourth chapter of his Epistle to the Ephesians: "When he ascended up on high, he led captivity captive, and gave gifts unto men. . . . And he gave some, apostles; and some, prophets; and some, evangelists; and some, pastors and teachers; for the perfecting of the saints, for the work of the ministry, for the edifying of the body of Christ."

This Church of the new dispensation (which is also the last), with its rich ascension gifts, its living ministry, its holy sacraments of baptism and the Lord's Supper, its completed canon of inspired Scriptures, its great commission to evangelize all nations, its indwelling presence of the Holy Ghost, and its prophetic word of promise—"Lo, I am with you alway, even unto the end of the world"—is itself the historical realization of the kingdom of God on earth.

It is a great mistake to think that kingdom belongs

alone to the future. That kingdom of righteousness and truth and peace has long ago been founded and is already in the world, filling it with glory. We are now in it, living in the midst of its triumphs; we are under the bright blaze of its culminating dispensation. The light from heaven is now shining over all the earth. Jesus Christ is already reigning, and has been reigning for eighteen centuries. There are great things behind us in all the past history of his reign, and doubtless still greater things before us in the near future. But we are now living amid the wonderful triumphs of his grace, and the manifestations of his presence and glory are visible in all parts of his kingdom. The Messiah has not abdicated his throne or abandoned his Church. Why should he? Wicked men may blaspheme and devils may rage, but are they likely to be too strong for the Lord? He who has all power in heaven and earth, and who said to his Church by the ancient prophet, "The nation and kingdom that will not serve thee shall perish; yea those nations shall be utterly wasted" (Isa. lx. 12), is not likely to desert her now after eighteen centuries of trial and triumph and progress.

There is something of the morally sublime in this perpetual and indestructible life of the Church of Christ. "Because I live, ye shall live also," is as true of the organic life of the Church as of the individual life of its members. The Church is the only governmental institution on earth that never dies. It has already outlived everything else in the world. It was well symbolized by the burning bush at Horeb. All the great world-powers of antiquity that in succession strove to crush her life have passed away. The Assyrian, the Medo-

Persian, the Græco-Macedonian, the Roman empire, rose around her, and raged against her, and then perished one after another at her feet. The most of the great nations of modern history have gone in the same way, except as they were in sympathy with Christ's kingdom. All earthly interests and institutions except those which had the true life of Christianity in them have died around her. The Church alone has stood fast amid the storms of time and the wrecks of nations. Built upon the Rock of ages and endued with the power of an endless life, she has always been safe, and is as safe to-day as ever. When these heavens shall be dissolved and the solid earth shall pass away, she will still stand fast, ready to be transferred to "the new heavens and the new earth, wherein dwelleth righteousness." Time has been when man counted it a great honor to say, "I am a Roman citizen." How empty the boast compared with that of the apostle when he said, "I am a fellow-citizen with the saints, and of the household of God"!

CHAPTER XXXIV.

THE GOSPEL MINISTRY.

PROMINENT among the ascension gifts of Jesus Christ to his Church stands the living ministry—an order of men called, qualified and appointed by himself to preach the gospel, expound the Scriptures, administer the sacraments and have the superintending care of his Church. From early times opinions have differed greatly, and do still differ, amongst the denominations into which the Church has been divided, as to the titles, prerogatives and functions of these officers, some making but one order in the ministry, and some making several with distinctly marked powers. But of the fact itself that a ministry separate from the body of the members exists in the Church by divine authority, dating from Christ's appointment of his twelve apostles, there can be no doubt. On this point there has been general agreement and consent in all the great churches of Christendom, Greek, Roman and Protestant. Even among Protestants, whether Lutheran, Reformed, Anglican, Presbyterian or Independent, there has been little or no controversy as to the fact of a living ministry in the Church, having a divine warrant for its existence and claiming succession from the apostles.

It would indeed have been strange had Christ appointed no such ministry. It is evidently so essential to the existence and perpetuity of a society which from the beginning had to be propagated by the preaching of the word and the telling of the story of the cross, that it should have a distinct class, charged with all the solemn responsibilities of the Christian ministry, that we can scarcely conceive how the Church could have made any headway in the world without this divine institution. Nothing, perhaps, more evinces the divine and far-reaching wisdom of the great Founder of Christianity than this ordination of a perpetual leadership of instruction and oversight and guidance, exemplified in the pastors, teachers and evangelists of the New-Testament Church. To a living ministry inducted into office from age to age under the most sacred of all vows, charged with the greatest of all interests—the care of souls—and endowed with the best spiritual gifts and the highest intellectual and moral culture, the Head of the Church has committed the great work of preaching his gospel to the ends of the earth and carrying forward the administration of his kingdom until he shall return. When he gave this grand commission of delegated and prescribed power, he said, " Lo, I am with you alway, even unto the end of the world."

Men may differ as to the names, titles and attributes of this ministry, but, with the New-Testament Scriptures in our hands, it is impossible not to see that Christ has appointed it, and that he has attached to it the utmost importance. In virtue of his own mediatorial and kingly office he had all power in heaven and earth to ordain a ministry for all time. He first called and trained and ordained his twelve apostles. To these he gave the keys of the kingdom, with plenipotentiary power and the gifts of the Holy Ghost to invest others with all the authority needful for the work of the ministry. When he had ascended to heaven we find them fulfilling this high commission in the ordination of the bishops, presbyters, deacons and evangelists of the New-Testament Church. What the apostles did they had authority to do, because Christ had fully invested them with it. Thus the New-Testament ministry began with Christ himself, and was transmitted to others through his inspired apostles, acting in his name. What they did he did; and so the ministry they ordained has come down through all the ages as his own divine institution.

The living ministry, therefore, is a part of the gospel itself. It can no more be set aside than the Church can be set aside. It is part and parcel of New-Testament Christianity. It is an indispensable part of all true evangelical Christianity. We can no more disparage it than we can disparage Christ's own word and Christ's own institution. If the Church is founded on a rock against which the gates of hell shall not prevail, the living ministry is founded on the same rock, for it is an integral part of the Church. Paul calls it the ministry of the word because its great distinctive function is to proclaim and expound the word of God, and he calls it the ministry of reconciliation because its great aim, through the preaching of the word, is to persuade and induce men to be reconciled to God: " Now then we are ambassadors for Christ, as though God did beseech you by us: we pray you in Christ's stead, be ye reconciled to God" (2 Cor. v. 20). The same apostle, in another significant passage, connects this living ministry directly with the salvation of men. He says, "Whosoever shall call upon the name of the Lord shall be saved. How then shall they call on him in whom they have not believed? and how shall they believe in him of whom they have not heard? and how shall they hear without a preacher? and how shall they preach, except they be sent? as it is written, How beautiful are the feet of them that preach the gospel of peace, and bring glad tidings of good things!" (Rom. x. 13-15).

It is foreign to the purpose of these pages to enter into any discussion of the conflicting views held by the different branches of the Christian Church as to the orders, titles and peculiar functions of the ministry. Each Church claims to follow the standard of the New-Testament Church on these differentiating points. Of course all cannot be right, but that Church is certainly nearest the truth which can show itself possessed of a ministry the most in accordance with the letter and spirit of the New Testament. It is sufficient here to maintain—what is admitted by all—that a separate official ministry, invested by regular ordination with the great functions of preaching and instruction, and charged with the pastoral care of the Church, is essential to the propagation of the gospel and to the spiritual edification of the body of Christ, and that such a ministry is of divine authority, as being instituted by Christ and his apostles. The existence of such a ministry through all the ages from the beginning until now is an unquestionable fact of Church history as patent as the Church itself, and the fact of its appointment and existence in the New Testament is as undeniable as its existence in all subsequent history. Hence, we are entitled to say that the fact of a living ministry constitutes one of the great distinctive doctrines of Christianity, which we are no more at liberty to reject or to ignore than Christianity itself.

In this light we may understand such passages as the following, which show how intimate is the connection between the work of the ministry and the spiritual edification of the Church: "And he gave some, apostles; and some, prophets; and some, evangelists; and some, pastors and teachers; for the perfecting of the saints, for the work of the ministry, for the edifying of the body of Christ: till we all come in the unity of the faith, and of the knowledge of the Son of God, unto a perfect man, unto the measure of the stature of the fullness of Christ" (Eph. iv. 11–13). Parallel with this is the passage in the First Epistle to the Corinthians (xii. 28): "And God hath set some in the church, first apostles, secondarily prophets, thirdly teachers, after that miracles, then gifts of healings, helps, governments, diversities of tongues." In his second letter to the Corinthian church the apostle discusses very fully the divine calling and the sacred functions of this ministry. Amongst other things he says, "For we are unto God a sweet savor of Christ, in them that are saved, and in them that perish: to the one we are the savor of death unto death; and to the other the savor of life unto life. And who is sufficient for these things? For we are not as many, which corrupt the word of God: but as of sincerity, but as of God, in the sight of God speak we in Christ. . . . But our sufficiency is of God; who also hath made us able ministers of the new testament; not of the letter, but of the spirit: for the letter killeth, but the spirit giveth life.... Therefore, seeing we have this ministry, as we have received mercy, we faint not: but have renounced the hidden things of dishonesty; not walking in craftiness, nor handling the word of God deceitfully; but, by manifestation of the truth, commending ourselves to every man's conscience in the sight of God" (2 Cor. ii. 15-17; iii. 5, 6; iv. 1, 2).

In like manner the apostle Peter says, "As every man hath received the gift, even so minister the same one to another, as good stewards of the manifold grace of God. If any man speak, let him speak as the oracles of God; if any man minister, let him do it as of the ability which God giveth: that God in all things may be glorified through Jesus Christ; to whom be praise for ever and ever" (1 Pet. iv. 10, 11). Again he writes: "The elders which are among you I exhort, who am also an elder, and a witness of the sufferings of Christ, and also a partaker of the glory that shall be revealed: Feed the flock of God which is among you, taking the oversight thereof, not by constraint, but willingly; not for filthy lucre, but of a ready mind; neither as being lords over God's heritage, but being ensamples to the flock. And when the chief Shepherd shall appear, ye shall receive a crown of glory that fadeth not away" (1 Pet. v. 1-4).

Paul has given us three Pastoral Epistles addressed specially to God's ministers—two to Timothy and one to Titus—containing the most explicit directions as to the qualifications and duties of those who enter the sacred office. He says, "If a man desire the office of a bishop, he desireth a good work," and he exhorts to the utmost faithfulness in the discharge of it: "But watch thou in all things, endure afflictions, do the work of an evangelist, make full proof of thy ministry;" "Study to show thyself approved unto God, a workman that needeth not to be ashamed, rightly dividing the word of truth;" "O Timothy, keep that which is committed to thy trust." Again he says, "Let the elders that rule well be counted worthy of double honor, especially they who labor in the word and doctrine."

No candid man can read these brief but weighty Epistles without feeling at every sentence how high is the calling, how sacred the office, how momentous the work, how solemn the responsibility, of the ministers of God. "Obey them," says Paul, " that have the rule over you, and submit yourselves: for they watch for your souls, as they that must give account, that they may do it with joy, and not with grief: for that is unprofitable for you" (Heb. xiii. 17); "And no man taketh this honor unto himself, but he that is called of God, as was Aaron" (Heb. v. 4).

CHAPTER XXXV.

THE CONVERSION OF THE WORLD.

OF the nine or ten most prominent systems of religion which have gained belief amongst men Christianity is the only one which has possessed the true missionary spirit and aimed at the moral conquest of the world. Mohammedanism has, in fact, extended over large portions of mankind of different races and nationalities, but its greatest triumphs were won by the sword, and but for the lust of power on the part of its first great military leaders there is little reason to think it would ever have spread beyond the home of its birth. The religion of Buddha, which gained so strong a foothold over the vast populations of Central, Eastern and Southern Asia, has been regarded as the nearest parallel to Christianity in its spirit of diffusion; but even this, after eighteen centuries of gradual expansion, has been confined to one quarter of the globe, and cannot properly be called a missionary religion in the sense that its direct aim from the first has been to bring the whole world under its influence.

On the contrary, the divine Founder of Christianity, when he sent forth his first apostles, sent them forth as missionaries to the ends of the earth. Breaking over the narrow boundaries of race and nation which had hitherto divided mankind, he gave his followers a commission as wide as the world, and a work to do which should not be ended till all mankind had acknowledged his dominion. He distinctly proclaimed the nature of the work, its universal extent and its progressive movement through all time when he said, "Go ye into all the world and preach the gospel to every creature." "Lo, I am with you alway, even unto the end of the world." No commission ever given to men, no task or duty ever assigned to human hands, can be compared with this in its vastness, its difficulty, its uniqueness of conception, its grandeur of design. It embraced all nations, all races, all ages, to the end of the world.

Before he suffered our Saviour had distinctly declared this idea of a universal reign over men, and this great purpose that his religion should prevail until it conquered the world. "And I," said he, "if I be lifted up from the earth, will draw all men unto me." Still more clearly did he set forth the grand conception of a universal diffusion of his religion when he met his disciples after rising from the dead, and uttered the memorable words, "Thus it is written, and thus it behoved Christ to suffer, and to rise from the dead the third day, and that repentance and remission of sins should be preached in his name among all nations."

From these impressive passages, taken in connection with what occurred on the day of Pentecost, it is manifest that our Lord not only contemplated the continual and universal proclamation of his religion among all nations to the end of the world, but that he organized his Church under this last dispensation, with all its high endowments of a living ministry, a completed inspiration of Scripture and an indwelling presence of the Holy Ghost, for the express purpose of bringing all men to the knowledge of the truth and of subduing all things to himself. In a word, he contemplated the conversion of the world to Christianity and the establishment of his universal reign of righteousness amongst men, and committed to his reorganized Church the task of accomplishing in his name that great end. According to his direction, his apostles did tarry in Jerusalem until the marvelous endowment of spiritual power came down from heaven in the cloven tongues and miraculous gifts of the Spirit on the day of Pentecost. Then the work began, and a new departure was inaugurated which has never ceased, but has been going forward with ever-increasing power and widening influence to the present hour.

We are living to-day under this great commission of the Son of God. We are living and acting our part in furtherance of this great endeavor of the Church of God—the most gigantic, the most august and inspiring, the most persevering and undying, that ever engaged the heart of man—the God-appointed endeavor to convert all men to the acknowledgment of the truth and belief of the gospel. How many heroic men and women through the ages have felt the inspiration of this lofty idea! How many have spent their lives and perished in the attempt to put it into actual realization! Has the great endeavor ever been abandoned? Not for one moment. Many of the noblest characters that have adorned the history of Christianity through the centuries belong to the annals of missions. Men and women of whom the world was not worthy, in all

Christian lands, have cheerfully endured all manner of privation and toil and faced death in a thousand forms in obedience to this charge of their ascended Lord.

It is the peculiar distinction of the Church of Christ to "attempt great things and expect great things." The cause of missions calls for, and at the same time warrants, this spirit of high endeavor. In carrying the gospel to all nations the Church is only acting under the command of her divine Head, only obeying the "marching-orders" of the Captain of our salvation. All the triumphs of the past, the whole progress of eighteen centuries, the sure promises of Christ and the predictions of ancient prophecy, unite their strong encouragement to urge forward the Church in her work of missions. No one can read the Messianic psalms or the glowing descriptions of Immanuel's kingdom in the Old-Testament prophets without seeing that Christianity, in attempting the conversion of the world, is aiming at an end which God himself has authorized, and to which he has set his own seal that it shall surely be accomplished. The time may be long deferred or it may be near at hand, but the promise of God cannot fail.

The inspired psalmist represents God as saying to the Messiah, "Ask of me, and I shall give thee the heathen for thine inheritance and the uttermost parts of the earth for thy possession;" "He shall have dominion also from sea to sea, and from the river unto the ends of the earth;" "All nations shall serve him;" "His name shall endure for ever: his name shall be continued as long as the sun: and men shall be blessed in him: all nations shall call him blessed" (Psalms ii. and lxxii.). The prophet Habakkuk speaks of a time when "the earth shall be filled with the knowledge of the glory of the Lord, as the waters cover the sea." Micah says, "He shall judge among many people, and rebuke strong nations afar off, and they shall beat their swords into ploughshares, and their spears into pruning-hooks: nation shall not lift up sword against nation, neither shall they learn war any more" (Hab. ii. 14; Micah iv. 3). The evangelical prophet devotes the last twenty-six chapters of his book to a description of Christ's kingdom in the last days, when the world shall be full of peace and righteousness, when there shall be nothing to hurt or destroy in all the holy mountain of the Lord.

It is in accordance with these ancient predictions of the universal extension of Messiah's kingdom, and the conversion of all nations to him under the preaching of the gospel and the outpouring of the Spirit in the latter days, that in the Apocalypse the last New-Testament writer beholds a mighty angel flying through heaven and having the everlasting gospel to preach to the inhabitants of the earth. This sublime vision from heaven symbolizes for all time what constitutes the peculiar glory and distinction of our Christian dispensation—namely, the universal proclamation of the gospel in all lands and in all nations by God's appointed heralds, the ministers, evangelists and missionaries of the Christian Church. This grand proclamation of the truth is now going on under the whole wide circuit of the heavens.

In the history of Christianity we may trace three distinct epochs of missionary zeal in the evangelization of the pagan world, each giving rise to a great aggressive movement which was destined to send its influence down through many centuries. These in succession mark the progress and triumph of Christianity over paganism in ever-increasing power and on an ever-widening area. It is impossible not to see in the whole progress of now nearly nineteen centuries that the spirit of missions has been the very life of the Church, and that the history of missions is the history of all aggressive Christianity. The first missionary epoch was that which began with the labors of the apostles and their immediate successors, first from Jerusalem, and then from Antioch, as its centre. It embraced all the nations represented on the day of Pentecost—Greek, Jewish, Roman, Scythian, barbarian—and did not cease until it had carried the gospel to the utmost bounds of the Roman empire, and had, in fact, so far evangelized the old Græco-Roman world that early in the fourth century Christianity had gained the throne of the Cæsars and was proclaimed the dominant religion. Little did the Romans who put to death the Prince of life, and the Jews who laid him in the sepulchre, dream of a resurrection like this. The Nazarene had gained his first great historic triumph, and he had gained it by the preaching of his gospel, by the story of his cross.

The second great epoch in which we find a widespread revival of the missionary spirit and a general aggressive movement of the Church for the conversion of the heathen is that which dates from the fifth and sixth centuries, after the incursion of the barbarian tribes and nations into Europe. This movement, whose chief point of departure was Rome, though it had other centres of influence, had for its great aim the evangelization of all those fierce, warlike peoples which one after another, after spreading desolation over the Roman empire, made their permanent home in Northern, Eastern and Central Europe. It was no light task to Christianize and civilize such races, but it was not too great for the gospel of Christ. The work was slow and often retarded, but it was ever aggressive and onward. It cost many noble lives, and much treasure, and long centuries of patient toil; it extended far down through the Middle Ages; but it was at last accomplished. Every tribe and every nation of Europe heard the gospel, received the gospel, renounced its pagan gods and its savage life, and before ten centuries were ended rejoiced in the pure light and civilization of Christianity. A continent of nations now the most powerful in the world had been won and reclaimed for Christ. It was his second grand historical triumph. The first had saved the Roman empire circling the Mediterranean and given the world Greek and Latin Christianity in place of the old mythology; the second evangelized and saved all Europe, giving us the Christianity of the great Teutonic, Scandinavian, German, Sclavonic and Anglo-Saxon nations in place of the religion of the fierce followers of Wodin and Thor. The second conquest had been longer, but it was greater, than the first, for the conquerors of the world's conquerors had now yielded to the divine power of Christianity.

The third great revival of the missionary spirit is that under whose influence it is our privilege to live.

It dates from the closing decade of the last century and the opening years of the nineteenth. It is as yet in its bright spring-time of promise. Compared with the other two great missionary ages, its epoch thus far has been brief; but the movement, on the part of the Church, has been far more general and the field of operations on a far wider scale. Its centres of influence are not in one country, but in many. They are the great commercial capitals of every leading nation of Protestant Christendom, our own included. The New World not less than the Old has caught the spirit across the waters and is fairly enlisted in the cause. The missionary enterprise is now the cause of universal Christendom—especially so with all Protestant churches amongst whom this last missionary epoch was inaugurated. Every evangelical body of Protestant Christians in the world is now engaged heart and soul in the work of foreign missions, having its band of Christian heralds on the field and contributing its treasure and its prayers to the cause. And what a field it is! It is the world for which Jesus died—the one world of human brotherhood; the world of nations nd races and tribes of pagan men. No longer the nar-.ow boundaries of Rome or of Europe, but all the continents and all the isles of the ocean, constitute the one missionary field now set before the combined Church of God for this third and greatest, and perhaps final, effort to bless and save the race.

What has been done during the century thus far, on both the home and the foreign field, is enough to demonstrate and to guarantee the success of all the rest. The increasing triumphs of the past and of the present, wherever the gospel has been preached and is now being preached, are sufficient to inspire all hearts with unspeakable joy at the near prospect of the hour when Christianity shall win its final, universal victory. We can have no hesitation in saying that the one most urgent duty to which God is now calling his Church, of every name and of every order, is that of giving the gospel to mankind in every pagan land. This is living Christianity—to preach the gospel to the poor, to send the gospel to those who still sit in the region and shadow of death. What is any Christian profession worth, and what is any organization under heaven, calling itself a Church, worth, if it fails to do this?

That venerable servant of God and noble type of the Christian missionary, Dr. Alexander Duff, expressed the sentiment just before his death that the cause of missions is the chief reason for the Church's continued existence in this world. Having closed his long and successful career in India and returned for the last time to his native Scotland, worn out in the service, he addressed a communication to the first General Council of the Presbyterian Church at Edinburgh, in 1877, in which he declared with great emphasis the one ruling conviction on which he had begun his missionary life, and with which he was now closing it, to be that " missions, in the large and comprehensive sense of the world's evangelization, are by appointment and decree of the glorious triune Jehovah the chief end of the Christian Church, and he expressed the belief that the Christian Church would accomplish its grand mission of converting the whole world to Christ only when it should enter heart and soul into the mission work.

CHAPTER XXXVI.

THE COMING OF THE LORD.

THE second coming of Christ holds very nearly the same relation to the New-Testament Scriptures and to the Church of this last dispensation which his first advent held to the Old Testament and the Jewish Church. It is the great unfulfilled prophecy of our period, to which all believing hearts unceasingly look forward as the absorbing object of Christian hope. Other grand events are associated with it in the New-Testament Scriptures, but the Lord's personal appearing in glorious majesty at the end of this dispensation is the one central fact of prophecy around which cluster all the other facts of the latter days. The second advent of Christ is so clearly revealed, both by himself and in the writings of his inspired apostles, that it must ever be regarded as one of the most prominent doctrines of Christianity. We could as soon set aside the historical fact that the Son of God was once manifested in the flesh to put away sin as we can the yet prophetic but revealed fact that he will come again in the clouds of heaven to raise the dead and to judge the world.

When our Lord stood arraigned before the judgment-bar of the Sanhedrim and was solemnly adjured by the high priest to declare who he was, he asserted his Messiahship and said, "Hereafter shall ye see the Son of man sitting on the right hand of power, and coming in the clouds of heaven." He had already, a few days before, as recorded in the twenty-fifth chapter of the Gospel by Matthew, made the same revelation of his coming kingdom and glory to his disciples: "When the Son of man shall come in his glory, and all the holy angels with him, then shall he sit upon the throne of his glory: and before him shall be gathered all nations; and he shall separate them one from another, as a shepherd divideth his sheep from the goats: and he shall set the sheep on his right hand, but the goats on the left." These sublime revelations are in accordance with what took place on the day of his ascension to heaven, as stated by Luke in the last chapter of his Gospel and in the first chapter of the Acts of the Apostles: "And he led them out as far as to Bethany: and he lifted up his hands, and blessed them;" "And when he had spoken these things, while they beheld, he was taken up; and a cloud received him out of their sight. And while they looked steadfastly toward heaven, as he went up, behold, two men stood by them in white apparel; which also said, Ye men of Galilee, why stand ye gazing up into heaven? This same Jesus which is taken up from you into heaven, shall so come in like manner as ye have seen him go into heaven."

If we turn to the subsequent writings of the New Testament, we find them everywhere filled with this glorious hope of the return of Jesus Christ to this world. He had promised to come again in great power and glory, and had exhorted them to stand always ready, watching and praying for his appearing: "Ye know neither the day nor the hour in which the Son of man shall come." In this spirit Paul writes to the Corinthians: "So that ye come behind in no gift; waiting for the coming of our Lord Jesus Christ" (1 Cor. i. 7). To the Thessalonians he says, "I pray God your whole spirit, and soul, and body, be preserved blameless unto the coming of our Lord Jesus Christ" (1 Thess. v. 23). To the Philippians he said, "Our conversation is in heaven; from whence also we look for the Saviour, the Lord Jesus Christ" (Phil. iii. 20). To Titus he wrote, "Looking for that blessed hope, and the glorious appearing of the great God and our Saviour Jesus Christ" (Tit. ii. 13). In the General Epistle to the Hebrews he says, "So Christ was once offered to bear the sins of many; and unto them that look for him shall he appear the second time, without sin, unto salvation" (Heb. ix. 28).

The last book of the Bible, the Apocalypse, opens and closes with this great promise of the second coming: "Behold he cometh with clouds; and every eye shall see him, and they also who pierced him: and all kindreds of the earth shall wail because of him;" "Behold, I come quickly: blessed is he that keepeth the sayings of the prophecy of this book;" "He which testifieth these things saith, Surely I come quickly: Amen. Even so, come, Lord Jesus" (Rev. i. 7; xxii. 7, 20). The apostle Peter, as if in anticipation of the long delay of this coming, says in the close of his Second General Epistle, "The Lord is not slack concerning his promise, as some men count slackness; but is long-suffering to us-ward, not willing that any should perish, but that all should come to repentance. But the day of the Lord will come as a thief in the night; in which the heavens shall pass away with a great noise, and the elements shall melt with fervent heat, the earth also and the works that are therein shall be burned up" (2 Pet. iii. 9, 10). The one passage, however, which gives us the fullest revelation of the Saviour's second advent is in Paul's First Epistle to the Thessalonian church: "I would not have you to be ignorant, brethren, concerning them which are asleep" (dead), "that ye sorrow not, even as others which have no hope. For if we believe that Jesus died and rose again, even so them also which sleep in Jesus will God bring with him. For this we say unto you by the word of the Lord, that we which are alive and remain unto the coming of the Lord shall not prevent them which are asleep. For the Lord himself shall descend from heaven with a shout, with the voice of the archangel, and with the trump of God: and the dead in Christ shall rise first: then we which are alive and remain shall be caught up together with them in the clouds, to meet the Lord in the air: and so shall we ever be with the Lord. Wherefore comfort one another with these words" (1 Thess. iv. 13–18).

Such is the clear testimony of Scripture on the subject of our Lord's second coming. In a matter which belongs wholly to the future, and on which we can have no possible information except what God has seen fit to reveal to us in his word, it is needless to speculate or to frame theories. We must await the hour of the grand apocalypse from heaven before we can know the full truth. As in all former generations, so also in our own, many learned and godly men have earnestly striven to penetrate the veil which hides the future. Such curiosity is as unwise as it is unavailing. The times and the seasons of all coming events God hath reserved to himself. We cannot tell beforehand the day or the hour of their arrival. On this very point the inspired apostle, who had once been caught up into paradise, was constrained to say, "Of the times and the seasons, brethren, ye have no need that I write unto you. For yourselves know perfectly, that the day of the Lord so cometh as a thief in the night" (1 Thess. v. 1, 2). How could he or they, and how can we, know anything as to the set time of his coming, when the Lord himself has so emphatically said, "Of that day and hour knoweth no man, no, not the angels of heaven, but my Father only"? (Matt. xxiv. 36).

Whether Christ's advent is now near at hand, as some think, or will be still longer deferred, and whether he will come before the millennial reign of righteousness and peace on earth or after that period of a thousand years has been fulfilled, are questions which learned and godly men are now anxiously debating. Of these deep problems of the future, which have so often been discussed through all the past centuries, back to the very times of the apostles, and which are now again exciting a wide interest in the Church, we shall attempt no elucidation and no decision, simply because we believe none is given in the word of God. Where we can neither know nor explain, our wisest course is to be silent, to watch and pray and wait for the salvation of God.

To the individual believer who loves the Lord it makes no special difference in the exercise of faith and love, hope and joy, whether he shall first see his

Saviour in this world or in the next. In either event the great and blessed promise is fulfilled that he shall see him and be for ever with him. Of the true believers of all ages and all lands, some have lived and toiled in the expectation of seeing his return to this world, of first seeing him here, and some have toiled and died in the expectation of meeting him first in heaven; but all alike have lived, labored and died in the assured hope that they shall certainly see him, for the Lord hath spoken it: "I go to prepare a place for you; and if I go and prepare a place for you, I will come again and receive you unto myself, that where I am there ye may be also."

While, therefore, we know nothing as to the precise time of our Lord's coming, there are some characteristics of it which are revealed in Scripture with great clearness. We know, first, that it is to be an actual and a personal advent. There can be no uncertainty on this point: "This same Jesus which is taken up from you into heaven, shall so come in like manner." Then, again, it is to be a sudden coming: "At such an hour as ye think not." He has himself compared it in suddenness to "the lightning which shineth out of one part of heaven to the other." Still further, it is to be glorious beyond anything ever before witnessed on earth: "Then shall they see the Son of man coming in the clouds with great power and glory." All the sublime revelations of the last judgment, the universal resurrection of the dead, the consummation of his mediatorial kingdom and the retributions of eternity gather around this great central fact of our Lord's second advent.

CHAPTER XXXVII.

THE FINAL RETRIBUTION.

OUR benevolent sympathies would prompt us to desire the salvation of all men through the gospel, and to hope that under the rule of a merciful and long-suffering God their eternal happiness might in some way be secured. But such is not the doctrine of the Scriptures; this natural prompting of the heart is not sustained by the testimony of God. When we listen to the repeated utterances of Christ and his inspired apostles in the New Testament, it seems impossible to resist the conclusion that, while some men shall be saved, some will irretrievably perish. No candid interpretation of these utterances, not to mention many similar ones in the Old Testament, can set aside the great fact which underlies them all—that there is to be a difference hereafter, even as there is now, between the righteous and the wicked, between "him that serveth God and him that serveth him not." Any explanation which would obliterate this fundamental distinction of the Scriptures, and make Christ and his apostles teach that the righteous and the wicked shall go to the same abode and share in the same blessed destiny, would nullify the clear and obvious import of all language. The plain doctrine of the Bible is that there is a difference now between the good and the bad, and that in the world to come the difference will become an actual and a final separation, a great gulf fixed between.

The time when this final separation and sentence of retribution on the wicked shall take place is described in the New Testament as the "day of judgment." It is to be at the end of the world, the close of the Christian dispensation and the consummation of all things. It is to be accompanied by the great events of Christ's second coming and by the general resurrection of the dead. In many passages of Scripture the three things are so intimately associated that it seems difficult, if not impossible, to divide them. Yet some able interpreters of the twentieth chapter of the Apocalypse and a few other texts have thought there will be two resurrections, one of the righteous dead and the other of the wicked dead, separated by a period of a thousand years, during which Christ will reign on earth, and at the end of which period the final judgment will take place. It may be so; but we shall not here undertake to unfold what seems to us as yet a deep mystery of prophecy. It is enough to know that the time will surely come; the King shall appear in his glory; the dead shall be raised and assembled before him; the throne shall be set; the books shall be opened; and the world shall be judged in righteousness.

The day of final judgment and retribution is often referred to by our Saviour in his parables and public discourses. He speaks of it as "that day," "the end of the world," "the coming of the Son of man." In the twenty-fourth and twenty-fifth chapters of the Gospel by Matthew he describes it with much fullness. The Son of man shall come in the clouds of heaven with power and great glory, and the holy angels with him, to separate the good from the bad. He shall sit upon the throne of his glory, and all nations shall be assembled before him. The righteous shall be grouped on the right hand of his judgment-seat, and the wicked on the left. The respective sentences of approval and condemnation shall be pronounced: "Then shall the King say unto them on his right hand, Come, ye blessed of my Father, inherit the kingdom prepared for you from the foundation of the world: for I was an hungered, and ye gave me meat: I was thirsty, and ye gave me drink: I was a stranger, and ye took me in: naked, and ye clothed me: I was sick, and ye visited me: I was in prison, and ye came unto me. Then shall the righteous answer him, saying, Lord, when saw we thee an hungered, and fed thee? or thirsty, and gave thee drink? When saw we thee a stranger, and took thee in? or naked, and clothed thee? Or when saw we thee sick, or in prison, and came unto thee? And the King shall answer and say unto them, Verily I say unto you, Inasmuch as ye have done it unto one of the least of these my brethren, ye have done it unto me. Then shall he say also unto them on the left hand, Depart from me, ye cursed, into everlasting fire, prepared for the devil and his angels: for I was an hungered, and ye gave me no meat: I was thirsty, and ye gave me no drink: I was a stranger, and ye took me not in: naked, and ye clothed me not: sick, and in prison, and ye visited me not. Then shall they also answer him, saying, Lord, when saw we thee an hungered, or athirst, or a stranger, or naked, or sick, or in prison, and did not minister unto thee? Then shall he answer them, saying, Verily I say unto you, Inasmuch as ye did it not to one of the least of these, ye did it not to me. And these shall go away into everlasting punishment: but the righteous into life eternal."

It is here to be noticed that the words "everlasting," in the first clause, and "eternal," in the second, are renderings of one and the same word in the original Greek text; so that the punishment of the wicked and the life of the righteous, as to duration, are placed upon the same basis. There is no indication that either the punishment or the life shall ever cease. Assuredly, there is nothing in all the word of God more solemn and momentous than this scene of judgment and these sentences of life and death. No rightly-constituted mind can thoughtfully ponder them without being deeply moved. No preacher of the gospel should declare them to his fellow-men without tears of sympathy such as his divine Master shed over lost Jerusalem. But no faithful preacher can yet hesitate to declare them as a part of God's message of warning and of love to dying men. While they stand in the New Testament amongst the most emphatic and reiterated sayings of our Lord they must be believed, and they must be preached in all their awful import by those who would not shun to declare the whole counsel of God. Our natural sympathies and our reasonings drawn from premises outside of the Bible must not be allowed to ignore or impugn what is obviously so prominent a doctrine of all Scripture, and especially of Christianity, as the doctrine of a judgment to come and the final, irreversible punishment of the wicked.

As to the time when this final judgment is to take place, nothing further is revealed than that it will be at the end of the world, after the gospel has been proclaimed among all nations. Our Saviour said, " This gospel of the kingdom shall be preached in all the world, for a witness unto all nations; and then shall the end come" (Matt. xxiv. 14).

Turning to the writings of the apostles, we find the doctrine of a judgment to come set forth with much distinctness. When Paul stood before the men of Athens on Mars' Hill and urged the command of God on all men to repent, his argument was, " Because he hath appointed a day, in the which he will judge the world in righteousness, by that man whom he hath ordained: whereof he hath given assurance unto all men, in that he hath raised him from the dead" (Acts xvii. 31). When writing to the Romans and the Corinthians, he declares the same great truth: " For we shall all stand before the judgment-seat of Christ;" " For we must all appear before the judgment-seat of Christ; that every one may receive the things done in his body, according to that he hath done, whether it be good or bad" (Rom. xiv. 10; 2 Cor. v. 10). How fully does this accord with what Solomon has said— " For God shall bring every work into judgment, with every secret thing, whether it be good, or whether it be evil" (Eccl. xii. 14)—and also with what our Lord says: " Every idle word that men shall speak, they shall give account thereof in the day of judgment. For by thy words thou shalt be justified, and by thy words thou shalt be condemned"! (Matt. xii. 36, 37).

The apostle Jude quotes the ancient prophecy of Enoch, the seventh from Adam, saying, "Behold, the Lord cometh with ten thousand of his saints, to execute judgment upon all, and to convince all that are ungodly among them of all their ungodly deeds which they have ungodly committed, and of all their hard speeches which ungodly sinners have spoken against him." The apostle Peter closes his Second General Epistle with an earnest exhortation to his fellow-Christians to stand always prepared for that great day of reckoning which shall witness the destruction of the world that now is and the inauguration of new heavens and a new earth: "Looking for and hasting unto the coming of the day of God, wherein the heavens being on fire shall be dissolved, and the elements shall melt with fervent heat. Nevertheless we, according to his promise, look for new heavens and a new earth, wherein dwelleth righteousness." But the apostle John, in the twentieth chapter of the Apocalypse, has given a most graphic and sublime revelation of the scene of the last judgment: "And I saw a great white throne, and him that sat on it, from whose face the earth and the heaven fled away; and there was found no place for them. And I saw the dead, small and great, stand before God; and the books were opened: and another book was opened, which is the book of life: and the dead were judged out of those things which were written in the books, according to their works. And the sea gave up the dead which were in it; and death and hell delivered up the dead which were in them:

and they were judged every man according to their works. And death and hell were cast into the lake of fire. This is the second death. And whosoever was not found written in the book of life was cast into the lake of fire."

From the Scriptures here adduced, and from other passages, it is evident that the judgment of the last day will be by Jesus Christ in person; that it shall be a judgment in righteousness and equity; that it will extend to all men, living and dead, great and small; that it shall bring all their actions and their words into remembrance, whether good or bad, known or unknown; and that it must finally determine the happiness or misery, the weal or woe, of all mankind. After death there is before all men the judgment of the great day, and after judgment the Bible reveals to us but two conditions, two destinies, two places of abode—the one expressed by the life and bliss of heaven, the other by all that is dark and dreadful in the word "hell."

CHAPTER XXXVIII.

THE RESURRECTION OF THE BODY.

IF we were asked to point out the one doctrine which more than any other differentiates Christianity from all other religious systems, we should name that which in the Apostles' Creed is styled "the resurrection of the body." If, again, we should single out the one doctrine of the Christian system which prior to all evidence it would be the most difficult to believe, as containing the greatest of all mysteries, we should name this doctrine of the resurrection. Yet, peculiar as it is to Christianity, and difficult as it must have been originally to be accepted, the doctrine has unquestionably won its way over all obstacles to a wellnigh universal belief among Christian nations. Of all the peculiar and distinctive tenets taught by Christ and his apostles, there is not one which holds its place more firmly as an accepted faith in the heart and mind of Christendom than this stupendous miracle, the final resurrection of the body.

The remarkable thing is that thousands of men and women outside of all our churches who make no profession of Christianity yet believe, or at least acquiesce in, this doctrine of the Church, and when they are called to bury their dead do it just as we do, in the assured hope of a blessed resurrection. It would seem, indeed, that the triumph of Christianity over the minds and hearts of men has been more general and complete on this point than on any other single dogma of its creed. Here, at least, they feel that it is far better to believe than to deny.

The doctrine of the resurrection of the body from the sleep of death was taught with more or less distinctness in many passages of the Old-Testament Scriptures, but it held there no such prominence as it assumed in the New Testament in the teachings of Christ and his apostles. In fact, nothing is more prominent in the utterances of our Lord, and of all the New-Testament writers, than this blessed assurance that the dead shall rise. How emphatically and how sublimely does he declare himself at the grave of Lazarus!—" I am the resurrection and the life: he that believeth in me, though he were dead, yet shall he live: and whosoever liveth and believeth in me shall never die." Is there a single passage in all the New Testament which impresses the reader with a more vivid conviction that he who speaks has the absolute certainty of a divine authority than when he declared on another occasion, "Verily, verily, I say unto you, The hour is coming, and now is, when the dead shall hear the voice of the Son of God; and they that hear shall live. For as the Father hath life in himself, so hath he given to the Son to have life in himself, and hath given him authority to execute judgment also, because he is the Son of man. Marvel not at this, for the hour is coming, in the which all that are in the graves shall hear his voice, and shall come forth; they that have done good unto the resurrection of life; and they that have done evil unto the resurrection of damnation"?

Since Christ himself rose from the sepulchre, it stands amongst the clearest and the sublimest revelations of God that there is to be a final resurrection of the dead, both of the just and of the unjust. In order to see how prominent a place this great doctrine held in the preaching of the apostles, we have only to read that inspired chapter of logical argument, scriptural argument, impassioned eloquence and exultant hope, the fifteenth chapter of the First Epistle to the Corinthians, which has become the very formula and liturgy of the burial-service of every Church under heaven. Indeed, so prominent was it that to preach "Jesus and the resurrection" became the descriptive designation of the gospel, as we learn when Paul reached the metropolis of the Grecian philosophy and delivered his first sermon on Mars' Hill to the Athenian sages and critics. How impressively are we taught on this occasion the wide antagonism between Christianity and all the antecedent paganisms, when we are told that the cultured audience heard him patiently until he broached the topic of the resurrection of the dead, and then broke up the assembly, unwilling to hear anything on a topic so absurd and so abhorrent to the reigning philosophy!

How could the gospel ever triumph over prejudices so deep-rooted and over opposition so fierce and unreasoning? But why need we discuss possibilities? We know that it did triumph, and that, too, within a century from the time when this Athenian audience laughed it to scorn. It is a remarkable fact that two of the earliest apologists for Christianity were philosophers of this most cultured, critical school. Two of the earliest defences of Christianity now extant were written in the second century and addressed to the Roman emperors, one by Justin Martyr, a native of Samaria, thoroughly educated in the Grecian and Roman as well as the Jewish philosophy, and the other by Athenagoras, the Athenian philosopher, a man versed in all the learning of the times.

It is worthy of special notice that each of these learned Christian philosophers, thus converted to Christ after the most patient investigation and on evidence which they found to be unanswerable, wrote fully on the resurrection and defended it against the attacks of the early adversaries. It is curious to notice how their arguments cover the very same ground which is taken to-day against the doctrine—namely, first, its alleged impossibility, as contrary to nature; and second, its alleged repugnance to reason and philosophy. One might read these ancient treatises with the feeling that, instead of being written for an emperor, they furnish an answer in point to much of the atheistic philosophy, the scientific materialism and the captious criticism of our own times.

When, therefore, we consider the prominence of this doctrine in the New-Testament revelations, how essentially characteristic it is of Christianity, how constantly it was upon the lips of the great Founder, how it cheered the hopes and inspired the zeal of the apostles, and how inestimably precious it has been to the hearts of God's children through all ages, we cannot wonder that it should form one of the twelve distinct doctrinal utterances of the Apostles' Creed. In the three sections of that ancient symbol, describing in turn the most important truths related to the personality and work of the adorable Trinity, we find this doctrine enunciated among the great closing words of the formula: "I believe in the Holy Ghost; the holy catholic Church; the communion of saints; the forgiveness of sins; the resurrection of the body; and the life everlasting." Here it will be perceived that the resurrection of the body is introduced as the very gate to the eternal inheritance, the final and perfect preparation for the full fruition of the life everlasting.

The inscriptions on the tombs of the early Christians, as found in the catacombs at Rome, represented death as a sleep and the new life as an awakening. This had been the favorite metaphor of Scripture. To die in the Lord was but to fall asleep in Jesus and to wake again in his image, their vile bodies fashioned like unto his glorious body. In this blessed hope the early Church buried its dead. In this confidence the early confessors and martyrs willingly laid down their lives for Jesus. With such a hope, how joyous and exultant are the words of the inspired apostle!—"So, when this corruptible shall have put on incorruption, and this mortal shall have put on immortality, then shall be brought to pass the saying that is written, Death is swallowed up in victory. O death, where is thy sting? O grave, where is thy victory? The sting of death is sin, and the strength of sin is the law. But thanks be to God who giveth us the victory through our Lord Jesus Christ."

CHAPTER XXXIX.

THE LIFE EVERLASTING.

THE last clause of the Apostles' Creed is like the grand *finale* of some lofty anthem. It swells across the ages, bearing the rich harmonies of all Christian doctrine to one sublime consummation in the life to come. The *credo* of the "holy catholic Church, the communion of saints, the forgiveness of sins, the resurrection of the body," is but the prelude and the preparation for this final note, "the life everlasting." All is well that ends well, and all here ends in the rest and the glory of the future unending life. It is beautifully significant that three things—this most ancient creed of the Church, the book of God, and the life of the righteous—all have one and the same ending in the rest and glory of heaven. Immortality, blessed and perfect, at God's right hand, is the one ideal, the one goal, of the Bible, of the Church, and of every faithful follower of Jesus Christ.

True, there is a higher end, a sublimer ideal of the future life. It is the glory of God as formulated in the Catechism. But then the life everlasting to the righteous will consist largely in the beholding and the enjoying of that divine glory. Whether on earth or in heaven, the word of Christ stands true: "This is eternal life that they might know thee, the only true God, and Jesus Christ whom thou hast sent." The end of salvation here is the life everlasting hereafter; but that endless life in heaven will find its highest blessedness in God, even as Christ prays: "Father, I will that they also whom thou hast given me be with me where I am; that they may behold my glory, which thou hast given me." How perfect is the economy of divine grace in the gospel and in the unfolding of the saint's everlasting rest in the life to come! First the cross and then the crown is Heaven's order, the life that now is only preparing for and ending in that which is to come. After toil, the rest; after strife, the peace; after pain, the pleasure; after defeat, the victory; after weeping, enduring for a night, the joy of the coming morning; after sin and death, the sinless life and the unending glory. Who would change it if he could? Who would reverse the conditions of Christianity and the promises of God?

It is eminently fitting that this ancient creed of the Church should reach its sublime doctrinal climax in the strong assurance of everlasting life. What could have been more cheering in the hour of trial, more inspiring in the day of persecution and death, to the suffering children of God, than this belief in a life to come, this blessed hope of an immortality to which death was but the portal? It was a compensation full and perfect for all the ills of this mortal existence, for all the losses and privations, the pains and penalties, which that suffering Church was enduring at the hands of an ungodly and infuriated world.

Never in all the history of man was any belief embraced with a deeper conviction of its truth and a heartier appreciation of its ineffable preciousness than was this grand doctrine of the life everlasting, with its cognate doctrine of the resurrection of the body, embraced by the ancient Church. The one was but the complement and consummation of the other, and the great hope of the life everlasting, comprehending both soul and body, was embraced, not as some vague and far-off anticipation of future good, but as a near and present reality, a daily living expectation of seeing Jesus and of being with him for evermore, which the believer might enter upon at any moment, and would assuredly enter upon at death.

It is instructive to notice what prominence—we might say what emphatic conspicuousness—this doctrine of the life everlasting holds in the teaching of our Saviour and his apostles throughout the New Testament. It forms one of the great themes of all Scripture. In each of the Gospel histories, but especially in that of John, the conception of a life to come—the life of the soul, the eternal or everlasting life—is continually present in the instructions, the parables, the revelations of our Lord, from the opening to the close of his ministry. This is so much the case that even one of his titles is "the Life." He is "the Bread of Life," "the resurrection and the Life." He is the Light of the world and the Life of men. "When Christ, who is our life, shall appear," writes Paul to the Colossians, "then shall ye also appear with him in glory." So strong is this feeling of the reality and the pre-eminent glory of everlasting life on the mind of the great apostle that he goes so far as to say to the Corinthians, "If in this life only we have hope in Christ, we are of all men most miserable;" and in another place, to the Philippians, " I am in a strait betwixt two, having a desire to depart and to be with Christ, which is far better." John says, with the utmost confidence, " We know not what we shall be, but we know that when he shall appear we shall be like him, for we shall see him as he is." How resplendently does the grand ideal of the life to come and the saint's everlasting rest shine forth through all the symbols and imagery of the Apocalypse, with its "book of life," its "tree of life," its "river of the water of life," and its New Jerusalem of light and life, from which sickness and sorrow and sin and death have fled for ever! We can scarcely say that there is any one thing more essentially characteristic of the Bible as a book, and of Christianity as a religion, than its precious doctrine of the life everlasting.

For what would the suffering child of God to-day exchange this blessed hope of the ancient creed? What earthly prize of wealth or station would be an adequate compensation to the humblest believer for the loss of it? Some tell us, in their ignorance and folly, that all the creeds and all the dogmas of the Church are now exploded. Is the life everlasting exploded? If so, what are our great thinkers prepared to give us in its place? Some highly-cultivated minds would perhaps give us the agnosticism and nihilism of modern speculation as the most fitting consolation for the last days of a philosopher. Some poetic souls, smitten with the newly-discovered beauties of hoary antiquity, seem inclined to console us with the pure morality of Confucius or the pantheistic Nirvana of Buddhism. Some, perhaps with less elevated thoughts, stand ready, like Esau or Judas, to sell their celestial birthright and their inheritance in the Son of Mary for a mess of pottage or for thirty pieces of silver.

But what arithmetic shall compute for us the loss and the gain of such a bargain? What words in human speech are so adequate to solve it as those of him who spake as never man spake?—" What shall it profit a man if he shall gain the whole world and lose his own soul? or what shall a man give in exchange for his soul?" One of the ablest sermons ever delivered was by that prince of preachers Robert Hall, on the theme " The Vanity of Man apart from his Immortality." Our generation has been discussing the question, " Is life worth living?" The true solution is found only by him whose life here, brief or long, ends in the everlasting life promised and made sure by the gospel of Jesus Christ. Without this all is vanity and vexation of spirit; with it all is blessedness and glory for ever.

The final abode of the righteous, where they shall enter upon this inheritance of everlasting life, is revealed to us with much fullness in the Scriptures, particularly in the closing book of the New Testament. It is described as the " new heavens and the new earth, wherein dwelleth righteousness." It is " the paradise of God," " the house of many mansions," " the city that hath foundations, whose Maker and Builder is God," " the New Jerusalem prepared as a bride adorned for her husband." It is a world of pure spiritual enjoyment in the presence of God, in the society of angels, in the companionship of just men made perfect. There shall be nothing to hurt or destroy in all the holy mountain of God. It is at once the saint's everlasting rest from sin and sorrow and everlasting employment in all that can make existence peaceful and joyous. With what emphasis did our Lord speak of it!—"I go to prepare a place for you: and if I go and prepare a place for you, I will come again and receive you unto myself, that where I am there ye may be also."

All the images of splendor and beauty which can be drawn from material nature are employed in the book of Revelation to give us an idea of the glory of this heavenly world to which Christ Jesus has ascended. There he now reigns on his mediatorial throne at God's right hand, surrounded by the cherubim and the seraphim and the innumerable hosts of the redeemed, "clothed in white raiment." Nothing could be more appropriate than that the canon of inspired Scripture should close with these sublime revelations of the Apocalypse, setting forth the ineffable glory of that home of the blessed, that enduring city, that house of many mansions, which the great Redeemer has gone to prepare for his people. When we speak of it as a home, a heaven, a Father's house, we have reached the highest, purest, noblest utterance of which either thought or speech is capable. In all literature and in all philosophy there is nothing higher, grander than this.

The very book of God has reached the climax of promise and its limit of delineation in the heaven of the Apocalypse: "And he carried me away in the spirit to a great and high mountain, and showed me that great city, the holy Jerusalem, descending out of heaven from God, having the glory of God: and her light was like unto a stone most precious, even like a jasper stone, clear as crystal. . . . And I saw no temple therein: for the Lord God Almighty and the Lamb are the temple of it. And the city had no need of the sun, neither of the moon to shine in it: for the glory of God did lighten it, and the Lamb is the light thereof. And the nations of them which are saved shall walk in the light of it: and the kings of the earth do bring their glory and honor into it. And the gates of it shall not be shut at all by day: for there shall be no night there. And they shall bring the glory and honor of the nations into it. And there shall in no wise enter into it any thing that defileth, neither whatsoever worketh abomination, or maketh a lie; but they which are written in the Lamb's book of life. And he showed me a pure river of water of life, clear as crystal, proceeding out of the throne of God and of the Lamb. In the midst of the street of it, and on either side of the river, was there the tree of life, which bare twelve manner of fruits, and yielded her fruit every month: and the leaves of the tree were for the healing of the nations. And there shall be no more curse: but the throne of God and of the Lamb shall be in it; and his servants shall serve him: and they shall see his face; and his name shall be in their foreheads. And there shall be no night there; and they need no candle, neither light of the sun; for the Lord God giveth them light: and they shall reign for ever and ever."

When the last voices at Patmos died away with these inspiring revelations of the coming and eternal glory of heaven, the Church of God had a great and blessed hope which should abide with her through all the ages.

In that hope she has lived, and in that hope all her sons and daughters have died. Nor shall they be disappointed: "There remaineth a rest for the people of God;" "Now we see through a glass, darkly; but then face to face; now I know in part; but then shall I know even as also I am known;" "Eye hath not seen, nor ear heard, neither have entered into the heart of man the things which God hath prepared for them that love him." But we shall enter in through the gates into that blissful abode,

> "Where the rivers of pleasure flow o'er the bright plains,
> And the noontide of glory eternally reigns;
> Where the saints of all ages in harmony meet,
> Their Saviour and brethren transported to greet;
> Where the anthems of pleasure unceasingly roll,
> And the smile of the Lord is the feast of the soul."

CHAPTER XL.

THREE EXPERIENCES: SIN, GRACE, GLORY.

TO every Christian believer belongs a career of three successive stages or states of being, each distinctly marked in the Scriptures as bringing to the soul in succession its own peculiar revelations and experiences. The first is the state of sin or natural depravity, ending at conversion; the second is the state of grace and partial sanctification, ending at death; and the third is the state of perfect and unending holiness and glory in heaven. On each the Bible gives us clear and unmistakable information. On two of them we have an actual knowledge derived from experience, additional to the light furnished by Scripture. On the third we have as yet no knowledge except God's own testimony revealed in the inspired pages. Nature, grace, glory—sin, sanctification, redemption—these are the three great periods of our individual existence, the three successive steps of our transit from time to eternity, or, as the Scriptures express it, what we were, what we are and what we shall be.

Every human life has its past, its present and its future. So here the Christian believer has his past, his present and his future as contemplated in the clear light of Scripture. And how distinctly marked is each period! In the first he is called to a perpetual remembrance of the bitter past—what he was under sin; in the second to a continued realization of what he is under grace—a mixed condition of good and evil, each struggling for the mastery; and in the third to a brighter future—a joyful anticipation, a great hope, of what he shall be. Standing in the midst of a career like this (which is, in fact, the career of every true believer), the great apostle of the Gentiles well describes the case (past, present and future) when he says, "Brethren, I count not myself to have apprehended; but this one thing I do, forgetting those things which are behind, and reaching forth unto those things which are before, I press toward the mark for the prize of the high calling of God in Christ Jesus" (Phil. iii. 13, 14).

It may be useful to young Bible-readers and others to bring together into one view some of the many passages which bear upon these three stages of our career. To group all the texts having reference to the subject would be to quote a large portion of the New-Testament Epistles, which are, in fact, full of descriptions of what we were by nature, what we become by grace and what we shall be in glory. But a few prominent passages may be presented.

1. *What we Were.*—In the second chapter of his Epistle to the Ephesians, Paul sets forth a vivid picture of what the believers among the Gentiles had been in their unconverted estate; and this description applies not only to Gentiles, but to all others in a state of nature. He says, "Who were dead in trespasses and sins; wherein in time past ye walked according to the course of this world, according to the prince of

the power of the air, the spirit that now worketh in the children of disobedience: among whom also we all had our conversation in times past in the lusts of our flesh, fulfilling the desires of the flesh and of the mind; and were by nature the children of wrath, even as others. . . . At that time ye were without Christ, being aliens from the commonwealth of Israel, and strangers from the covenants of promise, having no hope, and without God in the world." Substantially the same delineation of the character of the natural man is given in his letters to the Romans, the Corinthians, the Colossians, and to every other Gentile church, as well as in the Epistle to the Hebrews, respecting those converted from Judaism; for there is no difference: all, whether Jews or Gentiles, in their unconverted state are described as guilty, condemned, helpless and hopeless in the sight of God.

And this is still the condition of all men by nature, whether born in Christian or in heathen lands. The world is not so bad as it once was, and Christian lands are far better than heathen lands. All men, even the most ungodly, are more or less bound in Christian countries by the outward forms of law, the restraints of education, and the potent influences of the Church. Still, it is true that in the most highly-civilized Christian countries, under the full blaze of gospel light, all men come into the world sinners with an apostate, depraved nature. The original stock of humanity is not improved by our outward culture. Each new generation needs as much to be converted to-day as did the generation which witnessed the advent. By nature men are all born in sin, all start on the same low level of a sinful nature, and all must be regenerated in order to see God in peace. The wild-olive stock of our degenerate nature, after all its graftings and cultivation, is still a wild olive at the root. Not only the Bible, but the ten thousand facts of daily observation and experience, even as it regards the children of Christian parents, can leave us in no doubt as to the sinfulness of all humanity. If the cultivated philosopher of the nineteenth century has not yet discovered this truth, it must be because he is very unobserving.

2. *What we Are.*—The apostle Paul, writing to the Corinthians about their former condition of ignorance and sin, says, "And such were some of you; but ye are washed, but ye are sanctified, but ye are justified in the name of the Lord Jesus, and by the Spirit of our God" (1 Cor. vi. 11). Writing to the Ephesians, he says, "For ye were sometimes darkness, but now are ye light in the Lord: walk as children of light; (for the fruit of the Spirit is in all goodness, and righteousness, and truth;) proving what is acceptable unto the Lord" (Eph. v. 8–10). To the Romans he says, "For sin shall not have dominion over you; for ye are not under the law, but under grace;" "Being justified by faith, we have peace with God, through our Lord Jesus Christ;" "There is therefore now no condemnation to them which are in Christ Jesus, who walk not after the flesh, but after the Spirit" (Rom. vi. 14; v. 1, and viii. 1).

The apostle John, speaking of those who are in Christ, tells us that "as many as received him, to them gave he power to become the sons of God, even to them that believe on his name : which were born, not of blood, nor of the will of the flesh, nor of the will of man, but of God" (John i. 12, 13); "Behold what manner of love the Father hath bestowed upon us, that we should be called the sons of God" (1 John iv. 1). So also the apostle Peter, writing of the Christian Church, says, "Ye are a chosen generation, a royal priesthood, an holy nation, a peculiar people ; that ye should shew forth the praises of him who hath called you out of darkness into his marvelous light" (1 Pet. ii. 9).

By grace we are what we are, the redeemed, the sanctified in Christ Jesus, the heirs of promise, the sons and daughters of the Lord Almighty; no more foreigners and strangers, but fellow-citizens with the saints and of the household of God, built upon the foundation of apostles and prophets, Jesus Christ himself being the chief Corner-stone.

3. *What we Shall Be.*—" Beloved, now are we the sons of God," writes the venerable apostle, " and it doth not yet appear what we shall be: but we know that, when he shall appear, we shall be like him; for we shall see him as he is" (1 John iii. 2). Paul tells us that our life is hid with Christ in God ; that when Christ, who is our life, shall appear, then shall we also appear with him in glory ; and that he shall change our vile body, that it may be fashioned like unto his glorious body. In a moment, in the twinkling of an eye, shall this change be made. This corruptible shall put on incorruption, and this mortal immortality. So, when this corruptible shall have put on incorruption, and this mortal immortality, then shall be brought to

pass the saying that is written, Death is swallowed up in victory (Phil. iii. 21; Col. iii. 4; 1 Thess. iv. 16; 1 Cor. xv. 54).

After death is the glory. Life here is full of toil, full of sorrow, full of sin. Here we see through a glass darkly; there we shall see face to face. Now we know in part, understand in part; then shall we know even as we are known. Nor shall we await the resurrection to enter into this rest and glory. Paul tells us that to be absent from the body is to be present with the Lord. To depart and be with Christ is far better. For me to live is Christ, and to die is gain. For we know that if our earthly house of this tabernacle were dissolved, we have a building of God, an house not made with hands, eternal in the heavens (1 Cor. xiii. 12; 2 Cor. v. 1, 8; Phil. i. 21, 22).

The theme is a fruitful one. In the light of it the whole catechism of Christian experience and hope may be summed up in three questions and answered in three words: What were we? sin. What are we? grace. What shall we be? glory.

CHAPTER XLI.

THE SUPREME GOOD.

THE sages of this world's wisdom in their deepest meditations have been accustomed to discuss the question of man's supreme good. Where is the true rest of the soul to be found? How is substantial happiness to be attained? There is no weightier problem. How varied, conflicting, uncertain and unsatisfactory have been the answers given by the world's best philosophy! The great problem is solved by Christianity. The Bible sheds a light upon it nowhere else to be found. He who was in the bosom of the Father and who came forth from God tells us with no uncertain voice where and how the highest good is to be secured, and with his teaching all the sacred writers agree. The true rest of the soul, the supreme good for man, is in God—in knowing and doing his will, in being conformed to his character, in seeking his glory as the chief end of life. This is the best and highest good that can be proposed to a rational creature, and this is attainable through the grace of Jesus Christ and the operations of his Spirit.

When we turn to the Scriptures, they everywhere set before us God's service and glory as the true aim of human life, the supreme good of the soul. Eliphaz, in the book of Job, says, "Acquaint now thyself with him, and be at peace: thereby good shall come unto thee" (Job xxii. 21). Moses, after a long life of faithful service, in his parting counsels to the people of Israel said, "Their rock is not as our Rock, even our enemies themselves being judges" (Deut. xxxii. 31). The inspired psalmist asks the question, "Who will show us any good?" and answers it, "Lord, lift thou up the light of thy countenance upon us;" "Thou art my portion, O Lord;" "Whom have I in heaven but thee? and there is none upon earth that I desire besides thee;" "I shall be satisfied when I awake with thy likeness" (Psalms iv. 6; cxix. 57; xvii. 15; lxxii. 25). King Solomon sums up all instructions in one, saying, "Let us hear the conclusion of the whole matter. Fear God and keep his commandments, for this is the whole duty of man" (Eccles. xii. 13). Isaiah said, "Thou wilt keep him in perfect peace whose mind is stayed on thee: because he trusteth in thee" (Isa. xxvi. 3). The prophet Micah said, "He hath showed thee, O man, what is good; and what doth the Lord require of thee, but to do justly, and to love mercy, and to walk humbly with thy God?" (Micah vi. 8).

This unvarying testimony of the Old-Testament writers that the supreme good for man is found in God alone is abundantly confirmed by all the teachings of the New Testament. "And this is life eternal," cries the great Teacher, "that they might know thee the only true God, and Jesus Christ whom thou hast sent." "I am come," said he, "that they might have life, and that they might have it more abundantly." "Search the scriptures; for in them ye think ye have eternal life:

and they are they which testify of me" (John xvii. 3; x. 10; v. 39). When did oracle of human philosophy, or gifted bard of poesy, or founder of religious system, utter any voice of truth and consolation so adapted to the necessities of human nature and at the same time so tender and assuring to our hearts as that voice of the incarnate One?—" Come unto me, all ye that labor and are heavy laden, and I will give you rest. Take my yoke upon you, and learn of me: for I am meek and lowly in heart; and ye shall find rest unto your souls. For my yoke is easy, and my burden is light" (Matt. xi. 28-30).

We do not wonder that the apostles, who heard this voice of supernatural wisdom, whose very accent was the blessed tone of authority and love such as never man had uttered before, should be won by it. They had turned away from all other teachers to follow him, and on a certain occasion when the question was put, " Will ye also go away?" what could they do but reply with deepest emphasis, in the words of Peter?—" Lord, to whom shall we go? thou hast the words of eternal life. And we believe, and are sure that thou art the Christ, the Son of the living God" (John vi. 68, 69). No one can read the lives of these apostles after the day of Pentecost as recorded in the book of Acts, and listen to their instructions as given in the Epistles, without seeing how completely they had solved the great problem of life and found in Jesus Christ and in his blessed service the supreme good. Nor has the modern man, with all his science, literature and art, his treasured learning of the ages, and his great advance in everything that makes life desirable, ever been able to find a higher good, a truer wisdom, a purer source of happiness. Christianity, in setting before us God's service and glory as the chief good, the supreme joy, has reached the climax at once of human thought and of all human experience. This is the perfection of wisdom, than which no higher can be conceived. In this respect, of giving us an ultimate good to live for, Christianity commends itself to all men as a religion "worthy of all acceptation."

To the great question, so long and deeply pondered by the thoughtful, "What is the chief end of man?" no truer answer was ever given or ever can be given than the brief one of the Westminster Shorter Catechism: "Man's chief end is to glorify God and to enjoy him for ever." The merit of this brief definition is that it comprehends in one simple proposition the whole revelation of the Bible and the whole purpose of Christianity, in its relation both to God and to man. The ultimate aim of Christianity, as it relates to God, is to declare and to manifest the divine glory. As this is the highest conceivable excellence, so the highest end of Christianity is to reveal and promote God's glory. So far as it relates to man, the aim and end of Christianity is his salvation. But salvation is only a means to a higher end. Christianity seeks to save man in order to glorify God his Saviour. It is by and through the salvation of man that Christianity reaches its ulterior and supreme end of glorifying God. Christianity saves men from sin, restores them to God's image and favor, prepares them for heaven, and thus enables them to reach that noblest destiny for which they were originally created, and for which they are redeemed in

Christ, and this is to glorify God and to enjoy him for ever. It is only as they are redeemed in Christ and saved from sin that men are capable of attaining this exalted end of glorifying and enjoying God for ever. But that every true believer in Christ, even the humblest, will ultimately rise to this glory and fulfill this exalted destiny is as certain as that Christ has died and risen again.

"Now are we the sons of God," writes the apostle John, "and it doth not yet appear what we shall be: but we know that, when he shall appear, we shall be like him; for we shall see him as he is. And every man that hath this hope in him purifieth himself, even as he is pure" (1 John iii. 2, 3).

It is because God himself is the possessor of infinite moral excellence and is the source of all true blessedness to man that his glory is rightfully made the supreme end of our existence. In him is all perfection. "In his presence is fullness of joy, at his right hand are pleasures for evermore." When we aim to promote his glory, we seek the highest happiness of our own souls and the highest happiness of all moral and intelligent creatures. The one path to supreme happiness for rational beings lies in acquaintance and communion with God, in conformity to the will of God, in assimilation to the glorious character of God, and in holy and consecrated service in the presence of God and for his glory. The gospel of Christ, by reconciling and restoring us to God, makes this path possible to us and this life attainable. Every believer in Christ has this blessedness, and can say, "I must have all things and abound while God is God to me."

> "When all created streams are dried,
> His fullness is the same:
> May I with this be satisfied,
> And glory in his name."

We close these chapters where we began them—with God. The first sentence in the Bible is about God—the creative act of God, calling the heavens and the earth into being—and the last is about God, the Son of God coming in his glory. "Even so, come, Lord Jesus. The grace of our Lord Jesus Christ be with you all. Amen." The power of creation opens the book of God and the book of time, and the grace of redemption closes them. What a volume of truth, what a world of history, lies between the two points! Our whole Christian theology, beginning with God and ending with God, is unfolded here, for the Bible from first to last is a history of redemption, an unfolding of that scheme of divine grace through Jesus Christ which is to end in the conversion of the world and the salvation of the redeemed. "Then cometh the end, when he shall have delivered up the kingdom to God, even the Father; when he shall have put down all rule and all authority, and power, . . . that God may be all in all" (1 Cor. xv. 24, 28).

THE END.

www.ingramcontent.com/pod-product-compliance
Lightning Source LLC
Chambersburg PA
CBHW031906220426
43663CB00006B/786